Jewish Languages from A to Z

D1733080

Jewish Languages from A to Z provides an engaging and enjoyable overview of the rich variety of languages spoken and written by Jews over the past three thousand years.

The book covers more than 50 different languages and language varieties. These include not only well-known Jewish languages like Hebrew, Yiddish, and Ladino, but also more exotic languages like Chinese, Esperanto, Malayalam, and Zulu, all of which have a fascinating Jewish story to be told. Each chapter presents the special features of the language variety in question, a discussion of the history of the associated Jewish community, and some examples of literature and other texts produced in it. The book thus takes readers on a stimulating voyage around the Jewish world, from ancient Babylonia to 21st-century New York, via such diverse locations as Tajikistan, South Africa, and the Caribbean. The chapters are accompanied by numerous full-colour photographs of the literary treasures produced by Jewish language-speaking communities, from ancient stone inscriptions to medieval illuminated manuscripts to contemporary novels and newspapers.

This comprehensive survey of Jewish languages is designed to be accessible to all readers with an interest in languages or history, regardless of their background—no prior knowledge of linguistics or Jewish history is assumed.

Aaron D. Rubin is the Malvin E. and Lea P. Bank Professor of Classics and Ancient Mediterranean Studies, Jewish Studies, and Linguistics at Penn State University.

Lily Kahn is Professor of Hebrew and Jewish Languages at University College London.

Jewish Languages
from A to Z

Aaron D. Rubin and
Lily Kahn

Routledge
Taylor & Francis Group

LONDON AND NEW YORK

First published 2021
by Routledge
2 Park Square, Milton Park, Abingdon, Oxon OX14 4RN

and by Routledge
52 Vanderbilt Avenue, New York, NY 10017

Routledge is an imprint of the Taylor & Francis Group, an informa business

© 2021 Aaron D. Rubin and Lily Kahn

British Library Cataloguing-in-Publication Data
A catalogue record for this book is available from the British Library

Library of Congress Cataloging-in-Publication Data
Names: Rubin, Aaron D., 1976- author. | Kahn, Lily, author.
Title: Jewish languages from A to Z / Aaron D. Rubin, Lily Kahn.
Description: New York : Routledge, [2021] | Includes bibliographical
    references.
Identifiers: LCCN 2020014146 (print) | LCCN 2020014147 (ebook) | ISBN
    9781138487284 (hardback) | ISBN 9781138487307 (paperback) | ISBN
    9781351043441 (ebook)
Subjects: LCSH: Jews—Languages—History.
Classification: LCC PJ5061 .R83 2021 (print) | LCC PJ5061 (ebook) | DDC
    809/.933529924—dc23
LC record available at https://lccn.loc.gov/2020014146
LC ebook record available at https://lccn.loc.gov/2020014147

ISBN: 978-1-138-48728-4 (hbk)
ISBN: 978-1-138-48730-7 (pbk)
ISBN: 978-1-351-04344-1 (ebk)

Typeset in Times New Roman
by Apex CoVantage, LLC

Contents

Acknowledgements   viii
Introduction   ix

 1 Amharic   1

 2 Arabic, Medieval   4

 3 Arabic, Modern   10

 4 Aramaic, Ancient and Medieval   13

 5 Aramaic, Modern   18

 6 Armenian   21

 7 Catalan   25

 8 Chinese   29

 9 English   33

10 Esperanto   40

11 French   43

12 Georgian   48

13 German   52

14 Greek   59

15 Hebrew, Inscriptional   64

16 Hebrew, Biblical   68

17 Hebrew, Rabbinic and Medieval   75

18 Hebrew, Enlightenment   82

19 Hebrew, Modern   89

20 Hungarian   93

21 Israeli Sign Language   99

22 Italian   102

23 Karaim (and Krymchak)   110

24 Ladino (and Spanish)   117

25 Latin   125

26 Malay   131

27 Malayalam   135

28 Maltese   139

29 Papiamentu (and other creoles)   143

30 Persian   148

31 Polish (and Czech)   153

32 Portuguese   160

33 Provençal   164

34 Russian   169

35 Tajik (Bukhari)   173

36 Tat (Juhuri)   178

37 Turkish (and Uzbek)   183

38 Urdu (and Marathi)   189

39 Yiddish, Old and Early Modern   194

40 Yiddish, Modern Standard   202

41 Yiddish, Modern Hasidic   209

42 Zulu (Fanagalo)   214

    Bibliography   219

Acknowledgements

In our search for Jewish-language books and manuscripts, we have benefited greatly from the help of numerous librarians around the world. In particular, we would like to thank Jordan Finkin (Hebrew Union College), Rebecca Jefferson (University of Florida), and Ben Outhwaite (Cambridge University) for their generous assistance.

For answers to questions and other help with various issues, we are very grateful for the time and expertise of Sima Beeri, Zoë Belk, Dario Burgaretta, Riccardo Contini, Reuven Enoch, Steve Fassberg, Jami Fisher, Ophira Gamliel, François Guesnet, Nancy Hawker, Brad Sabin Hill, Geoffrey Khan, Agnes Korn, Julia Krivoruchko, Michael Legaspi, Deqi Liu, Magdalena Luszczynska, John McWhorter, Georgia Panteli, Claudia Rosenzweig, Kriszta Eszter Szendrői, Wheeler Thackston, Riitta-Liisa Valijärvi, Ben Whittle, and Sonya Yampolskaya.

Special thanks go to Gary Rendsburg for reading and giving invaluable comments on portions of the book.

Finally, we would like to express our deepest gratitude to James Holz and Kim Rubin for their endless support and encouragement, as well as for their many insightful suggestions for improvement. James also contributed the drawings of Proto-Sinaitic symbols that appear in Chapter 15.

Introduction

What is a Jewish language?

The first Jews, about whom we read in the Bible, spoke Hebrew. This was the language of ancient Israel, the language in which the Bible was written, and the language of the earliest rabbinic texts. Hebrew is thus the first and most important Jewish language, with a history spanning three millennia. But already in the biblical era, Jews migrated outside of the Land of Israel—either forcibly or by choice—and over a period of more than 2000 years have spread across the globe. In the course of their wanderings, Jews have almost always retained Hebrew as a language of scholarship and prayer, but in their everyday lives, they have adopted new languages that they have acquired along the way. In many cases, however, the languages of the Jews around the world were not exactly the same as those of their non-Jewish neighbours. And so we can say that Jews used specifically Jewish language varieties, and it is these that we can call Jewish languages. Broadly speaking, then, a Jewish language is any language used by Jews that has identifiable features distinguishing it from other related languages or dialects. Jewish languages have one or more of the following defining characteristics:

- The use of the Hebrew alphabet for writing
- The incorporation of Hebrew elements, especially vocabulary
- The incorporation of loanwords from other sources
- Distinctive features of pronunciation, grammar, and vocabulary.

Some languages, like Yiddish and Ladino, have all of the these features, and to a degree that makes them quite substantially different from their closest non-Jewish counterparts (German and Spanish, respectively). Others exhibit just one or two of the defining characteristics, and thus are far more similar to their non-Jewish counterparts. Medieval Judeo-French, for example, was likely to have been almost indistinguishable from the French spoken by Christians in the same period, except for the presence a small number of Hebrew words (connected to Jewish religious practices) and the fact that it was written with the Hebrew alphabet. Other Jewish languages vary considerably when it comes to just how distinctive they actually are.

Each of the chapters in this book will include some reference to one or more of the characteristic features of Jewish languages. But it is worthwhile to provide some general discussion of them here first.

The use of the Hebrew alphabet

Until the modern era, Hebrew was the primary written language of nearly all Jewish communities. Despite what language they might have been speaking at home—be it Greek, Arabic, Persian, French, or whatever—Hebrew was the language that most young Jewish children would have learned to read and write first. Hebrew is the language of the Bible and other classical texts, such as the Mishnah and Midrashim, the language of the famous commentaries of great medieval scholars like Rashi and Naḥmanides, and the language of nearly all the daily prayers. Hebrew was thus an enormous part of the life of any observant Jew, even one who may not have been particularly well educated. Given their intimate familiarity with the Hebrew alphabet, coupled with the fact that until the modern era Jews almost always remained somewhat outside the mainstream system of education—in places where there even was such a thing—it is not surprising that Jews very often used the Hebrew alphabet to write down whatever language they were speaking. Thus, we find Hebrew-letter texts in which the language is actually Arabic, Greek, French, Persian, or something else. All told, there are at least three dozen languages that have been written down at least once using Hebrew letters. The fact that a language was written in the Hebrew alphabet does not always mean that, when read aloud or spoken, it sounded any different from the non-Jewish variety of that language, but it does mean that on the page the language looked completely different and was recognizably Jewish.

For some languages, such as Malay, Urdu, and Zulu (Fanagalo), we have only just one or some very small number of texts written in Hebrew letters. For others, such as Yiddish, Ladino, or Judeo-Arabic, we have many thousands of texts, written over a period of hundreds of years. Nevertheless, all are examples of Jews using Hebrew letters to record their language.

In many cases, the Hebrew alphabet was modified to meet the needs of a particular language containing sounds that Hebrew historically did not have. For example, many Jewish languages have the sound corresponding to English *ch* (as in *church*), but Hebrew does not. Jewish languages have found different ways to represent this sound using the Hebrew alphabet, by repurposing existing letters, by combining letters, or by adding diacritical marks (accent marks). Yiddish represents the sound *ch* with the letters טש *t+sh* (e.g., טשײניק *chaynik* 'teapot'), while Judeo-Italian uses the letter צ *ts* with or without a diacritical mark (e.g., צינקווי or צ״ינקווי *cinque* 'five'), and Ladino uses the letter ג *g* with a diacritical mark (e.g., גיקו or ג״יקו *chiko* 'small'). Sometimes Hebrew letters have been used in very unexpected ways. For example, the letter ע ʿ (originally used for a guttural consonant that is generally not pronounced in Modern Hebrew) came to be used as the vowel *e* in Yiddish (e.g., ער *er* 'he'), while for some writers of Judeo-Turkish, the letter ה *h* was used for the same vowel. Most unusually, the same Judeo-Turkish writers used the Hebrew letter ך—which in Hebrew represents the sound *kh* and appears only at the ends of words—to represent the sound *h* in any position (e.g., Judeo-Turkish דהר *her* 'each').

Also, although most Jewish languages were written down, some were—and some still remain—purely spoken languages. Examples are Jewish Georgian, Jewish Malayalam, and Jewish Latin American Spanish. If these languages have ever been written down, they have used the native script rather than the Hebrew alphabet.

The incorporation of Hebrew elements

Another defining characteristic of Jewish languages is the incorporation of Hebrew vocabulary. When speaking about things pertaining to Jewish religious practices or Jewish culture, it is natural that these words should come from Hebrew. So words like *shabbat*, *shofar*, *mitzvah*, and *rabbi* are generally found in all Jewish languages. Typically, these borrowed Hebrew words were adapted to the local pronunciations. So we find, for example, Yiddish שבת *shabes*, Libyan Judeo-Arabic *shebbach*, and Judeo-Italian *sabad*, all of which mean 'Sabbath' and come from the Hebrew word שבת *shabbat*. However, besides these overtly Jewish words, Jewish languages also commonly contain various other kinds of vocabulary deriving from Hebrew, including all different parts of speech. We find nouns describing a wide variety of concepts (e.g., Judeo-Italian *hovod* 'debts', Yiddish גנב *ganev* 'thief', Judeo-Tat *shülḥon* 'table', Baghdadi Judeo-Arabic *sekkana* 'danger', modern Jewish Aramaic *gezel* 'robbery', and Ladino פרט *perat* 'detail'); as well as adjectives (e.g., Judeo-Italian *gadol* 'big', modern Jewish Aramaic *rasha* 'wicked', and Libyan Judeo-Arabic *'eshir* 'rich'); verbs (e.g., Judeo-Greek *daberizo* 'speak', Yiddish חתמענען *khasmenen* 'sign [a document]', Ladino דארשאר *darsar* 'preach', and Libyan Judeo-Arabic *bdeq* 'examine'); and particles (e.g., Yiddish אפשר *efsher* 'maybe', Moroccan Judeo-Arabic *'afillu* 'even', and Ladino ממש *mamash* 'really').

In addition to direct borrowings, we also find new creations based on Hebrew words, including nouns (e.g., Yiddish מאַרוויכער *marvikher* 'pickpocket', from the Hebrew verb להרוויח *le-harviaḥ* 'to earn'), adjectives (e.g., Yiddish חנעוודיק *kheynevdik* 'charming' and Ladino האנינו *hanino* 'graceful', both from the Hebrew noun חן *hen* 'grace'), and verbs (e.g., Judeo-Italian *ainare* 'to look at', from the Hebrew noun עין *'ayin* 'eye', and Israeli Russian хаморить *xamorit'* 'to work like a donkey', from the Hebrew noun חמור *ḥamor* 'donkey').

In some cases Hebrew words have taken on different meanings when they are used in Jewish languages. As you can see from the following examples, many such words have acquired euphemistic, ironic, or pejorative meanings:

Hebrew עולם *'olam* 'eternity; world' → Yiddish עולם *oylem* 'audience'
Hebrew רימונים *rimmonim* 'pomegranates' → Judeo-Greek *rimonim* 'breasts'
Hebrew מומר *mumar* 'apostate' → Algerian Judeo-Arabic *mumar* 'person with a tattoo'
Hebrew מקום *maqom* 'place' → Judeo-Italian *macom* 'toilet'

Hebrew חשיכה *ḥashekha* 'darkness' → Judeo-Greek *chashicha* 'church'
Hebrew פרחים *peraḥim* 'flowers' → Ladino פרחים *perahim* 'coins; money'
Hebrew חבר *ḥaver* 'friend' → Judeo-Italian *havèr* 'servant'
Hebrew תכשיט *ṭakhshit* 'jewel' → Yiddish תכשיט *takhshet* 'brat'
Hebrew הבטחה *havṭaḥa* 'promise' → Ladino הבטחה *aftaxá* 'hope'
Hebrew זקן *zaqen* 'old' → Jewish Georgian *zaqeni* 'bad'
Hebrew הרג *harag* 'kill' → Baghdadi Judeo-Arabic *haragh* 'beat'

The incorporation of loanwords from other sources

Another feature of many Jewish languages is the presence of words borrowed from languages other than Hebrew—languages that are not typically the source of borrowings for non-Jewish speakers of closely related languages and dialects. For example, Jewish English contains numerous loanwords from Yiddish (e.g., *zeyde* 'grandpa', *lox* 'smoked salmon', *shmate* 'rag', *ferklempt* 'choked up', and *nudnik* 'pest'), as do Jewish Latin American Spanish, Jewish Swedish, and several other modern Jewish language varieties. This is obviously due to the Yiddish-speaking roots of many members of these Jewish communities. Even though the great majority of the descendants of Yiddish-speaking immigrants have abandoned Yiddish in favour of the languages of their new home countries, Yiddish influence has persisted. Likewise, many Jewish speakers of Latin American Spanish have roots in Arabic-speaking countries, and so their Spanish is often peppered with borrowings from Judeo-Arabic.

Similar situations have arisen elsewhere in the course of Jewish history. For example, some of the Jews who were expelled from Spain in 1492 settled in Italy, where they largely assimilated and adopted the Italian language. However, the varieties of Spanish that had previously been spoken left their linguistic imprint on some varieties of Judeo-Italian. So in the Judeo-Italian dialect of Livorno, we find words like *nada* 'nothing' and *cabezza* 'head', which derive from Spanish. The Ladino word *negro* means 'bad, unfortunate' (in contrast with the Spanish word *negro*, which means 'black'), and this word was borrowed into many Judeo-Italian dialects as well.

In some cases, Jewish immigrants maintained the language of the land from which they had come, but then it was subsequently influenced by the language or languages of their new home. For example, Yiddish first emerged as one of many medieval German dialects in Central Europe, surrounded by other German dialects (see YIDDISH, OLD AND EARLY MODERN). But as its speakers moved into Eastern Europe and became largely cut off from German-speaking territories, Yiddish was influenced by Slavic languages (see YIDDISH, MODERN STANDARD), which only served to further distance it from German and its various dialects. Similarly, the Spanish spoken by Jews in medieval Spain was likely extremely similar to that of their Christian neighbours. But after the Jews were expelled from Spain in 1492, many brought the language with them to the Ottoman Empire (especially to the areas corresponding to modern Greece, Turkey, and the various Balkan states), where their language developed into what became known as Ladino. In those countries, Ladino borrowed many words from Greek and Turkish (see LADINO). As with Yiddish, these borrowings help make Ladino that much more distinct from Spanish.

Therefore, in addition to the borrowing of Hebrew words—which is rooted in the consistent use of Hebrew in Jewish communities throughout history—the unexpected influences from other languages serve to make the Jewish language varieties even more distinct from the speech of surrounding non-Jewish society. They also bear witness to the complex history of Jewish migration.

Distinctive features of pronunciation, grammar, and vocabulary

It is not just the use of Jewish elements—namely the Hebrew alphabet and borrowed Hebrew words, or the existence of words borrowed from other languages—that make Jewish languages distinct. Another defining characteristic of these languages is that they frequently have unique elements of pronunciation, grammar, and/or vocabulary. This can often be compared to how the many different regional dialects of English have their own distinguishing features. For example, English speakers from the American South pronounce many vowels differently than Northerners, and they often use the pronoun *y'all*; Brits and Australians say *it's got cold out*, while Americans say *it's gotten cold out*. As a generic term for a carbonated soft drink, an American from New York says *soda*, but a Midwesterner says *pop*, and a Southerner says *coke*. We find similar differences between Jewish languages and their closest non-Jewish counterparts.

A case in point is the Judeo-Arabic dialect of Baghdad. In that city, the once-numerous community of Jews spoke an Arabic dialect that was quite distinct from that of their Muslim neighbours. Some of the differences pertained to pronunciation. For example, the verb 'was' is pronounced *chan* by the majority Muslim population, but Jews pronounced this verb as *kan*. Other differences pertained to grammar. As an example, while a Muslim would say *da-yiktib* 'he is writing', a Jew would say *qa-yiktib* 'he is writing', with a different prefix (*da-* vs. *qa-*) used to indicate the present tense. (For differences in vocabulary, see further in ARABIC, MODERN.) Similarly, in the town of Sulaymaniya in northern Iraq, Jewish speakers of Aramaic (who lived there until the mid-20th century) pronounced the word for 'house' as *bela*, whereas their Christian Aramaic-speaking neighbours said *besa*. And the verb 'he is opening' was *paloxé* for Jewish speakers, but *bepatáxele* for Christians, illustrating just how different the structure of these Jewish and Christian dialects were.

Ladino contains a myriad of distinct grammatical forms and vocabulary items when compared with Spanish, a language to which it is closely related. Examples are Ladino סו *so* 'I am' vs. Spanish *soy*, Ladino ביירבו *biervo* 'word' vs. Spanish *palabra*, and Ladino פריטו *preto* 'black' vs. Spanish *negro*. As described earlier, the uniqueness of Ladino is a result of the fact that the Spanish language developed differently among the Jewish communities that were expelled from Spain in 1492 and resettled elsewhere in the Mediterranean, as compared with how the language developed within Spain. The same can be said for Yiddish compared to German. Both are Germanic languages that derived from medieval German dialects, but the independent development of Yiddish means that it has numerous features of pronunciation, grammar, and vocabulary—in addition to the Hebrew and Slavic elements discussed earlier—that make it quite distinct from German. (For examples, see YIDDISH, MODERN STANDARD.)

In sum, to say a language is a Jewish language does not just mean that the speaker merely uses words associated with Judaism or has a recognizable style of speaking. In many cases at least, Jewish languages have real structural differences when compared to their non-Jewish counterparts. Major differences in pronunciation, distinct ways of conjugating verbs, and other divergent grammatical features combine to make Jewish languages more than simply an "accent". Rather, each Jewish language is a unique linguistic system that does not precisely mirror any other language or dialect.

Why are Jewish languages important?

Jewish languages are not just curiosities, but rather they can add much to our understanding of Jewish life and history. Texts preserved in Jewish languages include great works of literature—from the eternal stories of the Hebrew Bible to the epic poems of medieval Judeo-Persian authors to the Yiddish novels of Nobel Prize-winning author Isaac Bashevis Singer. They preserve fascinating details of Jewish history, including the Jewish experience of major historical events like the Crusades and the Spanish Inquisition, as well as more obscure events that gained only local fame. For example, a Judeo-French poem commemorates a massacre that took place in Troyes in 1288 (see FRENCH); a Judeo-Greek poem celebrates the foiling of an anti-Jewish plot in Sicily in the late 1300s (see GREEK); and a Judeo-German document records the hardships faced by Jews during the Napoleonic Wars (see GERMAN).

Jewish languages also preserve details of Jewish communities and their members. For example, a Hebrew–Chinese manuscript documents the names of the members of the Jewish community of Kaifeng (China) over several generations (see CHINESE); Judeo-Arabic texts from Cairo describe dealings between the famous 12th-century scholar Moses Maimonides and his medical patients; a text in Papiamentu records a scandalous love affair within the Jewish community on the island of Curaçao (see PAPIAMENTU); and a 16th-century Yiddish letter found in Egypt preserves the complaints of a mother to her uncommunicative son (see YIDDISH, OLD AND EARLY MODERN).

Jewish languages are sometimes of great value to those who study the history of languages. For example, a number of Judeo-French glossaries contain obscure Old French words that help scholars better understand the history of French (see FRENCH); the earliest known texts in modern Persian were composed in the Hebrew script by Jewish writers (see PERSIAN); and Judeo-Greek texts provide evidence for the contemporary pronunciation of medieval and early modern Greek (see GREEK).

Sometimes texts in Jewish languages reveal surprising facts about Jewish life. For example, a Judeo-Provençal prayer-book from the 15th century contains a feminist blessing that is almost without parallel (see PROVENÇAL); a medieval

Hebrew version of the legend of King Arthur shows that Jews in the Middle Ages read some of the same popular stories as Christians; and Esperanto was so closely associated with Jews that it came under persecution by the Nazis (see ESPERANTO). Throughout this book, we have tried to showcase the full range of literary, linguistic, and historical treasures associated with Jewish languages.

The scope of this book

In this book we have taken a very liberal view as to what constitutes a Jewish language. Many of the chapters treat languages that are uncontroversially Jewish or have well-known Jewish varieties. Such are Hebrew, Aramaic, Yiddish, Ladino, Arabic, Persian, Tat, and several others. These languages have long and rich histories, and they exhibit many or all of the distinctive characteristics described earlier. Other languages have an obvious connection to Jewish literature and history, but their status as distinct language varieties is perhaps less secure. They may be known from only a small corpus of texts, or are known from only a short period of time. They also tend to show less of the distinctive features described earlier. Such is the case for the Jewish varieties of French, Portuguese, Catalan, Turkish, English, Georgian, and several others. The inclusion of a third group of languages appearing in this book may raise some eyebrows, because they have rarely, if ever, been discussed in the context of Jewish languages. Such are Armenian, Malay, Maltese, Zulu, and a couple of others. We have decided to include them because in each case there is an interesting Jewish connection to be explored, and in most cases there is at least one text written in the Hebrew alphabet. Every language included in this book, no matter how minor its distinguishing Jewish features or how tenuous its Jewish connection, tells us a story about the Jewish people and the many diverse places in which they have lived over the course of the last three millennia.

A handful of languages discussed in the book are not indicated in the chapter titles. These are Berber (discussed in ARABIC, MEDIEVAL), Bosnian (discussed in POLISH), Dutch (discussed in GERMAN), Gujarati (discussed in URDU), Lithuanian (discussed in LATIN), Saramaccan and Sranan (discussed in PAPIAMENTU), Swedish (discussed in GERMAN), and Syriac (discussed ARAMAIC, ANCIENT AND MEDIEVAL). All told, this book includes discussion of 48 languages with some Jewish connection; this number is even higher if we consider that some languages have historical varieties that are the subject of individual chapters (e.g., HEBREW, BIBLICAL and HEBREW, MODERN).

No prior knowledge of Hebrew or any other language is necessary in order to read this book, though we assume that you, the reader, have a general interest in languages. Each chapter in this book is designed to be independent, meaning that you can read the chapters in any order. We have added cross-references to other chapters where appropriate to facilitate this, and so that you can follow up on any particular points of interest. In some cases, especially where smaller or less widely known language varieties are concerned, we have aimed to be quite comprehensive in our discussion. For languages with a more extensive history (e.g., Hebrew, Arabic, Yiddish, and Ladino), we have aimed to provide a broad overview, rather than an exhaustive treatment, with a special focus on elements that we find particularly interesting or important. Every chapter includes a section at the end with suggestions for further study and reading, so that interested readers can investigate topics in greater depth.

In all chapters we have provided language samples, as well as book titles and other relevant information, in their original scripts (usually Hebrew but sometimes also others such as Arabic, Greek, Russian, etc.), but always along with a transliteration in English letters. The transliteration system used in this book is intentionally not technical, with the aim of making it user-friendly to all readers. Most chapters are accompanied by one or more images showcasing the rich variety of Jewish-language texts and other written materials discussed in the book. These range from ancient stone inscriptions to medieval illuminated manuscripts to modern books, newspapers, and websites.

References and further study

Kahn and Rubin (2017) and Benor and Hary (2018) are both comprehensive reference works on Jewish languages. Tirosh-Becker and Edzard (2021) is another important reference work. Myhill (2004) and Spolsky (2014) both provide historical and sociolinguistic discussions of Jewish languages. On the adaptation of Hebrew scripts for Jewish languages, see Daniels (2018). There are currently two websites devoted to Jewish languages, the Jewish Language Research Website (www.jewish-languages.org) and לשון הבית *Leshon ha-Bayit* (www.lashon.org/en). There have been three academic journals dedicated to the study of Jewish languages: *Jewish Language Review* (1981–87), *Massorot* (1984–present), and *Journal of Jewish Languages* (2013–present). Important collections of digitized manuscripts in Hebrew and other Jewish languages can be found on the following websites:

- *The National Library of Israel*
  web.nli.org.il/sites/nlis/en/manuscript

- *The British Library*
  www.bl.uk/manuscripts

- *Polonsky Foundation Digitization Project*
  (Oxford Bodleian Library and Vatican Library)
  bav.bodleian.ox.ac.uk/hebrew-manuscripts

- *Hebrew Union College*
  mss.huc.edu

- *The Friedberg Jewish Manuscript Society*
  www.genizah.org

1 Amharic

Jews have lived in Ethiopia for many centuries, though for exactly how long is the subject of much debate. The Ethiopian Jews themselves have varying accounts of their origins. According to one legend, they are the descendants of the biblical Tribe of Dan, while according to another, their ancestry can be traced to Menelik, the first emperor of Ethiopia, who is said to have been the son of the biblical King Solomon (who reigned from 970 to 931 BCE) and the Queen of Sheba. Scholarly views also vary quite significantly. Some scholars believe that the community has its origin in groups of Jews who were exiled from Judah with the destruction of the First Temple in Jerusalem by the Babylonians in 586 BCE. Others believe that the community is much younger, dating only as far back the 14th to 16th centuries CE. There have also been further proposals for origins between these two extremes.

Ethiopian Jews have traditionally lived mainly in northern and northwestern Ethiopia, in the Gondar and Tigrai regions, in villages that were inhabited mostly by Christians. They call themselves *Beta Israel*, meaning 'House of Israel'. In the past, they have been referred to by outsiders as *Falasha*, a term which they themselves consider highly derogatory. Almost all Ethiopian Jews have immigrated to Israel—most immigration took place in the 1980s, 1990s, and early 2000s—and there are now relatively few left in Ethiopia.

Ethiopian Jews long practised a unique form of Judaism based predominantly around the Bible; they did not have knowledge of the Mishnah, Talmud, or other rabbinic texts. And in contrast to most other Jewish communities, the Ethiopian Jews had completely lost knowledge of Hebrew. Like Ethiopian Christians, they read the Bible in Geʿez, a Semitic language distantly related to Hebrew that was used for almost two thousand years as the primary written language of Ethiopia. Ethiopian Jews also possess their own religious literature written in Geʿez, such as ሞተ ሙሴ *Mota Muse* ('The Death of Moses') and ሞተ አሮን *Mota Aron* ('The Death of Aaron'), which expand on the biblical stories about Moses and Aaron. This type of text, usually called *midrash*, is common in the Jewish world, but the particular stories contained in the *Mota Muse*, *Mota Aron*, and others, are unknown outside the Ethiopian Jewish community. Today, Ethiopian Jews in Israel have adopted normative Rabbinic Judaism.

As for spoken languages, most Ethiopian Jews used either Amharic, Tigrinya, or Qwara. Amharic, the national language of Ethiopia, and Tigrinya, the national language of Eritrea, are both Semitic languages closely related to Geʿez and are thus also related to Hebrew. By contrast, Qwara is a member of the Cushitic family, of which Somali is the most well-known member. The Amharic spoken by the Ethiopian Jews in Ethiopia was essentially identical to that of their non-Jewish neighbours, but occasionally there were slight differences in certain words and idioms. Jews were especially keen to avoid Christian references, so, for example, while the standard Amharic term for a certain type of grasshopper is የማርያም ፈረስ *ya-maryam faras* 'Mary's horse', Jews preferred the term የሙሴ ፈረስ *ya-muse faras* 'Moses' horse'.

There are currently around 135,000 Ethiopian Jews in Israel, at least a third of whom were born in the country. Those who were born in Ethiopia brought with them their various written and spoken languages, though Amharic is by far the most predominant among them (even the 8% or so who speak Tigrinya also usually know Amharic), and most have learned Hebrew. Those who were born in Israel speak Hebrew natively, and many of them have little to no knowledge of Amharic. In contrast to recent Russian immigrants, who are often very proud of their language and make a concerted effort to pass it down to their children (see RUSSIAN), many Ethiopian immigrants have not encouraged their children to learn Amharic, because they sometimes hold it in low esteem. In addition, Ethiopian Jews in Israel have suffered from widespread racial discrimination, and this has contributed to added pressure to assimilate into mainstream Israeli society by speaking Hebrew. However, because there were so many immigrants who arrived in Israel as children or young adults, there are still a large number of Amharic–Hebrew bilingual speakers, and the Amharic of these speakers has developed into a distinct Israeli variety. This is somewhat comparable to the distinctive variety of Russian that has developed in Israel since the 1990s (see RUSSIAN).

Not surprisingly, much of the Hebrew influence on Amharic in Israel consists of borrowed words. Many of these are terms that refer specifically to aspects of life in Israel and lack Amharic equivalents, but there are also Hebrew words that do have Amharic counterparts which have simply been replaced. The borrowed words have been incorporated into Amharic grammatical structure (e.g., appearing with Amharic plural endings). Occasionally, as a form of wordplay, Israeli Amharic speakers replace Israeli place names or words borrowed from Hebrew with Amharic words that sound similar but have quite a different meaning. For example, Amharic speakers sometimes replace the Hebrew word עובדת סוציאלית *ʿovedet sotsyalit* 'social worker' with the similar-sounding, and cutting, Amharic phrase ወፌ ጥልጥዋሊት *wofe t'olt'walit* 'my meddlesome bird'.

There is relatively little Amharic-language content produced in Israel for the Ethiopian community. Israeli radio broadcasts in Amharic for two hours a day, and there is a dedicated Ethiopian-language TV channel, but most of the programmes are taken from Ethiopia rather than produced locally in Israel. Until recently, there was a monthly Amharic-language newspaper called ידיעות נגט *Yediʿot Negat* (literally 'news of the dawn', from Hebrew ידיעות *yediʿot* 'news' and Amharic ንጋት *negat* 'dawn'), but it has closed down and there is currently no Amharic press in Israel. There is a burgeoning Ethiopian-Israeli literature, but it is almost exclusively written in Hebrew, even when the authors were born in Ethiopia rather than Israel. Some Ethiopian literature has also been translated into Hebrew for the benefit of Israeli-born members of the community. It remains to be seen what the future holds for the Amharic language in the State of Israel.

References and further study

For more on the history of the Jews in Ethiopia, see Kaplan (1992) and Quirin (1992). On the unique religious writings of the *Beta Israel*, along with some interesting cultural notes, see Leslau (1963). See Anbessa Teferra (2017, 2018) for overviews of Jewish Amharic in Israel. Mendelson-Maoz (2015) is an overview of Ethiopian-Israeli literature (which, as mentioned earlier, is generally written in Hebrew).

2 Arabic, Medieval

In the wake of the Islamic conquests of the 7th and 8th centuries CE, much of the population of the Middle East and North Africa adopted the Arabic language. There were even Arabic-speaking communities in parts of Europe, most notably in Spain, Sicily, and Malta (see MALTESE). Arabic became the vehicle of a thriving scholarly culture, and was used in the composition of huge body of literature encompassing many diverse genres. Like their non-Jewish neighbours, most of the Jews living in these areas adopted Arabic, largely abandoning the languages that they had previously been speaking, such as Aramaic in Iraq and Syria, Greek and Berber in North Africa, and Romance languages in Spain and Portugal. (In fact, some Jews did keep speaking these earlier languages; see ARAMAIC, GREEK, and LADINO. North African Jews, especially those living in the Atlas Mountains region of Morocco, kept on speaking Berber into the modern period.)

When writing Arabic, Jews did not generally employ the Arabic script, but rather used the Hebrew alphabet. This written language, which we call Judeo-Arabic, was in use for at least 1200 years, and probably even longer. During that time, Jews living in the Arabic-speaking world from Spain to Iraq composed a vast array of texts in Judeo-Arabic, including works on biblical interpretation, philosophy, law, medicine, history, astronomy, mathematics, grammar, and more. Jews made translations of the Bible, Mishnah, and other important Hebrew and Aramaic texts into Judeo-Arabic, and they also used the language for more mundane purposes relating to everyday life.

Tens of thousands of Judeo-Arabic texts have survived, some from as early as the 8th and 9th centuries CE. A substantial portion of the surviving texts were found in the so-called Cairo Genizah. A genizah is essentially a storeroom intended for the disposal of sacred Jewish texts. For example, Jews would either place a worn-out copy of the Torah in a genizah or ceremonially bury it, since it is against Jewish practice to simply throw away a text containing the name of God. One such genizah, in the Ben Ezra Synagogue of Cairo, turned into a depository for any discarded Jewish text—and even some non-Jewish texts—whether sacred or not. It is unclear why this genizah came to be used so frequently, but it is very fortunate that it did. Over the course of roughly a thousand years, a vast number of books and manuscripts were placed in the Cairo Genizah, where they remained until they were recovered by scholars in the late 19th century. Nearly 300,000 texts were removed and brought to Europe, the United States, and Israel. About two-thirds of the texts are now owned by the University of Cambridge—which has by far the largest collection in the world—while the rest are scattered among numerous other libraries and private collections. Most pages from the Genizah have now been digitized and can be found free online.

Many of the texts from the Cairo Genizah are, of course, in Hebrew, but a significant number are in other languages (see also ARMENIAN and YIDDISH, OLD AND EARLY MODERN). Of these non-Hebrew texts, the majority are in Judeo-Arabic, including many that tell us about the daily life of medieval Jews living in Cairo. We find things like personal letters, marriage and divorce contracts, business documents, and records of disputes between members of the community, all of which have dramatically enhanced our understanding of Jewish history in the Middle Ages. The content of the personal documents is by no means limited to events that took place in Cairo, but rather they include information about the wider Jewish world. For example, the Genizah tells us about Jewish suffering in the Holy Land during the Crusades, about maritime travel, and about business transactions in India.

One of the most famous Jewish residents of medieval Cairo was Moses Maimonides (1135–1204). Born in Spain, Maimonides settled in Egypt in his thirties, where he practised medicine and served as head of the Jewish community in Cairo. He wrote an impressive range of texts, both in Hebrew and Judeo-Arabic. His Judeo-Arabic works include his well-known *Guide for the Perplexed*, a commentary on the Mishnah, and a number of other religious, philosophical, and medical treatises. The Cairo Genizah not only preserves copies of many of his works but also in some cases his original, handwritten drafts! Some of his drafts even include the corrections he made as he wrote, enabling us to better understand the development of his work. The Genizah also contains some of his private letters, which allow us a window into his personal life that is rare to have for a medieval author or historical figure.

We also find in the Genizah some of Maimonides' responses to questions that were posed to him by fellow Jews, including both medical questions and legal-moral ones. Some of these describe situations that sound surprisingly modern. For example, in one letter, a concerned gentleman explains to Maimonides that an aged widow has accused a respected teacher of jokingly expressing a desire to sleep with her. There were no witnesses to the alleged incident, and the teacher had never before been accused of any such misconduct. The author of the letter believes that the woman's accusation is a deliberate attempt to damage the teacher's reputation and livelihood. He asks Maimonides if the woman's report should be considered credible, and if he should place a public ban on anyone repeating these allegations. Maimonides' reply, written on the same piece of paper as the letter that he received, is as follows:

כלאמהא גיר מקבול . . . ואלצואב פי הדّא אלנחו קטע אלכלאם ואן לא יוקע חרם ולא כלאם ברבים וכתב משה.

kalāmuhā ġayr maqbūl . . . w-al-ṣawāb fī hāðā l-naḥw qaṭ ʿ al-kalām wa-ʾan lā yūqa ʿ ḥerem wa-lā kalām ba-rabbīm. wa-katab mōše.

'Her testimony is not acceptable. . . . The proper way to proceed in this case is to silence the gossiping, but not to pronounce a ban and not to have any further discussion in public. Moses [Maimonides] wrote [this].'

There are a myriad of other documents in the Genizah that recount incidents to which the modern reader can easily relate, including cases of bullying, marriage disputes, arguments over money, loss of family members, and even complaining mothers (see YIDDISH, OLD AND EARLY MODERN). In one of the Judeo-Arabic documents recording a marriage dispute, a woman threatens her husband with a daytime hunger strike if he does not return home. The husband, who had been living with (and paying rent to) his wife's family, had moved out, returning only on Saturdays for brief conjugal visits. In his response to the wife's letter (likewise written in Judeo-Arabic), he wrote:

קד אקסמת אן לם תפטרי לא נזלת יום אלסבת פי אלדאר לא פיה ולא יום גיר יום אלסבת

qad ʾaqsamt ʾin lam tufṭirī lā nazalt yawm al-sabt fi l-dār, lā fīhā wa-lā yawm ġayr yawm al-sabt

'I swear, if you don't break your fast, I won't come to the house on Saturday or on any other day!'

Written Judeo-Arabic is not a uniform language, and we find a great deal of variation over the course of its 1200-year history. In some cases, the grammar and vocabulary of Judeo-Arabic were quite close to the written Muslim Arabic of the time, and the primary distinguishing feature of the Jewish variety was the use of the Hebrew alphabet. In other cases, however, especially with the non-literary texts (like personal letters), the language betrayed colloquial features and other grammatical peculiarities. These colloquialisms are important, since they give us an insight as to how these Jews were actually speaking Arabic. Oftentimes these colloquial features match what we know about spoken Judeo-Arabic dialects from the 20th century (see ARABIC, MODERN), and so these written texts provide a linguistic link between the medieval and modern Jewish communities of the Arab world.

In the modern period, Jews developed a culture of publishing in Judeo-Arabic, and a large number of printed books appeared in the 19th and 20th centuries, most notably translations of the Bible and other religious texts. Judeo-Arabic books were published not only in cities from the Arab world, but also in India and in European cities like Livorno and Vienna. Beginning in the late 19th century, Judeo-Arabic newspapers were printed in several Jewish communities around the Arabic-speaking world. At the same time, with the modernization of education in these countries, Jews shifted more and more to writing Arabic in the Arabic script, gradually abandoning their traditional use of the Hebrew alphabet.

With the emigration of almost all the Jews from Arabic-speaking countries following the establishment of the State of Israel in 1948 and the adoption by these immigrants of new languages, production of Judeo-Arabic texts quickly ceased, though reprints of some popular texts, like translations of the Passover Haggadah,

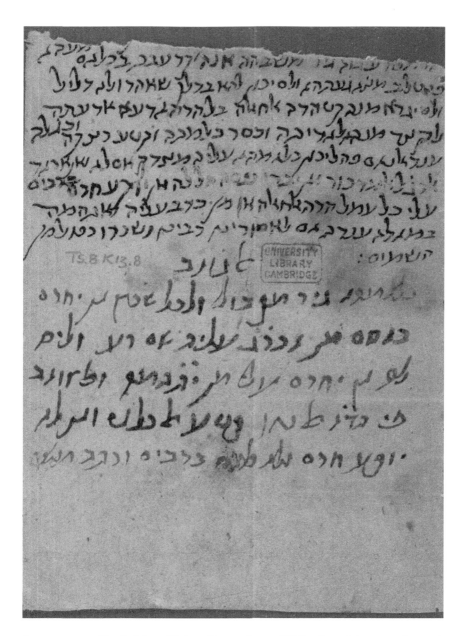

A responsum written by Moses Maimonides on the credibility of a certain woman's report. Cambridge University Library, T-S 8K13.8, fol. 1r. COURTESY OF THE SYNDICS OF CAMBRIDGE UNIVERSITY LIBRARY.

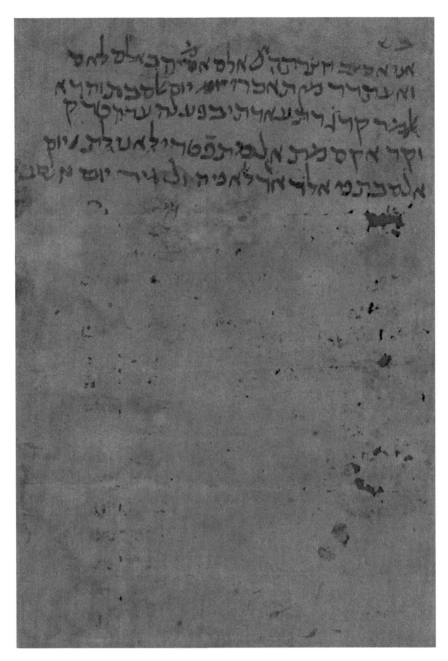

A Judeo-Arabic letter from an angry wife to her husband. Cambridge University Library, L-G Ar.2.51, fol. 1v. Courtesy of the Syndics of Cambridge University Library.

continued for several decades. Judeo-Arabic now lives on only in the spoken dialects, but even those are in danger of dying out in the near future.

References and further study

Khan (2017) provides a historical overview of Judeo-Arabic from all periods. On the Jewish variety of Berber, see Chetrit (2017, 2018). Hoffman and Cole (2011) and Glickman (2011) tell the history of the Cairo Genizah and its many treasures. The text by Maimonides cited in this chapter is in a manuscript held by the Cambridge University Library (T-S 8K13.8), and was published by Friedlaender (1908). The exchange between the unhappy husband and wife is also in Cambridge (L-G Ar.II.51), and was published by Zinger (2009). Both manuscripts are digitized and available, along with most other Genizah manuscripts, at www.genizah.org. Several Judeo-Arabic newspapers can be found on the Historical Jewish Press website:
https://web.nli.org.il/sites/JPress/English

3   Arabic, Modern

Arabic is currently the native language of over 300 million people across the Middle East and North Africa. However, there is not just one kind of Arabic, since the spoken language differs greatly across this vast region. For example, the Arabic spoken by a Moroccan is very different from that of an Egyptian, which is in turn very different from that of an Iraqi. In fact, spoken Arabic varies so greatly from place to place that Arabic speakers from those countries are often unable to understand one another. However, all educated Arabs share a common written language. What scholars call Modern Standard Arabic, the language of books and the media, is what Arabs learn to write and speak in school, and it differs quite substantially from the many spoken vernaculars. As a result, there is an interesting linguistic situation in the Arabic world: there is one standard written language, used also in formal spoken contexts (like news broadcasts, academic lectures, and political speeches), but dozens of mutually unintelligible colloquial varieties used for everyday speech. The situation is not unlike parts of Europe in the Middle Ages, when speakers of French, Italian, Spanish, and Portuguese all usually used Latin for academic writing.

Until the 1950s, there were large Jewish communities throughout the Arab world, in Iraq, Yemen, Syria, Lebanon, Egypt, Libya, Algeria, Tunisia, and Morocco. Like their non-Jewish neighbours, Jews from different regions spoke local dialects of Arabic, which varied significantly from place to place. This fact alone is not surprising. What is striking, however, is that the Jewish dialects of Arabic often differed from the non-Jewish dialects spoken in the same locales. So, for example, the Jews who lived in Tunis spoke an Arabic dialect distinct from that of their Muslim neighbours, though the differences were small enough that the two communities could still easily communicate with one another. The same can be said of the Jewish communities of Tripoli (Libya), Algiers, and many other places. In Baghdad, the situation was especially remarkable, in that the dialects of Jewish speakers, Muslim speakers, and Christian speakers were all distinctive. That is, there were three dialects of Arabic spoken in one city, and the dialect that a person spoke depended on his or her religion!

Some of the differences between the Jewish and non-Jewish varieties within a single location have to do with pronunciation. For example, in many parts of Morocco, Jews pronounced the consonant *k* as *t*. So the word for 'dog' among many Moroccan Jewish Arabic speakers is *telb*, while their Muslim neighbours would say *kelb*. In Baghdad, it is the Muslims who had a different pronunciation of *k*. Where Jews (and Christians) pronounced *k*, a Muslim would often have *ch* (as in the English word *child*), and so for 'dog' Jews would say *kalb* 'dog', Christians would say *kaleb*, and Muslims would say *chaleb*. As another example, the Jews of Tripoli (Libya) do not pronounce the sound *h*, whereas their Muslim counterparts do; thus, a Jew in Tripoli would say *āda* for 'this', while a Muslim would say *hāda*.

Such differences between Jewish and non-Jewish varieties of Arabic are not limited to simple matters of pronunciation, but rather can go deeper into the structure of the language. For example, the basic pronouns can have different forms. A Muslim speaker of Arabic in Algiers uses the form *enta* 'you' when addressing a man but *enti* 'you' when addressing a woman. By contrast, a Jewish speaker makes no such distinction but instead uses *enti* for both genders. A Muslim speaker of Arabic in Baghdad would say *āni* and *ehna* for 'I' and 'we', whereas Jews and Christians would say *ana* and *nehna*. A Jew in Baghdad would say *llenu* for 'to him', but a Muslim would say *ela*, and a Christian would say *elu*. Verbs can also be conjugated differently. For example, a Jew in Baghdad would say *ktabtu* for 'I wrote', while a Muslim would say *ktabet* or *ketabet*, and a Christian would say *katabtu*. A Baghdadi Jew would say *kel* for the command 'eat!' (as would a Christian), but a Muslim would say *ukul*.

The vocabulary used by Jewish Arabic speakers can also differ from that of their neighbours. Once again, the situation is Baghdad is especially interesting because of the fact that there is a local Christian dialect as well. Compare the following short list of lexical differences between the three different religious communities of Baghdad:

Jewish	Muslim	Christian	English
dūni	*mūzēn*	*mū malēh*	'bad'
ḍaww	*nār*	*nāgh*	'fire'
zōj	*rajel*	*zōj*	'husband'
enf	*khāshem*	*khashem*	'nose'
lbōhi	*lbārha*	*mbēha*	'yesterday'
ashkun	*shenu*	*shenu*	'what'
wnīki	*hnāka*	*hōnīki*	'there'

As can be seen from this sample list, sometimes the Jewish and Christian dialects have a word in common (like the word for 'husband'), while other times the Christian and Muslim ones do (like the words for 'nose' and 'what'), and still other times all three dialects have a unique word.

The differences between Jewish and Muslim Arabic dialects within the same city are roughly comparable to what we find in many American cities, in which black and white communities frequently speak recognizably different varieties of English, even though the two varieties are mutually intelligible. There are certain features of pronunciation that are distinctive to Black English (also sometimes called by linguists African American Vernacular English), just as there are distinctive features of grammar and vocabulary. Just by hearing someone speak, Americans can often successfully identify whether the speaker is black or white. Likewise, in cities throughout the Arabic-speaking world, Jews could be identified by their speech patterns alone.

As with other Jewish languages, Jewish dialects of Arabic incorporate vocabulary from Hebrew. Many of these, of course, are words that have to do with Jewish cultural or religious practices. So, for example, in the Jewish Arabic dialect of Algiers, we find words like *kasher* 'kosher' (from Hebrew כשר *kasher*), *metsva* 'good deed' (from Hebrew מצווה *mitsva* 'commandment'), and *resshāna* 'Rosh HaShanah' (from Hebrew ראש השנה *rosh ha-shana*). But we also find words borrowed from Hebrew that do not pertain to religion, like *kaʿas* 'anger' (from Hebrew כעס *kaʿas*), *ḥukhma* 'wisdom' (from Hebrew חכמה *ḥokhma*), and *afellu* 'even' (from Hebrew אפילו *ʾafillu*).

Muslim Arabic speakers rarely write their local spoken dialects. Instead, as noted earlier, they use Modern Standard Arabic. Jewish Arabic speakers very often wrote Arabic as well, but since they normally did so using Hebrew letters, they were less bound by the norms of standard written Arabic. Sometimes they did write standard Arabic, or something close to it, but often their writings reflect at least some of the characteristics of their spoken vernaculars (see ARABIC, MEDIEVAL).

Jewish Arabic dialects, some of which had been in use for over a thousand years, continued to flourish well into the 20th century. Following the establishment of the State of Israel in 1948, the vast majority of Arabic-speaking Jews emigrated (voluntarily or forcibly) from their respective homelands, and settled either in Israel or in other western countries. As a result, these many Jewish dialects of Arabic have already been or will soon be lost, because they are not being passed down to younger generations. Luckily, many of the dialects have been recorded and described by scholars, preserving our knowledge of this fascinating linguistic heritage.

References and further study

Khan (2017) provides a historical overview of Judeo-Arabic, including the modern period, and gives references for many studies of individual Jewish Arabic dialects. Descriptions of specific Judeo-Arabic dialects include M. Cohen (1912) on the dialect of Algiers, D. Cohen (1964–75) on the dialect of Tunis, Yoda (2005) on the dialect of Tripoli (Libya), and Bar-Moshe (2019) on the dialect of Baghdad. Blanc (1964) is a comparison of the Arabic spoken by Jews, Christians, and Muslims in Baghdad, while Heath (2002) is a comparison of Jewish and Muslim dialects in Morocco.

4 Aramaic, Ancient and Medieval

Although Hebrew is the language most typically associated with Judaism, Aramaic has been spoken and used by Jews for nearly as long. Aramaic is a Semitic language closely related to Hebrew; the two languages are about as similar to each other as Spanish is to Portuguese or as German is to Dutch. The close resemblance between Hebrew and Aramaic is illustrated in the following few examples.

Hebrew	Aramaic	English
גבר *gever*	גבר *gevar*	'man'
יום *yom*	יום *yom*	'day'
טוב *tov*	טב *tav*	'good'
כתב *katav*	כתב *ketav*	'he wrote'
כתבנו *katavnu*	כתבנא *ketavna*	'we wrote'

Like Hebrew, Aramaic is first attested in inscriptions on stone from around the 10th century BCE (see HEBREW, INSCRIPTIONAL). It was originally spoken in the region of Aram, which corresponds roughly to present-day Syria, but by the middle of the first millennium BCE it had become widely used across the entire Near East as the main language of politics and commerce. The importance and prestige of Aramaic became even greater when the successive empires of the Assyrians, Babylonians, and Persians, each of whom controlled almost the entire Near East region (including much or all of the region that is now Israel), adopted it as their language of administration. In the Persian Empire, which lasted from about 550 BCE until it was conquered in 330 BCE by Alexander the Great, Aramaic was actually the primary language of administration, despite the fact that the Persians themselves spoke a totally unrelated language.

Already in biblical times, when the Assyrian Empire was at its height, Aramaic was being used by some Israelites alongside Hebrew. In a story from the book of 2 Kings (18:26), which takes place around 700 BCE, some Judean noblemen are speaking to an invading Assyrian general, and they say to him, דַּבֶּר־נָא אֶל־עֲבָדֶיךָ אֲרָמִית כִּי שֹׁמְעִים אֲנָחְנוּ *dabber-na 'el-'avadekha 'aramit ki shom'im 'anaḥnu* 'Please speak Aramaic to your servants, for we understand it.' The Israelites staved off the Assyrians on that occasion, but a century later they were not so lucky: in 587/586 BCE the Babylonians conquered Jerusalem, destroyed the Great Temple, and deported much of the population of Judah to Babylon. After the period of the Babylonian Exile (586–537 BCE), during which time a significant portion of Judeans were living in an Aramaic-speaking environment, the use of Aramaic became much more widespread. Books of the Bible composed after this period show influence from Aramaic, and two biblical books, Ezra and Daniel, are even written partly in Aramaic. Interestingly, the alphabet that we today know as Hebrew was actually borrowed from Aramaic during this period. Before the Babylonian Exile, the forms of the Hebrew letters looked very different. For example, the name ישראל *yisra'el* 'Israel' was written ㄴＫ⊀⫟Ｗ⊣ in the original Hebrew script, which is today called 'Paleo-Hebrew' script (see HEBREW, INSCRIPTIONAL).

Use of Aramaic among Jews continued to increase in the post-biblical period, eventually replacing Hebrew altogether as the main spoken language of Roman Judea. It is believed that Jesus spoke Aramaic, and that portions of the Gospels were originally composed in Aramaic and then translated into Greek. Even in the Greek Gospels there are some Aramaic words from the mouth of Jesus. For example, in Mark 5:41, when Jesus raises a little girl from the dead, he says *talitha kum*, which is Aramaic for 'get up, little girl!'. Later, in Mark 15:34, when he is on the cross, Jesus cries out in Aramaic *Eloi Eloi, lema sabachthani*, which means 'my God, my God, why have You forsaken me?'.

Some of the most important texts of post-biblical Judaism are written in Aramaic, including much of the Talmud. Because many Jews in the early post-biblical period were no longer familiar enough with Hebrew to understand the Bible in the original, they began to translate it into Aramaic. These translations are known as Targumim. Some of the Targumim gained official status among Jews and were read alongside the Hebrew original in the synagogue; there are numerous references to the Targumim in the Talmud and other rabbinic works. The Babylonian Talmud (*Berakhot* 8a) even instructs that when reading the weekly Torah portion in synagogue, one should read it twice in Hebrew and once in the Aramaic Targum.

Some of the Targumim are very literal translations of the Hebrew Bible, while others are much looser and contain additional material. Sometimes this additional material expands on a story, providing details that are not present in the original. This can make the Targumim interesting texts in their own right. For example, the Targum known as Pseudo-Jonathan, whose exact date of composition is unknown (opinions range from the 3rd to 9th centuries CE, though the earliest physical copy that we have is from the 16th century), is especially rich in this type of expansive material. Sometimes the additions simply give a little more detail without adding much to the story. For example, in Genesis 1:2, where the Hebrew Bible says that the earth was "unformed and void" (תֹהוּ וָבֹהוּ *tohu wa-vohu*), Targum Pseudo-Jonathan says that the earth was "unformed and void, deserted of people, and empty of all animals". In many places though, the additions provide information unknown from the biblical text itself. For example, in Genesis 31:19, when Jacob is about to run away from his father-in-law with his wives Leah and Rachel, we read in the Hebrew original that "Rachel stole her father's idols"; no additional information about these idols is provided. Targum Pseudo-Jonathan, however, tells us much more about them. The corresponding passage in that Targum—the exact vocalization of which is uncertain—reads as follows:

וגנבת רחל ית צלמנייא דהוון נכסין גברא בוכרא וחזמין רישיה ומלחין ליה במילחא ובוסמנין וכתבין קוסמין בציצא דדהבא ויהבין תחות לישניה ומקימין ליה בכותלא וממלל עמהון ואילין הינון דהוה גחין להון אבוהא

we-genavat raḥel yat tsalmanayya de-hewon nakhsin gavra bukhra we-ḥazmin resheh we-malḥin leh be-milḥa we-busmin we-katvin qusmin be-tsitsa de-dahba we-yahvin teḥot lishaneh we-meqimin leh be-kutla we-memallel ʾimmehon we-ʾillen hennon de-hewa geḥen lehon ʾevuha

'Rachel stole the idols. They used to kill a first-born man, cut off his head, and sprinkle it with salt and spices. They would write incantations on a plate of gold, and put it under his tongue. They would put it (the head) up on a wall, and it would speak with them. And these were what her father (Laban) would bow down to.'

Because of all of this additional material, the Aramaic Targum Pseudo-Jonathan is much more than just a translation of the Bible. It tells us how some Jews in the first millennium CE were interpreting and explaining the Bible.

Aramaic remained in widespread use among Jews (and Christians) throughout the Near East for most of the first millennium CE, but after Islam began to spread across the Near East in the 7th century, Arabic gradually began to supplant Aramaic as the primary language of Jewish (and Christian) communities in the region (see ARABIC, MEDIEVAL). Likewise, Jews who migrated to Europe adopted the local languages. However, Aramaic remained an important language of study for Jews in both the Near East and Europe, and Jews have continued to study the Talmud and Targumim in the original Aramaic up to the present day. Moreover, although Hebrew was the primary written language among Jews in the medieval period, Aramaic was still sometimes used in the composition of new texts, especially certain kinds of very scholarly works. By the medieval period the language had become particularly associated with the Jewish mystical tradition known as Kabbalah. The most famous medieval Aramaic work is the Zohar, the central text of Kabbalah, which is thought to have been composed in 13th-century Spain.

Aramaic also remained important in some Middle Eastern Christian communities; the dialect of Aramaic known as Syriac remains the liturgical language of a variety of Christian denominations, including the Syrian Orthodox and Chaldean Catholic Churches. There is an enormous corpus of Syriac Christian literature, and it is likely that some medieval Jews living in various Near Eastern communities were familiar with Syriac writings. There is even a document from the Cairo Genizah (see ARABIC, MEDIEVAL) that appears to be Judeo-Syriac, i.e., Syriac written in Hebrew script. Another Judeo-Syriac text, a carefully copied version of the book of I Maccabees—a book only found in Christian Bibles, though it deals with the story of Hanukkah—was produced some time in the 19th century.

Targum Pseudo-Jonathan, Genesis 31:9–31:23. British Library, ms. Add. 27031, fol. 35r.
© THE BRITISH LIBRARY BOARD.

Just as Hebrew vocabulary was incorporated into later Jewish languages such as Yiddish and Ladino, so too was Aramaic a source of borrowed words in these languages. Some common Yiddish words deriving from Aramaic include אַוודאי *avade* 'of course', חגא *khoge* 'Christian holiday', מילא *meyle* 'never mind', חבֿרותא *khavruse* 'group of friends', and מסתמא *mistome* 'probably'. In modern Israeli Hebrew, Aramaic often serves as a source for specialized terminology. In the way that one might see Latin terms and phrases in highly technical legal or scholarly literature in English, one sees Aramaic vocabulary in Modern Hebrew works of this nature. For example, the standard Hebrew phrase for 'on the other hand' is מצד שני *mi-tsad sheni*, but in an academic paper one might see the Aramaic equivalent, מאידך גיסא *me-ʾidakh gisa*. The normal Hebrew word for 'only' is רק *raq*, but in legal parlance one might instead see the Aramaic גרידא *gereda*.

Aramaic is still used by Jews all over the world in various religious contexts. For example, the *ketubbah*, the marriage contract that is recited at a Jewish wedding ceremony, is written in Aramaic, as is the well-known Passover song *Ḥad Gadya*. Two of the most important and familiar pieces of Jewish liturgy are also in Aramaic, namely the *Kaddish*, which is recited daily, and *Kol Nidre*, which is heard on the eve of Yom Kippur.

While for most Jewish communities of the last thousand years, Aramaic has survived only as a written language, it has remained the spoken language of a small number of Jewish communities in the Near East into the 21st century. This modern type of Aramaic will be discussed in the next chapter.

References and further study

Fassberg (2017) provides an overview of Jewish Aramaic from all periods, and includes references to grammars and dictionaries of all varieties of Jewish Aramaic. English translations of the major Targumim have been published in twenty-two volumes by various authors by The Liturgical Press under the series title The Aramaic Bible. General introductions to the Targumim include Grelot (1992) and Flesher and Chilton (2011). The complete manuscript of Targum Pseudo-Jonathan (ms. Add. 27031) is available online via the British Library website; the passage cited in this chapter appears on folio 35r. Neusner (1994) and Strack and Stemberger (1996) provide introductions to rabbinic Jewish texts, including many that are written in Aramaic. On Judeo-Syriac, see Bhayro (2017). The Judeo-Syriac version of I Maccabees is housed in the British Library (ms. Or. 9926), and is also available online.

5 Aramaic, Modern

As discussed in the previous chapter, Aramaic was widely spoken across the entire Middle East by the first centuries of the Common Era, and would have been the first language of most Jews living both in the Land of Israel and abroad, in places like Syria and Iraq. But after the Islamic conquests of the 7th century, Arabic began to supplant Aramaic as the main language of the entire region. Most Jewish communities, including those of large cities like Baghdad, quickly switched to Arabic, as we know from the large corpus of texts in Judeo-Arabic (see ARABIC, MEDIEVAL). However, in the area that corresponds to present-day northern Iraq, northwestern Iran, and southeastern Turkey—roughly what is sometimes referred to as Kurdistan—many Jews and Christians continued to use Aramaic until the 20th century.

Before 1948, there were dozens of towns and villages in which Jews spoke Aramaic. Towns like Erbil in Iraq and Sanandaj in Iran, respectively the largest towns in Iraqi and Iranian Kurdistan, were once home to thriving communities of Aramaic-speaking Jews. In many of these places, the Aramaic dialects were very distinct, meaning that Aramaic-speaking Jews from one town may not have understood those from another town. In fact, there are dozens of different modern Jewish Aramaic dialects. In some cases the differences pertain to the structure of the language, including things like the conjugation of verbs, while other differences have to do with vocabulary. Often the differences in vocabulary are the result of a particular dialect having borrowed a given word from a neighbouring language, usually Kurdish or Turkish. Consider the following list of words from the Jewish Aramaic dialects of Sanandaj (Iran), Urmia (Iran), and Sulaymaniyah (Iraq) in order to get an idea of how different they can be.

Sanandaj	Urmia	Sulaymaniyah	English
gupa	*yanaqta*	*qulma*	'cheek'
ʿayza	*shbira*	*rek*	'good'
gyana	*jandag*	*lasha*	'body'
spalta	*sbelta*	*licha*	'lip'
qome	*baqatta*	*qadome*	'tomorrow'
lā garesh	*garoshle*	*garoshay*	'he is pulling'

In general, however, Jewish dialects from towns in a particular region resembled each other, and their speakers could understand one another. In fact, a Jewish dialect in one town was usually far more similar to the Jewish dialects of the surrounding towns—or even towns far away—than it was to the Christian dialect of that same town. For example, the word for 'house' was pronounced *bela* in the Jewish dialect of Sulaymaniyah in Iraq, as it was also in the town of Erbil (95 miles, or 150 km, to the northwest), in Urmia (110 miles, or 180 km, to the north), and in Sanandaj (180 miles, or 290 km, to the southeast), but the word was pronounced *besa* in the Christian Aramaic dialect of the same town. We find a similar situation when it comes to many Jewish and Muslim dialects of Arabic (see ARABIC, MODERN).

The grammar of the Jewish and Christian dialects can vary quite dramatically, even within a single small town. For example, in Urmia, a Jewish speaker would say *paloxé* to mean 'he is opening', while a Christian speaker would say *beptáxele*. Both of these verb forms come from the same historical root (*pth* 'to open'), but the sounds and verbal conjugations differ wildly. Similarly, a Jew in Sulaymaniyah would say *yay* to mean 'he is coming', but a Christian would say *kasele*. Again, both forms come from the same historical root.

The following list illustrates some additional differences in pronunciation, vocabulary, and grammar between Jewish and Christian dialects, in this case from the Iranian town of Sanandaj:

Jewish Sanandaj	Christian Sanandaj	English
'ilá	*'ida*	'hand'
pema	*kema*	'mouth'
zbota	*spesa*	'finger'
bronaxun	*'ebroxen*	'your son'
qetlale	*temqatella*	'he killed her'
kena	*kasenyen*	'I am coming'
hiyay	*gi'isele*	'he has come'

The last two sets of examples in the list, which are forms of the verb 'come', all derive from the same historical verbal root. They have come to look totally different in the two dialects because of sound changes and because of differences in the verbal prefixes and suffixes used for the various tenses.

Though there is abundant evidence of ancient forms of Jewish Aramaic (see ARAMAIC, ANCIENT), there has until recently been very little evidence of these later Jewish dialects of Aramaic that developed in the Middle Ages. The earliest text in a modern dialect of Jewish Aramaic is a manuscript from around 1650 that contains some discussion of three Torah portions. A small number of additional manuscripts exist from the following two centuries, but in large part our knowledge of modern Jewish Aramaic comes only from the latter part of the 20th century, when linguists began to document the many spoken varieties.

Almost all speakers of modern Jewish Aramaic immigrated to Israel in the 1950s, and none are left in their original homelands. The dialects are quickly dying out, because speakers have not typically passed them on to the younger generations. Some of the dialects are already extinct, and most others will be so very soon. Aramaic survived among these Jewish communities, against all odds, for over two thousand years, but soon that legacy will be gone.

Many substantial grammatical descriptions of modern Jewish Aramaic have been published, but since nearly all of these come from the last twenty years, it is really only very recently that scholars have gained a decent understanding of the various dialects. And there are still some dialects that have yet to be described. Scholars have also collected a substantial number of oral texts—folktales, biographical stories, descriptions of cultural practices, and the like—and through these texts some of the cultural history of these communities will be preserved. The following is an excerpt from a Jewish Aramaic speaker's recollection of life in Sulaymaniyah, recorded by the British scholar Geoffrey Khan of Cambridge University:

> *sulemani jwan-yela. sulemani ma-hītwala? dar-u dashti hītwala. nashe ruwwe hītwala. kenwa yatwiwa, haqenwa, tanenwa, gaḥkiwa. kulle hīt. gezixwa ta-ʾena, gezixwa ta-maʿe, gezixwa-wa ta-baruxawale. yale baxew kolixwa. kulle ʾanye-ʾasxàe kulle kolixwalu. nashe dawlamande hītwa. nashe faqire hītwa. nashe rek-ish hītwa. qrawe harawe lītwa.*

'Sulaymaniyah was beautiful. What did Sulaymaniyah have? It had country-side outside. It had great people. They used to sit, talk, tell stories, and laugh. There was everything there. We used to go to the spring, we used to go to the water, and we used to go to visit friends. We used to look after children. We used to do all such things. There were rich people. There were poor people. There were also good people. There were no fights or quarrels.'

References and further study

Fassberg (2017) provides an overview of Jewish Aramaic from all periods. Two book chapters by Khan give excellent overviews of modern Jewish Aramaic dialects (2011, 2018), while others cover both Jewish and Christian dialects (2019a, 2019b, 2019c). Some comprehensive descriptions of modern Jewish Aramaic dialects, including texts, are those of Khan (1999) for Erbil, Khan (2004) for Sulaymaniyah, Khan (2008) for Urmia, and Khan (2009) for Sanandaj. The excerpt in this chapter comes from Khan (2004).

6   Armenian

As discussed in a previous chapter (ARABIC, MEDIEVAL), the Cairo Genizah, discovered in the late 19th century, is a massively important cache of texts that contains texts from a period spanning nearly a thousand years. The Genizah documents are a window into the religious and everyday life of Jews in medieval Cairo and beyond and as such are of enormous value for scholars of Jewish history and literature. They also contain much of value to those interested in Jewish languages.

The Cairo Genizah contains texts from a wide variety of genres in a broad range of languages. The vast majority of the documents are in Hebrew, Judeo-Arabic (see ARABIC, MEDIEVAL), and Aramaic, but at least eight other languages are attested in the Genizah. These include some languages that have a well-known Jewish pedigree, such as Yiddish (see YIDDISH, OLD AND EARLY MODERN) and Judeo-Persian, but a few of the languages are more unexpected. One such language is Armenian, which is attested in just a single document out of the roughly 300,000 found in the Genizah.

Armenian is spoken today by nearly all of the three million inhabitants of Armenia, as well as by another couple of million Armenians living in diaspora communities. It is a member of the Indo-European language family, and so it is a distant relative of English, French, and Russian. However, within the Indo-European family it does not have any close relatives. So while English is a member of the Germanic subfamily of Indo-European (which also includes languages like German, Dutch, and Swedish), French belongs to the Romance subfamily (along with languages like Spanish, Italian, and Portuguese), and Russian is part of the Slavic subfamily (like Polish and Czech), Armenian stands alone as the only member of a distinct branch of Indo-European. Armenian is written in its own unique alphabet, which was invented in the early 5th century CE, around the same time that the Bible was translated into Armenian. (Incidentally, the Kingdom of Armenia was the first country in the world to adopt Christianity as its official religion, having done so in the early 4th century CE.)

Jewish settlers came to Armenia in the 1st century BCE, and there are records of sizeable Jewish communities there in the following few centuries. However, in the 4th century CE, most of the Jews were driven out of Armenia by an invading Persian king and resettled in Persia. From then on, there were no significant Jewish communities in Armenia until the relocation of several thousand Russian Jews to the country in the modern Soviet period. These 20th-century Jewish settlers in Armenia were part of the greater Russian Jewish community, and therefore, it is not really accurate to speak of a distinct Armenian Jewish community with its own local cultural traditions and long history. This can be contrasted with the long-standing Jewish communities in surrounding countries, such as the Jewish communities of Persia (see PERSIAN) and Georgia (see GEORGIAN), the Mountain Jews of Azerbaijan and Dagestan (see TAT), and, somewhat further away, the Bukharan Jews of Uzbekistan and Tajikistan (see TAJIK). The historical absence of Jews in Armenia is consistent with the fact the Armenia has long been an ethnically homo-geneous country, unlike its neighbours. There are currently only a few hundred Jews living in Armenia, mostly in the capital city, Yerevan.

To return to the Cairo Genizah, it was already mentioned that the collection contained a wide variety of text genres. In addition to all the literary, economic, and religious texts, letters, and other types of prose and poetry, there are texts that contain dictionaries and other kinds of word-lists. Most of these were designed for helping readers better understand biblical and other religious texts, but a small number of word-lists are closer to modern phrase books—that is, lists of words intended to help people communicate with speakers of other languages. Such phrasebooks might have been written in order to help Jews in their business deal-ings and travels (see also MALAY and TURKISH).

The single Armenian document found in the Cairo Genizah is one such word-list. It consists of only part of a single sheet of paper, on which there is a list of about twenty different Judeo-Arabic words and one phrase, each with an Armenian equivalent written in Hebrew script. (Recall that Judeo-Arabic was the native language of the Jews in Cairo.) The author of the word-list is unknown, as is the exact date and place of composition, but the paper and the handwriting style sug-gest that it was written between the 10th and the 12th centuries CE. The following words appear in the list: *bread, meat, water, wine, apple, pear, woman/wife, virgin, mother, father, beautiful face, singer, white, black, policeman, come up!, go away!, sit down!,* and *how are you?*. The included image shows the complete word-list. The first line of the list reads as follows:

Judeo-Arabic	*al-nabid* אלנביד	*al-ma* אלמא	*al-laḥm* אללחם	*al-khubz* אלכבז
Judeo-Armenian	*kini* כיני	*shur* שור	*mis* מיס	*hads* הַדְס
meaning	'wine'	'water'	'meat'	'bread'

From this list we can see that the words refer mostly to items of food and drink, as well as some family terms and colours. These can be described as everyday words. The verbal commands 'come up!', 'go away!', and 'sit down!' are also somewhat common phrases used in conversation, as is the expression 'how are you?'. However, a few of the words stand out as somewhat surprising along-side these more ordinary words, especially 'singer' and 'policeman'. The word 'policeman' is an approximate translation of the Judeo-Arabic word גלועז *jilwa ʿaz*, which is a variant form of Arabic جلواز *jilwāz*, a very obscure word that can mean

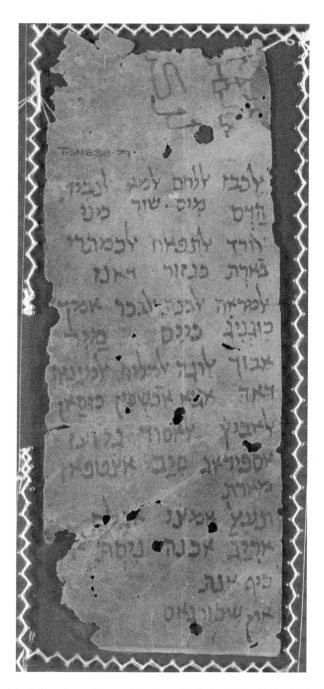

A Judeo-Arabic–Judeo-Armenian word-list from the Cairo Genizah. Cambridge University Library, T-S NS 38.79. COURTESY OF THE SYNDICS OF CAMBRIDGE UNIVERSITY LIBRARY.

'policeman' or 'tax collector'; however, the exact meaning of the Judeo-Armenian equivalent is less clear. One scholar of Armenian has suggested that the word is best translated as 'goat-herd man'. This is clearly a strange word to use as the equivalent of 'policeman', but the same scholar suggests that the correspondence might have to do with a costume mocking the hated policeman or tax collector at a holiday celebration. The connection to some kind of festival or celebration might also explain the appearance of the word 'singer' in the word-list. Regardless, the words that appear in this list indicate that there was social interaction between Jews and Armenians in medieval Cairo.

Like Jews, Armenians had been living in Egypt since antiquity. And we know from a few other Genizah documents that Jews had business dealings with Armenians in Cairo. However, evidence of Armenian–Jewish interaction is overall quite sparse, and so the existence of this word-list documenting a social interaction between the two communities is of both linguistic and socio-historical significance.

The Genizah document is only one of two Armenian texts written in the Hebrew alphabet that we know of. The other one is found in an Armenian manuscript (using the Armenian alphabet) from 1892, which has marginal notes in Hebrew and Ladino, as well as a list of the Armenian names of the zodiac signs transliterated into Hebrew characters (e.g., חֶזְקֶדִין *hezqedin* for Armenian խեցգետին *xec'getin* 'Cancer'). The marginal notes make it clear that the Armenian text—which was not a Jewish text—was being studied by a Jew; the fact that the manuscript is now housed in a Jewish institution (the Jewish Theological Seminary in New York) is also a testament to its previous Jewish ownership. This second example of Armenian in Hebrew script, like the Genizah document, is still just the product of one individual rather than evidence of Jews habitually speaking and writing Armenian.

References and further study

The Armenian word-list in the Genizah is held by the Cambridge University Library (shelfmark T-S NS 38.79). Shivtiel (2005), Clackson (2008), and Russell (2013a) all contain analyses of the text. Russell (2013a) discusses the difficulties in interpreting the connection between the Judeo-Arabic word 'tax collector' and its Armenian equivalent. The other text with Armenian in Hebrew characters is held by the library of the Jewish Theological Seminary in New York (ms. 10558). Russell (2013b) is a study of that text.

7 Catalan

In the year 1263, in Barcelona, the Jewish scholar Moses ben Naḥman, also known as Naḥmanides or Ramban (1194–1270), famously engaged in a debate with a Jewish convert to Christianity named Pablo. The debate was set up at the request of King James I of Aragon, who was sure that the Christian faith could be proven correct by logical arguments. Over the course of four days, the two men debated various issues, such as whether the Messiah had already come, and the opinion of the Talmud on this subject. Two records of this debate survive. One was written in Hebrew by Naḥmanides himself and ends with a decisive victory for the author. Naḥmanides claims that though the king thought him wrong, he was so impressed with his arguments that he rewarded him with three hundred pieces of gold. The other account, a much shorter work in Latin that bears the seal of the Crown of Aragon, tells of the defeat and humiliation of Naḥmanides. It is perhaps not surprising that the two versions, written by the opposing sides, each tell a very different story.

In the Hebrew version of Naḥmanides, there is a moment in the debate in which the two adversaries are arguing about the meaning of the Hebrew word יום *yom*, which normally means 'day'. The word relates to a passage in the book of Daniel (12:11–12), which discusses the coming of Messianic redemption in 1290 'days' (Hebrew ימים *yamim*, the plural of יום *yom* 'day'). Naḥmanides wants to show that the word יום *yom* can, in certain contexts, mean 'year', while Pablo asserts that every Jew knows that the word means 'day'. To prove his point, Pablo wishes to ask the opinion of an uninvested third party. As Naḥmanides tells it, Pablo said the following:

אין יהודי בעולם שלא יודה כי פירוש יום יום ממש. אלא שהוא משנה דברים כרצונו. וצעק למלך והביאו יהודי אחד שמצאו ראשון ושאלוהו: מהו יום בלשונכם. אמר דיאה.

'en yehudi ba-'olam she-lo yode ki perush yom yom mamash. 'ela she-hu meshanne devarim ki-rtsono. we-tsa'aq la-melekh we-hevi'u yehudi 'eḥad she-mats'u rishon we-sha'aluhu: mahu yom bi-lshonkhem. 'amar dia.

"There is no Jew in the world who would not confess that *yom* really means 'day'. Rather, he is changing the meaning (of the word) to match his want".

> And he [Pablo] cried out to the king, and they brought in the first Jew they
> found (from the street) and asked him, "What is *yom* in your language?"
> And he [the other Jew] said, "*Dia*."

Though the foregoing passage was written in Hebrew, the unidentified man says
dia, which is the word for 'day' in Catalan, the language that the man would have
spoken. It is used to make the man's opinion unambiguous, since the Hebrew term
for 'day' is itself in question.

Catalan is the vernacular language spoken in the Catalonia region of Spain,
including its capital, Barcelona. It was the native tongue of Naḥmanides and his
adversary Pablo, and likely the language of the debate itself, despite the fact that
the written accounts are in Hebrew and Latin. Today, Catalan has over twelve million native speakers, mainly in Spain, but because it is not the national language
of any one country, it is largely overlooked and unknown by outsiders. Before the
Expulsion of the Jews from Spain in 1492, there was a large community of Jews
in Catalonia, and Naḥmanides' home town of Girona was one of its centres. Jews
there spoke Catalan, like their Christian neighbours.

A few other Catalan words appears in the account of the 1263 debate written
by Naḥmanides. In addition to these, there exists a small number of original compositions in Catalan in Hebrew script. For example, there are five Judeo-Catalan
songs about marriage, which survive in two manuscript copies from the 15th century. Four songs contain advice to newlyweds and were perhaps sung at wedding
celebrations, while the fifth song is a cautionary tale about a marriage between an
old man and a much younger girl. One rhyming four-line stanza from a wedding
song reads as follows:

de la dona vaja memrant	די לדונא ווגא ממראנט
nuit o jorn son dret salvant	נוייט או גורן שונדריט שלווטן
dret es que nuvi el prim'an	דריט איש קי נובי אל פרימאן
lo yanum we-lo yishan	לא ינום ולא יישן

'Always remember your wife,
night and day guarding her right.
It is right that in the first year the groom
should not slumber and not sleep.'

Note that the first three lines of the stanza are in Judeo-Catalan, but the fourth is
in Hebrew, as is typical of these wedding songs.

Another important text was a Judeo-Catalan version of a Provençal epic romance
about the adventures of King Jaufre (also known as King Griflet in English), who
was one of the knights of King Arthur's Round Table. Though it was originally
quite lengthy, the Judeo-Catalan version survives only in very fragmented form
from around the year 1500. Still, the surviving portion is proof that at least one
text of significant length was composed in Judeo-Catalan.

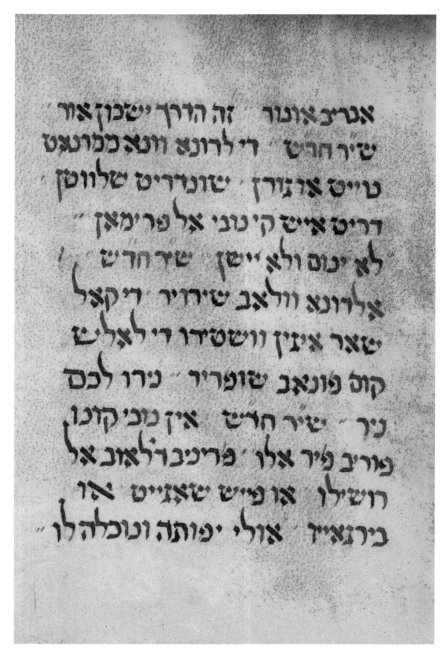

אגרצאונו ׳ זה הדרך ישכון אור ׳
שיר חדש ׳ די לרונצ וטא כמועט
טייט אוזרן ׳ שונדריט שלווטן ׳
דריט איש קי טני אל פרימאן ׳
לא ינום ולא יישן ׳ שר חדש ׳
אלדונצ וולאב שירור ריקאל
שאר איזן וושטידו די לאלש
קוש פונאב שופריר ׳ נרו לכם
ניר ׳ שיר חדש ׳ אין מכי קונו
פוריב פיר אלו ׳ פרימכדולאוב אל
רושילו ׳ או פיש שאזייט אור
בירנאייד ׳ אולי יפותה וטמלה לו ׳

A Judeo-Catalan wedding song. National Library of Israel, ms. 8°3312, fol. 33v. The stanza cited in the chapter begins on line 2. COURTESY OF THE NATIONAL LIBRARY OF ISRAEL.

Additional Judeo-Catalan words are found in a handful of official Hebrew documents and account books, as well as in Hebrew texts related to medicine or botany. One 15th-century Hebrew document, totalling less than 700 lines of text, contains as many as sixty-nine Judeo-Catalan words, mostly names of plants and animals. It is a Hebrew translation of a Latin medical treatise originally written by a Catalan-speaking Christian, translated into Hebrew by a Catalan-speaking Jew.

The Catalan language is very closely related to Provençal (see PROVENÇAL), and although today they are quite distinct, in the Middle Ages they were much more similar. Therefore, when we find apparently Judeo-Catalan words in Hebrew texts, it is not always possible to identify them as Judeo-Catalan or Judeo-Provençal. The Jewish communities of Catalonia and Provence also had long-standing historical connections. Nevertheless, it is clear that for several centuries before the Expulsion from Spain there was an important Catalan-speaking Jewish community, and there are a number of texts that we can confidently identify as Judeo-Catalan. After the Expulsion, the Jews of Catalonia integrated with the rest of Spanish Jewry that resettled in the Balkans, Turkey, Greece, and elsewhere in the Ottoman Empire and North Africa, and the Jewish use of Catalan thereby ceased. There may be some traces of Catalan influence in the Ladino language that developed in the newly formed communities in the Ottoman Empire and elsewhere (see LADINO), but the Expulsion ended the historical Jewish connection with the Catalan language.

References and further study

There is very little scholarship on Judeo-Catalan, and what little exists is mostly in Catalan or Spanish. One excellent overview of the subject, which happens to be in English, is Feliu and Ferrer (2011); additional references can be found therein. The text of the wedding song was taken from Baum (2016). The romance of King Jaufre is discussed by Baum (2019), the 15th-century medical text was published by Feliu (2006–07), and discussion of Hebrew in economic texts can be found in Valls i Pujol (2014).

8 Chinese

Of all the world's varied and diverse Jewish communities, one of the most intriguing and little known is that of China, where Jews have lived for over a thousand years. The earliest Jews arrived in China via two major routes. Some, primarily from Persia, entered China overland as merchants along the Silk Road trade route, which connected the Middle East with India and China. There is evidence of such Jewish traders in the far western part of what is now China as early as the late 8th century CE (see PERSIAN). Other Jews came to China as sea traders from either India or Persia and settled in eastern coastal cities such as Hangzhou and Quanzhou. There are reports of these settlements from between the 9th and the 14th centuries. Marco Polo, who travelled in China in the late 13th century, reported the existence of Jews in China, including the presence of Jewish traders in Beijing.

More recently, in the early 20th century, Russian Jews established communities in northern Chinese cities, chiefly Harbin and Tianjin. The Harbin Jewish community grew as large as 12,000 people by the 1920s, though nearly all had left by the time of the Communist Revolution in 1949. The coastal cities of Hong Kong and Shanghai have had a Jewish presence going back to the mid-19th century, when small numbers of Jews arrived in the wake of the expanding British Empire. Those in Shanghai were joined by Russian Jews in the early 20th century and then by around 20,000 German and Eastern European Jews who fled eastwards from the Nazis at the outbreak of World War II. The Japanese occupied Shanghai during the war, and in 1941 they instituted a ghetto for the Jewish population. However, despite Nazi requests, the Japanese did not hand the Jews over to the Germans. After the war, nearly all of the Jews living in Shanghai left China and settled elsewhere.

By far the most prominent and lasting Jewish community in China was that of Kaifeng, a city in the Henan Province along the Yellow River. Kaifeng was the capital of China during most of the years 913–1127 and was at that time one of the largest cities in the world. It was also during this period that Jewish traders first settled in the city. Like the other Jews in medieval China, they were originally Persian speaking; in fact, among the few surviving documents produced by the community are some lines in Judeo-Persian. However, they eventually adopted Chinese as their primary spoken language. (Like other Jewish communities, they used Hebrew for prayer and Torah reading in the synagogue.)

Only scant written evidence survives from the Jewish community of Kaifeng. The main records include a handful of stone inscriptions dating from the 15th and 17th centuries. However, even some of these no longer survive in the original, but only in copies made by early European visitors. There is also a bilingual Memorial Book in Hebrew and Chinese, which was completed in the middle of the 17th century. This manuscript records the names of more than 700 individual members of the community, who lived between the mid-15th and 17th centuries. The Kaifeng Jewish community was divided into seven clans, each of which had a Chinese family name (Ai, Gao, Jin, Li, Shi, Zhang, and Zhao), and the Memorial Book is divided by clan. It also separates the lists of men and women. The names are a curious mix of Hebrew and Chinese. On the whole, the Hebrew names are written in the Hebrew alphabet, while the Chinese names are written in Chinese characters. So the book is both bilingual and biscriptal. We find, for example, names like רבי זהָאָנג כוּן בֶן יִשׂרא'ל 坤張 *rabbi zhāng kūn ben yisra'el* 'Rabbi Zhang Kun son of Israel' and 氏高 בת יוסף *gāo shì bat yosef* 'Miss Gao daughter of Joseph'.

In a small number of cases, for reasons that are not apparent, Chinese names—especially women's names—were written in Hebrew script. Examples are לי שה *lǐ shì* 'Miss Li' and גן שה *zhāng shì* 'Miss Zhang'. Note that women are referred to either by their Hebrew first name (with names like לאה *le'a* 'Leah' and דבורה *devora* 'Deborah') or by their Chinese maiden name (*shì* = 'maiden name'). Even more interesting is that sometimes we find Hebrew abbreviations for a handful of Chinese phrases, indicating sibling birth order. For example, דז *d-z* stands for Chinese 大姐 *dàjiě* 'big sister' and עש '*-sh* stands for Chinese 二兄 *èr xiōng* 'second brother'. Despite these occasional Chinese names or parts of words in Hebrew script, there is no indication that there was any real tradition of Judeo-Chinese writing.

In the stone inscriptions, we find some Hebrew names written in Chinese characters, giving us evidence of how the local Jews actually pronounced Hebrew. For example, in the inscription from 1512, we meet 阿呵聯 *ā-hē-lián* for אהרון *'aharon* (Aaron) and 阿無羅漢 *ā-wú-luó-hàn* for אברהם *'avraham* (Abraham). Several European visitors to Kaifeng also recorded local pronunciations of Hebrew. According to one such traveller, who visited Kaifeng in 1721, the name ירמיהו *yirmiyahu* (Jeremiah) was pronounced as *Ialemeiohum*, while דברים *devarim*, the Hebrew name of the book of Deuteronomy, was pronounced as *teveliim*. These spellings are those of the 18th-century traveller rather than modern transliterations, so they may not be completely accurate, but at least they give us an idea of what the Kaifeng Jewish pronunciation of Hebrew was like at that time. (The large number of mistakes in some of the community's Hebrew texts suggests that their knowledge of Hebrew was generally poor.) One noteworthy feature present in both the stone inscriptions and in the eyewitness accounts is that Hebrew ר *r* tended to be pronounced as the consonant *l*. Rare cases of the confusion of ר *r* and ל *l* can also be found in some of the community's other Hebrew writings. For example, in a Hebrew inscription copied out for a western visitor by the community's chief rabbi in 1721, we find the spellings מַרְהוּתוֹ *marhuto* for מַלְכוּתוֹ *malkhuto* 'his kingdom' (also with *h* for *kh*) and רְעֹרָם *re-'oram* for לְעֹלָם *le-'olam* 'for eternity'.

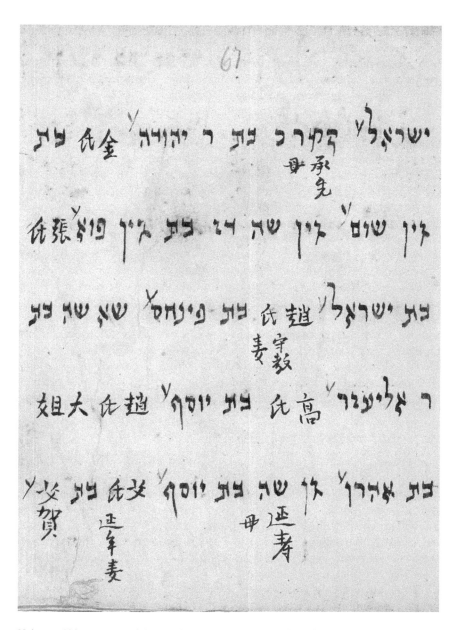

Hebrew–Chinese Memorial Book from Kaifeng. Among the Judeo-Chinese names is גין שה
דז בת גין פוא *jīn shì dàjiě bat jīn fú* 'Miss Chin, the elder sister, daughter of Chin Fu'. Hebrew
Union College, ms. 926 (Chinese 4), p. 67. COURTESY OF THE KLAU LIBRARY, CINCINNATI, HEBREW
UNION COLLEGE—JEWISH INSTITUTE OF RELIGION.

The Kaifeng Jewish community reached its peak in the 17th century, when it numbered perhaps a thousand souls. Then, in 1642, a devastating flood in Kaifeng destroyed the synagogue, along with most of the scrolls and books belonging to the Jewish community. At least one Torah scroll and the Memorial Book survived the flood. The community rebounded, and later stone inscriptions commemorate the flood and subsequent restoration of the synagogue.

In 1704, there are believed to have still been around a thousand Jews living in Kaifeng, but by 1850 this number had decreased to only a few hundred, in part due to another terrible flood that took place in 1841. In 1850, the Kaifeng synagogue still stood, though it was in disrepair. The community was scattered in 1857, during the Taiping Rebellion (1850–1864), and it never rebounded. It was during this period that the synagogue ceased to exist. All of the community's extant texts (most written after the flood of 1642), including a number of Torah scrolls, prayer-books, and the Memorial Book, were acquired by Europeans and taken out of China.

By the early 20th century, the remaining Jews of Kaifeng had acculturated into the surrounding Chinese society and stopped practising Judaism. They had by then abandoned all Jewish religious and cultural traditions except for the avoidance of pork, which continued to distinguish them from their non-Jewish neighbours. Because of the high rates of intermarriage in previous centuries, the remaining Kaifeng Jews already looked identical to the majority of the Chinese population, and this made it easy for them to move away from Kaifeng and lose the last remaining connections to their Jewish heritage. While there is no longer any real Jewish presence in Kaifeng, in recent decades some descendants of the city's Jewish community have attempted to reconnect with their roots, and a small group of them has even immigrated to Israel.

References and further study

White (1966) and Leslie (1972) both provide overviews of the history, culture, and writings of the Jews of Kaifeng. Leslie (1963–66) is a thorough study of the Memorial Book, while White (1966) includes a translation with commentary, as well as translations of the other major texts. Leslie (1972) includes the Hebrew inscription copied by the Rabbi in 1721, and Wexler (1985) discusses additional linguistically interesting features of the Jewish Chinese texts. The Memorial Book and most of the other surviving texts from the Kaifeng community are now owned by Hebrew Union College in Cincinnati. The manuscripts have all been digitized and are freely available online. A Kaifeng Torah scroll owned by the British Library is also available online. There is a miniature model of the Kaifeng synagogue at the Diaspora Museum in Tel Aviv.

9 English

The first Jewish communities in England were established after the Norman invasion of 1066. The Jews came mostly from France (like the Normans themselves), and those who came remained French speaking for a long time. However, during the course of the 12th and 13th centuries, many of them likely shifted from speaking French to English, or at least became conversant in both languages. Several hundred documents from this community have survived, almost all of which are documents connected to the sale of land or moneylending, an occupation that was dominated by Jews at that time. However, all of these documents are in Latin or Hebrew, with only the occasional English personal or place name appearing in Hebrew script. For example, various Hebrew documents from the 13th century mention places like ניוהוש נ 'Newhouse' (also spelled ניוהושא), נוטינגהם 'Nottingham', and גלוצהטר 'Gloucester', and several mention המלך הנרי בן המלך יוהן *ha-melekh henri ben ha-melekh yoh(a)n* 'King Henry [III] son of King John' (the latter name also spelled יואן or יהן).

There is also evidence of Hebrew literary production in England at this time, such as a famous manuscript of the Torah and Five Scrolls (including both Hebrew and an Aramaic translation) that was completed in 1189. In the margin of one page of this manuscript is a list of words (the names of unclean birds listed in Leviticus 11) in Judeo-French, a testament to the fact that at least some members of the Jewish community in England still preferred that language. Another remarkable Jewish document from 12th-century England is a Hebrew prayer-book, at the back of which we find a record of some loan transactions written in Judeo-Arabic. The Judeo-Arabic text, which specifically mentions transactions made with Englishmen 'here in England' (הונא פי אנגלטירה *hunā fī 'ingiltera*), was probably written by a Jew who had come to England from Spain. In short, the Jewish community of medieval England was multilingual, and some documents of real linguistic interest have been preserved, but there is nothing in the English language. Contemporary Jews in other countries were writing French, Italian, Arabic, Persian, and other languages in Hebrew script, but there is no indication that medieval English Jews ever wrote English in that way.

In 1290, all Jews were expelled from England. Only in 1656/1657 were they allowed to return, and there has been a vibrant Jewish community in England ever since. Jews also established communities in overseas British colonies: in North

America, Australia, South Africa (see ZULU), and elsewhere. The earliest Jewish settlers in what would become the United States began arriving in the 1650s. They were Sephardic Jews who came mainly from colonies in the Caribbean or Brazil (see PAPIAMENTU), or from Western European cities like Amsterdam and London. By the time of the American Revolution, the Jewish population was still quite small—only about 2500 people—but by the American Civil War it had increased to about 150,000, thanks to the immigration of large numbers of German and other Central European Jews. Thus the Ashkenazi Jewish population of the United States came to vastly outnumber the earlier Sephardic communities, even before the mass waves of Eastern European Jewish immigrants that came between the 1880s and 1920s.

Today, the United States is home to around six million Jews, around 40% of the world's Jewish population, and the largest community of any country besides Israel. Adding in the Jewish populations of Canada (roughly 350,000), the United Kingdom (roughly 250,000), and Australia (about 100,000) means that almost half of the world's Jews now live in an English-speaking country.

In the United States today, there is a particular accent that is recognizable as Jewish, best illustrated by celebrities like Mel Brooks, Jackie Mason, Woody Allen, and Larry David, though this accent is particular mainly to Jews from New York City. More applicable to Jews around the entire country is the Jewish use of particular words that come from Hebrew or Yiddish. In fact, many of the Hebraisms and Yiddishisms that today we think of as indicative of Jewish English were present in the language already by the 19th century, and some surely earlier. In an article from 1890, William Sproull, one-time president of the University of Cincinnati, wrote a scholarly article on Hebrew words in colloquial use by English-speaking Jews. Many of these words are still very familiar today, even to secular Jews, including *goy* 'Gentile' (< Hebrew גוי *goy* 'nation'), *mazal tov* 'good luck' (< Hebrew מזל טוב *mazzal ṭov*), *mamzer* 'bastard' (< Hebrew ממזר *mamzer* 'bastard'), *mitsvah* 'a noble act' (< Hebrew מצווה *mitsva* 'commandment'), *mishpokhe* 'family' (< Hebrew משפחה *mishpakha* 'family'), and *shikse* 'Gentile girl' (< Hebrew שקץ *sheqets* 'abomination'). One of the most interesting words that Sproull cites, and a word that was long in use among both American and British Jews, is *beytsimer* 'Irishman'. This derives from the Hebrew word ביצים *betsim* 'eggs'. In Yiddish, 'eggs' is אייער *eyer*, which sounds very close to the first syllable of English *Ireland* or *Irish*. So Yiddish-speaking Jews in England and the United States translated the element *Ire-* with the Hebrew word ביצם *betsim*, and added to it the suffix *-er*, which in Yiddish is used to denote an inhabitant of a place (e.g., אַן ענגלענדער *an englender* 'an Englishman' and אַן אַמעריקאַנער *an amerikaner* 'an American'). The word *beytsimer* has an added element of humour, since Yiddish ביצים *beytsim* is also slang for 'testicles', a usage that has been carried over into Modern Hebrew.

There is almost no evidence of English written in the Hebrew script, with just a couple of notable exceptions. One example is a Judeo-English translation of the Gospel of Matthew, published in London in 1902 under the title דהע גאספעל אקקארדינג טו סיינט מאטטהעו *The Gospel According to Saint Matthew*. But this was published by a convert named Joseph Solomon Davidson (born Davidowitch), with the goal of bringing the Gospel to a Jewish readership. The same individual privately published a Judeo-English version of the British National Anthem, 'God Save the King', in 1917 and 1919. A more organic example of Judeo-English comes from Benjamin Safer (1872–1959), a Lithuanian Jew who immigrated to the United States to become the first rabbi of an Orthodox synagogue in Jacksonville, Florida, a position which he held from 1902 to 1933. Among Safer's surviving papers are several sermonettes written in Judeo-English, which he presumably delivered to his congregation. The following is an excerpt from one of these:

אין סאָם סיטיס אוו דהי יונאײטעד סטײטס אוו אמעריקא, מעני אוו אור דזשואיש יוטה העוו
ביגאָן טו פערסיוו דהאַט דהיי לעק סאָממטהינג. איוון דהאוז הו אַ-ר נײטיווז אוו דהי יונאײטעד
סטײטס אוו אמעריקא, אוו דהי בלעסד לענד הוז לאָ-ז גרענט פרידאם ענד איקוועליטי טו אָל
מען . . . ענד סאָ דהי בעטטער קלעס אוו אַור יאַנג מען ענד וימן העוו ביגאַן טו ריעלאײז
דהאט ווהאײל ווי מי בי אײבל טו פול אורסעלוװז טו אימעדזשין ווי אַ-ר דזשאסט יומן
ביאינגז ענד טו דינאַי אור דזשואיש אַ-רידזשאן, ווי קעננאט פול דהי וואירלד. אין דהי אײעז
אוו דהי וואירלד ווי רימעין דזשועס; ענד איף ווי רימעין דיװאָיד אוו דזשואיש קאָנשאסנעס
ענד נײשאנעל סעלף ריספעקטס, ווי קאט אַ סאָררי פיגור. ווי לעק אינער פרידאם; ווי אַ-ר
איגער טו אימיטײט אדהערז אין אָרדער טו פליז דהעם; ענד ווי קעננאט פליז דהעם, ביקאָז
דהאוז הו קעננאט ריספעקט דהעמסעלוװז וויל סאירטעינלי נאט בי ריספעקטעד באי אַדהערז.
דהערפאָר דהער העז בין באָרן אין אור יאַנג פיפל אַ דיזאײר טו ליוו אַ מאָר נאָרמעל לאײף.
דהיי וויש טו דראָ- נירער טו דהייר פיפל, דהיי וויש טו אנדערסטענד דזשודײאיזם בעטטער
ענד טו אימבאײב דהי דזשואיש ספיריט.

'In some cities of the United States of America, many of our Jewish youth have begun to perceive that they lack something. Even those who are natives of the United States of America, of the blessed land whose laws grant freedom and equality to all men. . . . And so the better class of our young men and women have begun to realize that while we may be able to fool ourselves to imagine we are just human beings and to deny our Jewish origin, we cannot fool the world. In the eyes of the world we remain Jews; and if we remain devoid of Jewish consciousness and national self-respect, we cut a sorry figure. We lack inner freedom. We are eager to imitate others in order to please them, and we cannot please them, because those who cannot respect themselves will certainly not be respected by others. Therefore, there has been born in our young people a desire to live a more normal life. They wish to draw nearer to their people. They wish to understand Judaism better and to imbibe the Jewish spirit.'

At present, there is also a more distinct variety of Jewish English used by many Orthodox and ultra-Orthodox Jews, who tend to live in much more isolated communities. Because these communities are more regularly involved with the study of Hebrew religious texts, and because Yiddish is still widely spoken in some of them (see Yiddish, Modern Hasidic), their variety of Jewish English makes greater use of words from Hebrew and Yiddish. Thus, one is likely to hear words like *daven* (from Yiddish דאַוונען *davnen*) instead of 'pray' or *kallah* (via Yiddish from

St. Matthew II.

ST. MATTHEW II.   .II סיינט מאטטהעו

| CHAPTER II. | צהעפטער II. |

1 Now when Jesus was born in Bethlehem of Judæa, in the days of Herod, the king, behold, there came wise men from the east to Jerusalem,

2 Saying, Where is he that is born King of the Jews? for we have seen his star in the east, and are come to worship him.

3 When Herod the king had heard these things, he was troubled, and all Jerusalem with him.

4 And when he had gathered all the chief priests and scribes of the people together, he demanded of them where Christ should be born.

5 And they said unto him, In Bethlehem of Judæa: for thus it is written by the prophet,

6 And thou Bethlehem, in the land of Juda, art not the least among the princes of Juda: for out of·thee shall come a Governor, that shall rule my people Israel.

7 Then Herod, when he had privily called the wise men, inquired of them diligently what time the star appeared.

8 And he sent them to Bethle-

1 נאו ווהען דזיזאס ווהאז באָרן אין בעטהלעהעם אָוו דזודאָ אין דהע דעים אָוו הירָאד, דהע קינג, ביהאָלד דהער קיים ווהייַז מענן פראָם דהע איסט טו דזערוזאַלעם,

2 סייאינג, ווהער איז היא דהעט אין באָרן קינג אָוו דהע דזוס ? פאָר ווהי האָוו סיאין היס סטאַר אין דהע איסט ענד אַר קאָם טו ווהאָרשיפ הים :

3 ווהען הירָאד, דהע קינג, העד העַרד דהיז טהינגס היא ווהאָז טראָאבלד ענד אָלל דזערוזאַלעם ווהיטה הים :

4 ענד ווהען היא העד גאדהערד אָלל דהע ציף פריסטס ענד סקרייבם אָוו דהע פיפל טוגערדהער היא דעמאַנדערד אָוו דהעם ווהער קרייסט שוד בי באָרן :

5 ענד דהיי סעד אַנטו הים, אין בעטהלעהעם אָוו דזודאָ ; פאָר דהאַס איט איז ריטמָן ביי דהע פּראָפּעט :

6 ענד דהאו בעטהלעהעם אין דהע לענד אָוו דזודאָ אַרט נאָט דהע ליסט אַמאַנג דהע פרינסעס אָוו דזודאָ ; פאָר אַט אָוו דהי שעלל קאָם אַ גאָווערנאָר דהעט שעלל רול מיי פיפל איזראַעל :

7 דהען הירָאד, ווהען היא העד פרייוויילי קאללד דהע ווהייז מענן, אינקווייַרד אָוו דהעם דיליגענטלי ווהאָט טיים דהע סטאַר אַפּפּירד :

8 ענד היא סענט דהעם טו

7

The Gospel of Matthew (2:1–2:8) in Judeo-English. Published in London, 1902.

דהי בריטיש נאשיאָנל אַנטהעם.

.1

גאָד סייוו אַר גרעשאַס קינג,

לאָנג ליוו אַר נאָבל קינג,

גאָד סייוו דהי קינג!

סענד הים וויקטאָריאַס,

האַפּפּי ענד גלאָריאַס,

לאָנג טו רעַין אָווער אַס,

גאָד סייוו דהי קינג!

.2

אָ לאָרד, אַר גאָד, אַרייז,

סקאַטטער היס ענעמיס,

ענד מייק דהעם פאַלל;

קאָנפאָונד דהעיר פּאָליטיקס;

פראַסטרעיט דהעיר נייוויש טריקס:

אָן דהי, אַר האָופּס ווהי פיקס,

גאָד סייוו דהי קינג!

.3

דהי צהאָיסעַסט גיפטס אין סטאָר,

אָן הים בי פּליזט טו פּור;

לאָנג מעי הי רעַין!

מעי הי דיפּענד אַר לאָוס,

ענד עווער גיוו אַס קאָוז

טו סינג ווהיט האַרט ענד וואָיס:

גאָד סייוו דהי קינג!

The British National Anthem in Judeo-English. Published in London, 1919.

A Judeo-English Sermon of Benjamin Safer, Sermon 1, p. 4. THE REVEREND BENJAMIN SAFER AND FAMILY PAPERS, ISSER AND RAE PRICE LIBRARY OF JUDAICA, GEORGE A. SMATHERS LIBRARIES, UNIVERSITY OF FLORIDA.

Hebrew כלה *kalla*) for 'bride' from Orthodox or ultra-Orthodox Jews, but not from the majority of American Jews. In this dialect of ultra-religious Jews, which some have dubbed Yeshivish, we also find syntax that mirrors Yiddish. For example, a speaker might say 'he's eating by us' (mirroring Yiddish ער עסט ביי אונדז *er est bay undz*) instead of 'he's eating at our place' or 'I want that you should come' (mirroring Yiddish איך וויל אַז דו זאָלסט קומען *ikh vil az du zolst kumen*) instead of 'I want you to come'. Still, this more marked variety of Jewish English is spoken by only a small percentage of English-speaking Jews, and it is not likely to be encountered by outsiders very often.

References and further study

For a history of Jews in England, see Roth (1964) and Endelmann (2002); on America, see Diner (2004) and Sarna (2019). On the Hebrew and Latin documents of the medieval Jewish community in England, see Olszowy-Schlanger (2015). On the Hebrew Bible that was completed in England in 1189, see Beit-Arié (1985); that manuscript (Codex Valmadonna 1) is now owned by the Museum of the Bible in Washington D.C., where it is on public display. Appendices in Beit-Arié's volume discuss the Judeo-French glosses, as well as the Judeo-Arabic text from England. On the Hebrew words in English in the 19th century, see Sproull (1890). Copies of the Judeo-English texts of Joseph Solomon Davidson are held by the British Library. Rabbi Benjamin Safer's Judeo-English sermonettes are available online as part of the University of Florida Digital Collections (ufdc.ufl.edu/iufjudrev). On contemporary Jewish English in the United States, see Benor (2018). Weiser (1995) is a dictionary and description of Yeshivish.

10 Esperanto

It may be surprising to see a chapter on Esperanto in a book about Jewish languages. After all, Esperanto is an artificial language that was the invention of one man, and it has never been the native language of any ethnic or regional community. But Esperanto, arguably the world's most well-known and successful invented language, actually has legitimate Jewish credentials. Its inventor, Ludwig Lazar Zamenhof, was Jewish, as were a significant portion of its early supporters, and some of the earliest Esperanto texts were translations from Hebrew and Yiddish. The language's Jewish roots have even made it the target of persecution by antisemites in the past.

Zamenhof was born in 1859 in the city of Białystok, then part of the Russian Empire, but now part of Poland. His grandfather and father were both language teachers, and Białystok was a multilingual town. Zamenhof grew up hearing Polish, Russian, Belarusian, and Yiddish, and was educated in Hebrew, French, German, Latin, and Greek. In his youth he wrote one of the earliest grammars of Yiddish, and he was interested in the revival of Hebrew as a spoken language. However, he soon became convinced that multilingualism was the source of much of the ethnic tension that he saw around him. The widespread antisemitism that he witnessed as a child, culminating in the violent pogroms that swept Russia in the early 1880s, had a profound effect on his worldview. He decided that the world needed a universal language to unite all humankind. His story is comparable to that of Theodor Herzl, whose experience with antisemitism in France, Germany, and Austria in the same period inspired his manifesto for the creation of a Jewish homeland. The major difference between the two is that Zamenhof's vision was for a universal solution rather than a uniquely Jewish one.

Zamenhof first began working on his idea for a new universal language when he was a teenager, but put it aside for several years while he studied medicine. He became a practising ophthalmologist, eventually settling in Warsaw. But his true passion was always for his linguistic project, and in 1887 his first book on the subject appeared, introducing his new language to the world. He published the book under the pseudonym Dr. Esperanto, meaning 'Dr. Hopeful', and in time the language itself came to be called Esperanto. This first book was written in Russian, but within a year had been translated into several languages, including Hebrew and Yiddish. This is a testament to the fact that Jews featured prominently among the early supporters of the new language.

Zamenhof wanted his language to be as easy to learn as possible. To achieve this, he designed a simple grammatical system with only sixteen basic rules and no irregularities. The spelling of Esperanto is also very easy, since every word is pronounced exactly as it is written. As for the vocabulary, Zamenhof took words from various European languages with which he was familiar and which he thought would be the most familiar to others. The great bulk of the vocabulary comes from Romance and Germanic languages, particularly French, Latin, and German, which Zamenhof knew from childhood. For example, anyone who has a basic familiarity with French or Spanish can probably recognize many of the words in the Esperanto translation of the first verse of the biblical book of Genesis: *En la komenco Dio kreis la ĉielon kaj la teron* 'In the beginning God created the heavens and the earth'. All the words in this verse are plainly Romance, with the exception of *kaj* 'and', which comes from Greek και *kai* 'and'.

Given the fact that Zamenhof spoke fluent Yiddish and was proficient in Hebrew, we might expect some Hebrew and Yiddish vocabulary to show up in Esperanto. However, there is surprisingly little. This may have been an intentional omission, both because Yiddish was often regarded in the period as a substandard variety of German and because Zamenhof wanted Esperanto to be a universal language free of particular cultural or religious associations. However, occasional influences from Yiddish can be discerned. One of the most interesting is the Esperanto word *superjaro*, which means 'leap year'. This is a direct translation of the Yiddish compound word עיבוריאָר *iberyor*, which is itself based on the Hebrew phrase שנת עיבור *shenat 'ibbur*. The Yiddish element יאָר *yor* corresponds to the Hebrew שנת *shenat* 'year', while the Yiddish עיבור *iber* is a borrowing of Hebrew עיבור *'ibbur* 'leap (in the context of calendars)'. However, because the Yiddish word עיבור *iber* sounds identical to another Yiddish word, איבער *iber*, which has a slightly different spelling and means 'over' (like the related German word *über*), many Yiddish speakers assumed that *iberyor* was based on this second איבער *iber* and literally meant 'over-year'. It is exactly this belief that led Zamenhof to create the Esperanto word *superjaro*, which is a compound of *super*, meaning 'over', and *jaro*, meaning 'year'. No other language with which Zamenhof was familiar has a similar construction, so Yiddish must be the source of this Esperanto word.

Esperanto quickly developed a following, spreading across Europe and even further afield. The first international Esperanto Congress was held in France in 1905 and had nearly 700 participants from twenty countries. Although Zamenhof's linguistic vision appealed to Jews and non-Jews alike, a substantial number of early Esperantists were Jewish, perhaps as many as one quarter. Some enthusiasts sought to downplay or even hide Zamenhof's Jewishness, but Zamenhof never denied his heritage. He himself once wrote,

> Every Esperantist in the world knows full well that I am a Jew, because I have never hidden the fact, although I do not shout it chauvinistically from the rooftops. Esperantists know that I have translated texts from the Yiddish language; they know that for more than three years I have devoted all my free time to translating the Bible from the Hebrew original; they know that I have

always lived in an exclusively Jewish quarter of Warsaw. . . . They know that I have always had my works printed by a Jewish printer.

(cited in Korzhenkov 2010: 58)

Zamenhof published numerous books in and on Esperanto, including both original works and translations, but as he got older, he began to focus more on the greater philosophical questions of universalism. Eventually he developed a philosophy that he first called Hillelism, after the Talmudic rabbi Hillel (died ca. 10 CE), who famously said that the whole essence of Judaism is treating others as one would wish to be treated oneself. Later, fearing that the name Hillelism sounded too Jewish, Zamenhof renamed the philosophy Homoranism, meaning something like 'humanism' (based on the Esperanto word *homaro* 'humankind'). His philosophical teachings never really garnered a following, but Esperanto has remained widely studied until the present day. Even though Zamenhof's dream of Esperanto becoming a universal language has not come true, the language has had millions of students and has been far more successful than any other similar attempt. Esperanto has even had native speakers, including Zamenhof's own children. Today there are an estimated 2000 native speakers of the language worldwide, including the famous Hungarian-American billionaire George Soros.

Zamenhof died in 1917. His linguistic movement continued, but there were dark days ahead for its adherents in Europe. The Nazis had a special hatred for Esperanto, both because of its universalist message of tolerance and because of its Jewish associations. Hitler wrote in *Mein Kampf* that Esperanto was part of a secret Jewish plot to rule the world, and under the Nazi regime, Esperantists of all backgrounds were persecuted. When the Nazis invaded Poland, Zamenhof's family was specifically targeted by the Gestapo, and all of his children were killed in the ghettos or concentration camps. However, one grandson, Louis-Christophe Zaleski-Zamenhof (1925–2019), survived to carry on the family legacy. Zamenhof never intended for Esperanto to be a Jewish language, but its Jewish roots are undeniable.

References and further study

There are several histories of Zamenhof and the Esperanto movement, including Boulton (1960), Centassi and Masson (2001), Korzhenkov (2010), and Schor (2016).

11 French

By about the 7th century CE, the spoken Latin language no longer sounded like the written version. The language had spread around most of Western and Southern Europe thanks to the Roman Empire, but in each different area it had continued to evolve in different ways. The written language remained essentially the same as it had been many hundreds of years earlier, but there was no longer just one spoken variety. In the northern half of the territory that the Romans called Gallia, which Julius Caesar conquered around 50 BCE, Latin developed into the language that we know now as French.

The earliest documents that contain a language recognizable as French come from the early 9th century. From that time, until about the mid-14th century, scholars refer to the language as Old French. Old French is closer to Latin than Modern French is, and the differences between the two are roughly comparable to the differences between Chaucer's English and Modern English. There was no standard version of Old French, but rather there were a number of competing dialects. It was not until about 1300 that the dialect of Paris, the basis for what became standard French, began to gain prestige at the expense of other regional dialects. There exists a large body of Old French literature, of which the most famous works are epic poems like the 11th-century *Song of Roland*.

Rashi (1040–1105), an acronym for *Ra*bbi *Sh*lomo *Yi*tshaki, is one of the most famous Jewish scholars of all time, and it so happens that he was also a native speaker of Old French. Rashi lived in France, in the town of Troyes, where he ran a school for biblical and Talmudic studies. He is most famous for the commentaries that he wrote on the Bible and the Talmud, which are still widely read today. Rashi wrote his commentaries in Hebrew, but sometimes he included brief glosses (definitions or explanations) in Judeo-French—that is, in Old French in Hebrew letters. He did this for the benefit of his contemporary readers, usually in order to clarify the meanings of obscure or potentially unfamiliar Hebrew words. For example, the names of several species of tree are mentioned in Genesis 30:37. One of the Hebrew names is עֶרְמוֹן *'ermon*, a word that occurs only twice in the Bible, in this verse and in Ezekiel 31:8. In his commentary to this verse, Rashi glossed the Hebrew word with the Judeo-French term קשטנייר *castenier*, which is the ancestor of Modern French *châtaignier* 'chestnut tree', in order to better convey its meaning to his French-speaking audience.

There are thousands of such Judeo-French words in Rashi's commentaries. And Rashi was not the only medieval French scholar to include Judeo-French glosses in his work. Hundreds more Judeo-French words can be found in the Hebrew commentaries of other scholars, like Rashi's student and colleague Joseph Kara (ca. 1050–ca. 1125), Rashi's grandson Samuel ben Meir, also known as Rashbam (ca. 1080–1158), Rashbam's student Eliezer of Beaugency (active in the 12th century), Joseph Bechor Shor (also active in the 12th century), and several other scholars writing in the 11th–13th centuries. As another example, Isaiah 51:21 contains the phrase שְׁכֻרַת וְלֹא מִיָּיִן *shekhurat we-lo miy-yayin* 'drunk but not from wine'. In his commentary on the book of Isaiah, Joseph Kara explains this with the Judeo-French phrase אִיבְּרָא דְּאַלְטְרָא קוֹשָׁא יָן דְּבִין *ivre de altre chose ja ne de vin* 'drunk from something other than wine'. Judeo-French glosses also appear in other kinds of Hebrew texts from around the same period, like prayer-books and scientific works (see ENGLISH).

In addition to the many words and short phrases contained in these various biblical commentaries and other Hebrew texts, there also exist several long Hebrew–Judeo-French glossaries. These are all from the 13th and 14th centuries, and again the Old French is all in Hebrew characters. Six glossaries survive more or less complete, as do about a dozen fragments of other glossaries. The glossaries are not usually arranged alphabetically like a typical dictionary, but rather are mostly organized according to the order of the biblical books, and give translations for only select words. For example, the biblical book of Haggai contains 496 Hebrew words (many of which repeat, of course), but one Hebrew–Judeo-French glossary (ms. hébr. 301 from the National Library of France) contains only twelve words from Haggai. In total, however, the number of Old French words contained in these glossaries runs into the thousands, making them a substantial source of information on Old French vocabulary. The glossaries are often quite sizeable: for example, ms. 1099 from the University of Leipzig has around 460 pages of text, including over 22,000 entries!

One of the reasons that these glossaries are so interesting is that a number of the Old French words in them are not found in any other sources. Some of these are words that derive directly from Latin but are not found in other forms of French. An example is the word שִׁיטְרִיש *sitres* 'tribes', which derives from the Latin word *sceptrum* 'sceptre' but in the glossaries is used as a translation of the Hebrew term שבט *shevet*, which can mean either 'staff' or 'tribe', depending on the context. (Modern French *sceptre* is a later borrowing from Latin, rather than an inherited form that developed naturally.) Most of the unique Judeo-French words in the glossaries are new coinages that use known French roots in innovative ways. For example, in multiple places in the glossaries, we find forms like פְּרִינְצוֹיְיָארוֹנְט *prinçoyeront* 'they will rule', from a verb *prinçoyer* 'to rule'. The noun *prince* is known from Old and Modern French, but the derived verb *prinçoyer* does not appear outside of Jewish texts. Another example is the word קְרִימוֹרוֹש *cremoros* 'terrifying'. The noun *cremor* 'fear' is found elsewhere in Old French, but the adjective *cremoros* appears only in Judeo-French.

The great majority of the Judeo-French material that has come down to us is contained in the glossaries and in the individual glosses found in Hebrew texts like the commentaries of Rashi. However, a small number of original texts in Judeo-French are known. These include poetic pieces, such as liturgical hymns and a wedding song, some sermon fragments, and a lengthy medical treatise. The most famous of these original texts is a poem known as the Elegy of Troyes. In March of the year 1288, the Jews of Troyes were accused of a ritual murder, after a dead body was planted in the house of a prominent member of the community named Isaac Châtelain. As a result of this accusation (a classic example of a blood libel), thirteen Jews were burned alive, including Isaac, his pregnant wife, and his children. The Elegy of Troyes—a poem of seventeen four-line, rhyming stanzas—commemorates this tragic event. The third stanza reads as follows:

De la tré male felone jant sofro[n]s	דלטרימלא פֿלונא גֿאנט שופֿרוש
sete dolor	שיטא דולור
Bein nos fo[n]t changer e muer la color	בֵּיין נוס פֿוט קֿנגֿיר אימואר לקולור
Gé, prent en pité e enten cri e plor	גֿי פֿרנטן פיטי אי אנטן קרי איפֿלור
Car por nie[n]t a[von]s perdu mei[n]t	קר פֿור נייט א[ון]ש פֿירדו מיט
ome de valor	אומא דֿולור

'At the hands of the very evil people, we suffer this pain;
Indeed they make us switch and change colour.
God, take pity on us and hear our call and cry!
For we have for naught lost many a man of worth.'

This original poem is a fascinating window into the dangerous world in which French Jews lived in the 13th century, and is an important source of information about the events of the time. It is also a beautiful and moving piece of poetry.

The Judeo-French corpus of texts is of great interest to linguists. As already mentioned, many of the words preserved in these texts are otherwise unknown. In addition, the fact that the texts are written in the Hebrew alphabet gives us some insight as to how Old French was pronounced, sometimes more so than the Roman alphabet equivalents. Christian speakers of Old French were often influenced by Latin in their spelling practices, but Jews were not. Therefore, Judeo-French is in some ways a more accurate representation of the sounds of Old French. For example, the verb 'we suffer' in the first line of the excerpt from the elegy is spelled שופֿרוש <sufros>, which tells us that the *n* was not pronounced, but that the final -*s* was. The Old French spelling *soufrons* (like the Modern French spelling *souffrons*) is more ambiguous. As another example, consider the Old French word *vin* 'wine'. We know that originally this was pronounced [vin] (rhyming with English *clean*) and that at some point it came to be pronounced [vã] (like a nasalized version of English *van*), as it is today in Modern French. But the spelling *vin*, which is the same in both Old French and Modern French, does not tell us when this change occurred. The Judeo-French spelling בֿ֪ין *vin*, found in the commentary of Joseph Kara mentioned earlier, which dates to about the year 1100, shows us clearly that the word still rhymed with English *clean* at that time. Also, while the Hebrew-letter texts are unique to Jewish authors, there

A Hebrew–Judeo-French Biblical Glossary from the 13th century, showing glosses from Zeph. 3:3–19, all of Haggai, and Zech. 1:8–2:4. Bibliothèque nationale de France, ms. 301, fol. 58r.

is no evidence that the Jews themselves spoke a dialect any different from their Christian neighbors.

Production of texts in Judeo-French declined and then stopped as the 14th century wore on, no doubt as a result of the continuous persecutions and numerous expulsions suffered by the Jews throughout northern France. After the 14th century, there is no evidence of any French texts written by French Jews in Hebrew characters. However, in the 19th century, following the colonization by France of Algeria, and later Tunisia and Morocco, French exerted influence on the local Arabic dialects, including Jewish varieties (see ARABIC, MODERN). In some Judeo-Arabic texts of the late 19th and early 20th centuries—in newspapers, for example—we find borrowed French words written in Hebrew script. For example, in one Judeo-Arabic newspaper published on March 16, 1896 in Oran, Algeria, we find the phrase מוסיו לפריזידאן דלאריפובליק *musyu l-prezidan d-la-republik* (for French *monsieur le président de la république* 'Mr. President of the Republic'). As in the medieval texts, these Judeo-French words are spelled phonetically. Unlike the medieval Judeo-French texts, which add to our understanding of the phonetic and lexical history of the French language, the Judeo-French words and phrases appearing in 19th- and 20th-century North Africa are interesting mainly as evidence of the shifting cultural ties of North African Jewry to France.

References and further study

A general overview of Judeo-French can be found in Kiwitt and Dörr (2017), along with an extensive bibliography and guide to further reading. Works on the Judeo-French glosses appearing in Rashi include Darmesteter (1909) and Gruber (2004). On the glosses found in Joseph Kara's commentary on Isaiah, see Fudeman (2006). The sample from the Elegy of Troyes is based on the text presented in the study of Fudeman (2008). Other major works on Judeo-French include Banitt (1972, 1995–2005), Fudeman (2010), Kiwitt (2013), and Staller (2019). Benbassa (1999) is a general survey of French Jewish history, while Chazan (1973) and Golb (1998) are more detailed studies of Jews in northern France in the Middle Ages. French in the Judeo-Arabic of Algerian Jews is discussed by Tirosh-Becker (2011). On the use of French in modern Israel, see Ben-Rafael and Ben-Rafael (2018). The Judeo-Arabic newspaper from 1896 can be seen on the Historical Jewish Press website: https://web.nli.org.il/sites/JPress/English/Pages/maged-mesharim.aspx.

12 Georgian

The small country of Georgia in the Caucasus Mountains is home to one of the world's oldest Jewish communities, dating back to at least the 2nd century BCE. In fact, according to a medieval Georgian historical account, the Jews first arrived in the country even earlier, following the conquest of Jerusalem by the Babylonians in 586 BCE. The tradition of the Georgian Jews themselves holds that they are the descendants of the Lost Ten Tribes exiled from biblical Israel in the 8th century BCE. These earliest Georgian Jewish communities—however old they really are—were later joined by Jews who came to the Caucasus region from Armenia, Persia, and various places in the Byzantine Empire.

The Georgian Jews lived as serfs for about 500 years, from the late 14th century until the 19th century. During this period, they were controlled by the king, the church, or feudal masters and worked chiefly in fabric weaving and dyeing or in agriculture. As serfs, the Georgian Jews were often isolated from each other, with the result that traditional Jewish knowledge declined in many cases.

Over the course of the 19th century, Georgian territories gradually became part of the Russian Empire. In the 1860s and early 1870s, serfdom was outlawed in Georgia, and upon gaining their freedom, the Jews rapidly relocated to the country's urban centres, where they established synagogues and other Jewish institutions. Ashkenazi Jews from other parts of the Russian Empire began to settle in Georgia around the same time, but relations between the new arrivals and the local Georgian Jews were generally cool. The two groups remained distinct from each other, though there was certainly religious and cultural interaction between them.

The earliest Jews to arrive in Georgia probably spoke Hebrew and/or Aramaic, but at some point they adopted the local language, Georgian. Georgian is the most widely spoken member of the small family of languages known as Kartvelian, which is one of several language families confined to the Caucasus. Georgian has no relatives outside of the region. Striking features of Georgian include its large inventory of consonants and its tendency to have long strings of consonants. Examples include words such as მშვიდობით *mshvidobit* 'goodbye', თქვენ *tkven* 'you (plural)', and ცხრა *tskhra* 'nine'. Georgian is also quite unusual among the languages of the world in that it has its own native alphabet (rather than a borrowed one), which dates back to around 400 CE.

In contrast to many Jewish languages, Jewish Georgian was not generally written in the Hebrew alphabet but rather in the Georgian script. The spoken language of Georgian Jews seems to have differed a bit from that of their non-Jewish counterparts, although not to any significant degree; Georgian Jews could communicate with other Georgian speakers without any problems. Jewish Georgian had a few distinctive features of pronunciation and grammar, but its most prominent characteristic was the use of Hebrew and Aramaic vocabulary. Most of the Hebrew and Aramaic words found in the speech of Georgian Jews refer to Jewish holidays, rituals, and other aspects of Jewish culture. This can be contrasted with some other Jewish languages, such as Yiddish and Ladino, which use Hebrew and Aramaic vocabulary to refer to all kinds of everyday objects and concepts which do not have specific links to Jewish culture. Examples of words of Hebrew origin in Jewish Georgian are *misva* 'mitzvah, religious commandment' (from Hebrew מצוה *mitsva*) and *qolam* 'universe, world' (from Hebrew עולם *'olam*).

In some cases, words of Hebrew origin in Jewish Georgian can take on a different meaning than the one they have in Hebrew; for example, the Jewish Georgian word *keleb*, which comes from Hebrew כלב *kelev* 'dog', can be used to mean 'policeman'. The Georgian Jews also had a secret language called *qivruli* (literally meaning 'Hebrew') that they used when they did not want to be understood by non-Jewish speakers of Georgian. *Qivruli* was based on Georgian grammar, but its vocabulary contained a large amount of Hebrew words mixed with Georgian ones, which made it incomprehensible to outsiders.

Jewish Georgian was primarily a spoken language and was not typically used for written literature. There was a vibrant tradition of folktales, proverbs, and jokes in Jewish Georgian, and there were also a number of Georgian translations of classic Jewish texts that were passed down orally from generation to generation and recited on the Sabbath and other Jewish celebrations. One of the most famous of these is called the *Tavsili*, which is the Jewish Georgian translation of the Torah. In Georgian synagogues, it was traditional to recite the *Tavsili* orally alongside the weekly Torah reading in Hebrew. The language of the *Tavsili* reflects an older form of Georgian that was preserved over the centuries through oral transmission. There is also a Jewish Georgian Passover Haggadah, which, like the *Tavsili*, was not committed to writing; it was recited by Georgian Jews every year within the ritual context of the Passover seder. As in the case of the *Tavsili*, the Haggadah has some interesting linguistic features that reflect its older origins. This use of archaic forms is a distinctive feature of a number of Jewish language varieties (see, for example, LADINO).

We only know of one case of a text written in Georgian using the Hebrew script. The text, a book called ספר חנוך הנערים *sefer ḥinukh ha-ne'arim* 'The Book of the Education of the Youth', is a Hebrew–Georgian phrasebook with the Georgian printed in the Hebrew alphabet. It was written by Siman Rizhinashvili and published in 1892 in Jerusalem. This phrasebook seems to be unique, as books composed in Georgian by Georgian Jews were not otherwise written in Hebrew letters. The fact that this volume is a phrasebook suggests that, in the late 19th century, Georgian Jews wanted to be able to speak conversational Hebrew, even though Hebrew was not yet firmly established as an everyday spoken language in Ottoman Palestine, as it would become over the subsequent decades. The existence of this phrasebook also reflects the fact that there was a relatively large interest in Hebrew among Georgian Jews in that period. For example, in at least one community in Georgia—Tskhinvali—Hebrew was actually used as a spoken language in the 1890s and early 20th century—again, before Hebrew had become a widely established native spoken language in Palestine. This was because the town's chief rabbi was an Ashkenazi Jew from Lithuania, and Hebrew was the only language that he had in common with the congregation. Moreover, in the first two decades of the 20th century, Hebrew was the language of instruction in a number of Georgian Jewish schools.

There were no specifically Jewish Georgian periodicals until 1918, when a Georgian-language newspaper called ხმა ებრაელისა *khma ebraelisa* 'The Jewish Voice' was established. However, the newspaper lasted only about a year. In the late 1920s and early 1930s, Jewish Georgian writers translated Jewish works into Georgian from other languages. For example, there were Georgian translations of the Yiddish author Sholem Aleichem, who wrote the stories that would later become famous in English as the play and film *Fiddler on the Roof*, among many others (see YIDDISH, MODERN STANDARD). Another example is the Georgian version of the very popular modernist Yiddish play *The Dybbuk*, which was produced at the State Theatre in Georgia's capital, Tbilisi. There were also some Jewish authors who wrote original novels in Georgian about Georgian Jewish life.

This cultural activity did not have long to flourish before it was eradicated by repressive Stalinist policies in the late 1930s, as was the case for Jewish and other minority languages throughout the Soviet Union in the same period (see TAJIK and TAT). The last official remnant of Soviet Jewish cultural life in Georgia was the Georgian Jewish Museum in Tbilisi, which was established in the early 1930s and remained open until 1951. In this period, Georgian Jewish cultural and religious life in general was subjected to severe attacks by the Stalinist regime; many synagogues were closed, rabbis and writers were arrested and executed, and sacred books were destroyed. Despite this oppression, Georgian Jews generally continued to observe Jewish customs, such as keeping kosher and going to synagogue, and some even continued to study in secret, illegal Jewish schools.

The late 1970s saw the re-emergence of Georgian Jewish literary and cultural activity for the first time since the beginning of the Stalinist oppression several decades earlier. The first Georgian-language book on a Jewish topic to appear at this time was a translation of medieval Hebrew poetry by the Georgian Jewish writer Jemal Ajiashvili (1944–2013), who went on to write other books in Georgian on Jewish themes; in 1984, he received the Shota Rustaveli Prize, Georgia's most prestigious literary award, in recognition of his work. Since the late 1970s, other Georgian Jewish literary figures have contributed to the revitalization of Georgian Jewish culture by composing plays, poetry, and novels in Georgian about Jewish topics, such as Israel, Jewish life in Georgia, and the relationship between Georgian Jews and Christians. Despite this cultural renaissance, however, Jewish life in Georgia has been significantly affected by emigration over the past forty years. Beginning in the 1970s, and increasing with the collapse of the Soviet Union in the early 1990s, many Georgian Jews immigrated to Israel. Israel is where the bulk of the Georgian Jewish community now lives, with only a few thousand remaining in Georgia. Some Georgian Jews in Israel still speak Georgian, but the younger generations who have grown up in Israel often do not learn the language.

References and further study

Enoch (2017) is an overview of Jewish Georgian. Zand, Neishtat, and Beizer (2007) provide a concise survey of the history of the Jews in Georgia. Soltes et al. (2004) is a short cultural history of the Georgian Jews, accompanied by images of Georgian Jewish material culture. Zand (1991) contains some information on the history of the Georgian Jews in the context of the non-Ashkenazi Jewish communities in the Soviet Union. The *Tavsili* and oral translation of the Haggadah have been recorded and published by Enoch (2008, 2009, 2014), but these are very academic editions in Hebrew.

13 German

Jews began to move into Germanic-speaking areas of Central Europe in the first millennium of the Common Era, at which point they adopted local German dialects. We have evidence of the speech of German-speaking Jews from as early as the 11th century, and their language developed into what came to be called Yiddish (see YIDDISH, OLD AND EARLY MODERN). Early Yiddish in German-speaking areas of Western and Central Europe was not very different from local German dialects. Its most distinctive characteristics were the use of the Hebrew script and some items of Hebrew vocabulary. By the 17th and 18th centuries, the centre of the Yiddish-speaking world shifted to Eastern Europe, and the vast majority of Yiddish speakers ended up in the Russian Pale of Settlement (see RUSSIAN). There, largely cut off from German speakers, Yiddish continued to diverge from German. Yiddish declined in Western and Central Europe in the 18th century, as local Jews abandoned Yiddish in favour of non-Jewish languages like German and Dutch, and it more or less died out in the 19th century. Some pockets of the Western varieties of Yiddish did remain; as regional varieties, they were still noticeably distinct from the written standard German language, as well as from non-Jewish German dialects.

The much greater adoption of standard German by Jews that started in the late 18th century was the result of two main factors. The first was the promotion of German-language education by the great 18th-century monarchs Frederick the Great of Prussia (reigned 1740–1786) and Joseph II of Austria (reigned 1765–1790), especially the German-language schools established by the latter throughout Habsburg territories. The second and most important factor was the establishment of the Jewish Enlightenment movement, known as the Haskalah, in the last quarter of the 18th century. Central to this movement was the secular education of Jews, and, especially in Germany and elsewhere in Western Europe, their linguistic assimilation. Many Maskilim (adherents of the Haskalah) saw Yiddish as a corrupt form of German, which served to alienate Jews from mainstream society. Yiddish was also seen as a corrupting force within Jewish religious learning, taking the rightful place of Hebrew. As such, the promotion of standard German for secular learning, and Hebrew for religious learning, was also an important tenet of the Haskalah (see also HEBREW, ENLIGHTENMENT).

The name most closely connected to the Haskalah is undoubtedly Moses Mendelssohn (1729–1786), the renowned Jewish-German philosopher and scholar. His most influential publication was a five-volume edition of the Torah called ספר נתיבות השלום *Sefer Netivot ha-Shalom*, published in Berlin in 1783. This edition included, besides the original Hebrew text, a translation into Judeo-German—that is, standard German written in Hebrew characters. His translation, which was based on Jewish scholarship, was intended to provide a Jewish readership with an accessible entry into the standard German language. Mendelssohn found German translations by Christians unacceptable; as he saw it, they ignored Jewish interpretive traditions, emended the original Hebrew text as they saw fit, and introduced a Christian bent. Mendelssohn was explicitly framing his translation in opposition to the ideas of contemporary German scholars like Johann Michaelis (1717–1791) and Johann Eichhorn (1752–1827), whose works were hugely influential on later biblical scholarship. Mendelssohn's Judeo-German translation was accompanied by a lengthy Hebrew commentary, which itself was very influential on the use of Hebrew as a language of modern scholarship in the Haskalah. The commentary was innovative, but also drew heavily from the major medieval Jewish commentators, like Rashi (see FRENCH) and his grandson Samuel ben Meir (also called Rashbam). Following is Mendelssohn's translation of the beginning of the book of Genesis (from the first edition), followed by a transcription in standard German spelling:

אים אנפֿאנגי ערשוף גאטט דיא הימֵל אונד דיא ערדי. דיא ערדי אבר ווּאר אונפֿערמליך אונד פֿרמישט. פֿינסטרניס אויף דר פֿלעכّי דש אבגרונדש, אונד דר געטליכֿה גייסט ווּעבנד אויף דען ווּאסרן. דא שפֿראך גאט עש ווּערדי ליכֿט זא ווּארד ליכֿט. גאטט זאהי דש ליכֿט דש עש גוט זייא.

Im Anfange erschuf Gott die Himmel und die Erde. Die Erde aber war unfermlich und vermischt. Finsternis auf der Fleche des Abgrundes, und der göttliche Geist webend auf den Wassern. Da sprach Gott es werde Licht so ward Licht. Gott sahe das Licht dass es gut sei.

'In the beginning, God created the heaven and the earth. But the earth was unformed and confused. Darkness (was) over the surface of the abyss, and the Holy Spirit was hovering over the water. Then God said, "Let there be light!" So there was light. God saw that the light was good.'

Mendelssohn's translation and commentary were published in numerous subsequent editions in the 19th and 20th centuries. The Judeo-German spelling varied quite a bit among the editions, and so in other editions we find spellings like וואסער in place of וואסר for German *Wasser* 'water', גאָטט in place of גאטט for *Gott* 'God', and געטליכע in place of געטליכֿה for *göttliche* 'holy'. Note that Judeo-German spelling is typically imitative of German spelling, and so we find, for example, repeated letters (e.g., גאטט for German *Gott* 'God') or silent letters (e.g., איהר for German *ihr* 'her'); these features are not typical of other Jewish languages written in Hebrew script (except for some types of Yiddish spelling, which likewise attempted to imitate the German model). Sometimes, however, Judeo-German betrays some Yiddish influence. This is most obvious in the case of the German vowel *au*, which is spelled in Judeo-German with the Hebrew letters יו, no doubt in imitation of cognate words in Yiddish, in which this combination is typically pronounced *oy*. For example, in the foregoing text, we see the spelling אויף for German *auf*. Another well-attested example is the word בוים 'tree', for German *baum* (cf. Yiddish בוים *boym* 'tree').

In the 19th century, there was a surge of publishing in Judeo-German, not only in the territory corresponding to modern Germany, but also in parts of Poland, Hungary, and the Czech Republic, among other places. There were translations of biblical books, the Passover Haggadah, the Mishnah, *siddurim* (daily prayer-books), *maḥzorim* (holiday prayer-books), and important medieval works of Jewish literature. There were also original Judeo-German texts, including both academic and literary works. For example, the highly influential journal ביכורי העתים *Bikkurei ha-ʿIttim* (published annually from 1821 to 1832), was largely in Judeo-German in its first few years (with some articles in Hebrew), though later it shifted to a much greater percentage of content in Hebrew. Its Ukrainian-born founder, Shalom Cohen (or Salomon Kohn; 1772–1845), published several Judeo-German books, including a Hebrew grammar for schools called תורת לשון עברית *Torat Leshon ʾIvrit* (Berlin, 1801) that went through numerous later editions. He also published a book of rhyming fables in both Hebrew and Judeo-German called משלי אגור *Mishle ʾAgur* (Berlin, 1799), aimed at children learning Hebrew. Having both Hebrew and Judeo-German on opposite pages was typical of most Judeo-German works. For example, the book נהר מעדן *Nahar Me-ʿEden* (Breslau, 1837), a history of Jews in biblical times by David Samoscz (1789–1864) that is over 200 pages long, is almost entirely bilingual, with Hebrew on the right-hand page, and Judeo-German on the left-hand page. There were even Hebrew–Judeo-German dictionaries.

One very interesting Judeo-German text is a proclamation by the Jewish communal authority of the Kingdom of Westphalia (a political entity located in the northwest of present-day Germany that existed only from 1807 to 1813), issued in 1810. Part of this text reads as follows:

דאָ בערייטז זעהר אָפֿט פֿאָן זאָלדאַטען יידישער רעליגיאָן בייא אונז מינדליכע אַנפֿראָגע געמאַכט וואָרדען איזט: אָב איהנען ניכט געשטאַטטעט ווערדען קאָננע זיך אַם פֶּסַח דער הילזענפֿריכטע, אלז: ערבזען, באָהנען, לינזען, דעזגלייכען אויך דעז רייזעז אונד הירזען צו איהרעם לעבענזאונטערהאַלטע צו בעדינען, אינדעם איהנען . . . דיא מַצֹוֹת נור שפֿאַרזאָם מיטגעטהיילט ווירדען, אונד זיא גענאָטהיגט וואָרען, אַן דיזעם פֿעסטע . . . ענטוועדער צו הונגערן, אָדער חַמֵץ צו סען.

Da bereits sehr oft von Soldaten jüdischer Religion bei uns die mündliche Anfrage gemacht worden ist: Ob ihnen nicht gestattet werden könne, sich am Pesah der Hülsenfrüchte, als: Erbsen, Bohnen, Linsen, desgleichen auch des Reises und Hirsen zu ihrem Lebensunterhalte zu bedienen, indem ihnen . . . die matsot nur sparsam mitgeteilt würden, und sie genötigt wären, an diesem Fest . . . entweder zu hungern, oder hamets zu sehn.

'Since very often the request has been made to us by Jewish soldiers: whether or not they could be permitted to make use during Passover of legumes, such as peas, beans, lentils, as well as rice and millet, for their subsistence, since . . . *matzah* had been so sparingly distributed to them, and they have been compelled on this festival . . . either to starve or to look for *chametz*.'

This text is interesting not only as a real-world (non-literary) example of the use of Judeo-German, but also as an early example of what would come to be Reform Judaism. In this case, the issue of eating *kitniyot* (beans, peas, lentils, etc.), which had traditionally been forbidden among Ashkenazi Jews during Passover, is not merely a scholarly debate but rather a necessary consideration born out of the hardships resulting from the Napoleonic Wars. (Incidentally, the question of the eating of *kitniyot* during Passover is still debated among some Reform and Conservative Jews in the 21st century, though most Reform rabbis have declared *kitniyot* to be permissible.)

It was the wish of scholars like Mendelssohn that Jews would assimilate into the German-speaking world, and by the end of the 19th century there were a great many Jewish scholars writing in standard German (no longer in Hebrew characters). Famous Jewish German-language authors of the 19th and early 20th centuries include historian Heinrich Graetz (1817–1891), psychoanalyst Sigmund Freud (1856–1939), sociologist Franz Oppenheimer (1864–1943), writer Franz Kafka (1883–1924), physicist Albert Einstein (1879–1955), political theorist Hannah Arendt (1906–1975), and a myriad of others. Jews were very well represented in German academic circles until the rise of the Nazi regime.

Many of the early immigrants to Palestine were German speaking, especially those who came in the 1930s. When the cornerstone for Israel's first university was laid in Haifa in 1912, it was to be called the Technikum (a German word), and it was funded by a German-Jewish organization. Its administration decided that the language of education would be German; after all, German was an international language of scholarship, whereas Modern Hebrew was only in its infancy. This caused an uproar among the Jews of Palestine, especially among the non-German-speaking Jews that had come from Eastern Europe. The administration capitulated and decided in 1914 to make Hebrew the sole language of education, and the Technikum was given the Hebraized name Technion; the Technion is today an internationally well-respected institution. The whole episode—known later as the Language Wars—shows not only how important the German language was to many Jews, but also how it was instrumental in cementing the prestige of Hebrew in Palestine.

The long history that Jews have had speaking German has made an impact on the German language itself. Non-Jewish Germans borrowed many words from Hebrew (usually via Yiddish) during the many centuries of contact they had with their Jewish neighbours. Despite the loss of nearly all the Jewish population of Germany in World War II, many of these loanwords survive today. Most of these words have no overt connection to Judaism, and the average German speaker does not have any knowledge of their Jewish origins. So, for example, in

Genesis 1:6–1:8 in the first edition of Moses Mendelssohn's Judeo-German Bible (Berlin, 1783), with text in Hebrew and Judeo-German.

— 118 —

צוױיטער אבשניט.

פֿאָן דען

איבריגען בעשטיממונגען אים פֿעל.

§ 110.

אונסער דען ערװעהנטען המכדלונגסװערטען לאסטען זיך מיט פעל נאָך
פֿאָלגענדע פֿינף בעשטיאאװונגען מיטגעבען:

1) **הָאוֹפֶן** מָדער **הַדֶּרֶךְ** (דיא מַרט, אַמָדוס), נעהאױך מױך װעל־
לע מרט חונד װייגע דער בעגריף דעם לייטװערטעם דעם סוביעקטע ביים
געװעגט װירד.

2) **הַזְּמָן** (דיא לייט, טעאפוס), מין װעלכֶער לייט דיא בייחװעגונג
געטיעהט.

3) **הַגּוּף** (דיא פֿערזָןן, פֿערזָאנם),

4) **הַמִּין** (דמ: געטלעבט, גענוס), דעם סוביעקטעס

5) אונד **הַמְּסְפָר** (דיא לְמַהל, נואמרוס),

§ 111.

אוֹפַנִים (מרטען) װיא דער בעגריף דעם לייטװערטעם דעם סוב־
יעקטע בייאמגעװעגט װירד, זינד פֿאָלגענדע דרייא:

1) **אוֹפֶן הַהֶחְלֵט** (דיא בעשטיאאטע מאליגענדע מרט, אַמָדום
אינדיקמֶטיפֿום), װען דיא המכדלונג מיט דעם סוביעקטע געדמכלט אונד מיהן
בעשטיאאט אונד געװים גען ל1» מָדער מֶבגעטערמֶטען װירד, מאָס: **כָּתַבְתָּ**
(דיא המסט געטריעבען), **לֹא כָתַבְתָּ** (דיא המסט ניללט געטריעבען).

מינדעם לייגט דיעזער אופן מױך אױך אייגע מוהגעװיסםע מָדער פֿערבינדענדע
מרט (אַמָדום קאָניונקטיפֿום) מן, (עם מיז נעהאױך אין דיעזער טפרמכֶע
דיא מאליגענדע מרט, מיט דער פֿערבינדענדען גלייך, מאָס: **הָיִינוּ
שְׂמֵחִים** קמן ומ«וחהו הייסען: װיר װערען פֿרמה. מלם מױך
װערען פֿרמה. **אָבַדְתִּי בְּעָנְיִי** קמן הייסען: מיך פֿערלװיײ־
פעלטע מין אייגעם עלענדע, מונד מױך מיך װירדע מין

modern German one hears *Mischpoche* or *Mischpoke* 'family' (< Yiddish משפחה *mishpokhe* < Hebrew משפחה *mishpakha* 'family'), *zocken* 'to gamble' (< Hebrew שחק *saḥaq* 'play'), *Moos* 'money' (< Yiddish מעות *moes* 'money' < Hebrew מעות *maʾot* 'coins'), *Macker* 'boyfriend' (< Yiddish מכר *maker* 'partner' < Hebrew מכר *makkar* 'acquaintance'), *mies* 'bad' (< Yiddish מיאוס *mies* 'ugly, odious' < Hebrew מיאוס *miʾus* 'abomination, repulsiveness'), and many other such words. A common New Year's greeting is *Guten Rutsch*, the second element of which likely derives from Hebrew ראש *rosh*, the first element of the phrase ראש השנה *rosh ha-shana* 'New Year', even though it appears on the surface to be German *Rutsch* 'slide'. The enigmatic phrase *Hals- und Beinbruch*, literally 'neck and leg fracture', is used to wish someone luck in German, exactly like English 'break a leg!', and many believe that this German phrase (along with the English equivalent) comes from a misinterpretation of Yiddish הצלחה וברכה *hatslokhe u-vrokhe* 'success and blessing' < Hebrew הצלחה וברכה *hatslakha u-vrakha* 'success and blessing'.

Jews in other Germanic-language countries have had linguistic histories similar to the Jews of Germany. For example, in the Netherlands, Jews largely abandoned Yiddish before the 20th century, but they left a lasting impression on the Dutch language. In Sweden, which does not have a long history of Jewish settlement, Jewish immigrants from elsewhere in Europe abandoned Yiddish in favour of Swedish. There are some distinctive characteristics of the Swedish used by Jews, though it is probably a stretch to speak of a real Jewish variety of the language.

References and further study

On the history of Jews in medieval Germany, see Haverkamp (2018), and on the early modern period, see Hertz (2018) and Silber (2018). Background on Mendelssohn's translation of the Bible, along with an English translation of his lengthy introduction, can be found in Breuer (2018). A copy of the circular from the Kingdom of Westphalia is preserved at the library of Hebrew Union College in Cincinnati, and an edition with discussion was published online by Jordan Finkin (huc. edu/research/libraries/blog/2016/07/21/early-plea-passover-legumes). On Hebrew loanwords in German, see Wagner (2013). Several books on German words with Jewish origins have been published by Althaus (2014, 2015, 2019). On Jewish loanwords in Dutch, see van de Kamp and van der Wijk (2006), and on Jewish Swedish, see Klagsbrun Lebenswerd (2017, 2018).

14 Greek

After Alexander the Great conquered the Near East in the 330s BCE, Jews liv-ing throughout the Mediterranean—in places like Egypt, Asia Minor (Turkey), and Syria—adopted Greek in large numbers. Even in the Land of Israel, where Hebrew and Aramaic were the primary languages used by Jews, Greek culture and education soon became widespread, and knowledge of Greek became a marker of prestige. Hellenized Jews studied Greek literature and philosophy, and many highly influential Jewish texts were composed in Greek. For example, the famous Jewish philosopher Philo (ca. 25 BCE–50 CE), who lived in Alexandria (Egypt), composed all of his works in Greek. Josephus (37 CE–ca. 100 CE), the Jewish historian whose works are indispensable for our knowledge of Jewish history in Roman times, wrote his histories in Greek. But by far the most important text written by Jews in Greek is the Bible translation known as the Septuagint. (This is not counting the Christian New Testament, written in Greek, which was largely the product of Jewish authors.)

In the 3rd century BCE, Greek-speaking Jews living in Alexandria translated the Torah from Hebrew into Greek. Some traditions hold that the project began on the initiative of the Egyptian ruler Ptolemy Philadelphus II (285–247 BCE), but it may simply be that the local Jews, who no longer spoke Hebrew, wanted to be able to read the Torah in their own language. Over the next two centuries, the remaining biblical books were translated into Greek. The Greek translation later came to be known as the Septuagint, from the Latin word *septuaginta* 'seventy', because legend has it that the translation of the Torah was made by seventy-two Jewish scholars. The Hebrew Bible itself was not yet completed by the 3rd century—for example, the book of Daniel was most likely written in the mid-2nd century BCE—which means that the Greek translation of the Torah actually predates some Hebrew biblical material.

The Septuagint remained the standard Bible used by Greek-speaking Jews into the 1st century CE. It was read even in the Land of Israel, as proven by the fact that fragments of it have turned up among the Dead Sea Scrolls (see HEBREW, BIBLICAL). Because most of the early Christians were Greek-speaking (and often converts from Judaism), the Septuagint was the version of the Bible used by that community; they referred to it as the Old Testament, since it was supplemented by their New Testament.

Up until the 1st century CE, the Hebrew Bible itself remained a somewhat fluid collection of books. Different versions of some books were in circulation, and it was not agreed upon which books should be considered sacred. The Bible was, in fact, not yet one book but a collection of many books, and these books were produced individually, on scrolls. But in response to the political and religious upheavals of the 1st century CE, most notably the destruction of the Second Temple and Jerusalem in 70 CE, the Jewish Rabbis decided that they needed to agree on a set biblical canon. The Rabbis determined which books, and which versions of those books, were to be considered sacred. Of course, the Rabbis were concerned with the Hebrew Bible, and not the Septuagint translation.

The Septuagint contains additional books—books written in or translated into Greek by Jews—that are not in the Hebrew Bible. Over time, because it came to be associated with Christianity and because the Rabbis had deemed these extra books to be non-canonical, Jews stopped reading the Septuagint. After this happened, Jews thus lost awareness of those extra books. And because of this, some Jewish Greek works have been preserved only in the Christian tradition. The most well-known of these are the books of First and Second Maccabees, which include the story that gives us the holiday of Hanukkah. Of course, the Hanukkah tradition is preserved in later Jewish works like the Talmud, but with much less detail than in the books of Maccabees. And nowhere is Hanukkah mentioned in the Hebrew Bible.

When Jerome made his Latin translation of the Hebrew Bible in the 4th century CE, he also translated the extra books found in the Septuagint, but he referred to them as the "apocryphal" books. The Catholic Church adopted Jerome's translation, known as the Vulgate, as its official version of the Bible, and so these apocryphal books continued to be read by Christians into modern times.

It is not clear if the Greek spoken by Jews in the Hellenistic and Roman periods (4th century BCE–4th century CE) was different from that of their non-Jewish neighbours. The Septuagint does show some distinctive features, probably reflecting the fact that the text is a direct translation from Hebrew. But the language of authors like Philo and Josephus is no different from the standard Greek of the era.

As Greek influence in the Mediterranean waned, Jews living in the region gradually abandoned the language in favour of other vernaculars. However, a number of Jewish communities remained Greek speaking throughout the Middle Ages and into the 20th century, especially in cities on the Greek mainland and on Mediterranean islands like Corfu and Crete. Jews continued to write in Greek as well, although we find nothing like the grand literary creations of the ancient period; instead, we mostly find shorter texts, like hymns, letters, glossaries, and Bible commentaries. There is some evidence of other Bible translations as well, but these survive mostly in fragmentary form. During the medieval period and up until the late 19th century, Jews preferred to write Greek in the Hebrew alphabet, a style which we can call Judeo-Greek. What makes Judeo-Greek texts very interesting to linguists is that they often reflect the spoken vernacular rather than the literary standard of the time. As with other Jewish languages, Judeo-Greek is not bound by the conventional spelling rules of the standard language (as spelled in the Greek alphabet) but rather reflects actual pronunciation (see also FRENCH). For example, the Greek phrase οἱ υἱοι *oi uioi* 'the sons' contained three distinct vowel sounds in classical Greek, but all three (*u, i,* and *oi*) came in the medieval period to be pronounced by Greek speakers—both Jewish and non-Jewish ones—like the vowel in English *see*. While standard Greek spelling continued to reflect the classical pronunciation, in one 19th-century Judeo-Greek text (shown in the accompanying image of *Shir ha-Shirim Rabba*), we find the phrase 'the sons' spelled phonetically as אִיאִיאִי *iii.*

Noteworthy Judeo-Greek texts include a complete translation of the Book of Jonah from the 14th century, a translation of the entire Torah that was printed in Constantinople in 1547, and a number of original poems. One poem commemorates 'Little Purim', a holiday instituted by the so-called Sicilian Jews, who had come to Greece from Syracuse in Sicily. The poem describes how the Syracusan Jews were miraculously saved in the late 1300s from a plot by an apostate called Marcus, who betrayed the community and tried turn the king against them. The following is an excerpt from this captivating poem.

o markos o ksilothrimenos	אוֹמַרְקוֹס אוֹקְסִילוֹתְרִימֵינוֹס
ox to yisrael sparagmenos	אוֹחְטוֹ יִשְׂרָאֵל סְפַּארַאגְמֵינוֹס
ipagise na tus prozdosi	אִיפַּאגִ'יסִי נַאטוּס פְּרוֹזְדוֹסִי
se piriklo na tus dosi	סֵיפִּירִיקְלוֹ נַאטוּס דוֹסִי
tu vasilea na fanerosi	טוּ בַאסִילֵיַא נַאפַאנֵירוֹסִי
o thios na ton plirosi	אוֹתִיאוֹס נַאטוֹן פְּלִירוֹסִי
. . .	. . .
i ovrei i timimeni	אִי יוֹבְרֵיִי אִיטִימִימֵינִי
sta vasilia ksaikuzmeni	סְטַא וַאסִילֵיַא קְסַאיִקוּזְמֵינִי
susti ke imbistimeni	סוּסְטִי קֵי אִינְבִּיסְטִימֵינִי
tu theu ksidialigmeni	טוּתֵיאוּ קְסִידְיַיאלִיגְמֵינִי
ton ikremasan ton marko	טוֹן אִיקְרֵימַאסַאן טוֹן מַארְקוֹ
osan to skili to zarko	אוֹסַאן טוֹסְקִילִי טוֹ זַארְקוֹ
tsitsiliani me tin ya sas	צִיצִילְיַאנִי מֵיטִין יַאסַאס
fate piete me kali kardia sas	פַאטֵי פְּיֵיטֵי מֵי קַאלִי קַארְדְיַיאסַאס
ke me tin kali khara sas	קֵימֵיטִין קַאלִי חַארַאסַאס
na zisun ta pedia sas	נַאזִיסוּן טַא פִּידְיַיאסַאס

'Marcus, the wicked one, / Alas, who had broken away from Israel, He went to betray them, / To put them in danger, To expose [them] to the king. / May God pay him back! . . .

The Jews are honoured, / Renowned to the king, Just and righteous, / Chosen by God. Then Marcus was hung, / Like a wretched dog.

O Sicilians, cheers! / Eat and drink merrily, In your gladness and joy, / May your children have a long life!'

שִׁיר הַשִּׁירִים . לְיוֹם א

א

א יְשִׁיר הַשִּׁירִים, אֲשֶׁר לִשְׁלֹמֹה:
פֵּינֵיסִיס קֵי פִּינֵימָטָא. פּוּ אִיפֵּי אוֹ שְׁלֹמֹה אוֹ פְּרוֹפִיטָּיִס
בַּסִילֵיוָֹס טוּ יִשְׂרָאֵל. מֵי פְנֵימָא פְּרוֹפֵיטִיאָֹס.
אֶמְבְּרְסְתָּן טוֹן אַפֵּנְדְרִין אוֹלוּ טוּ קָזְמוּ זָל: רֵיקָא פֵּינֵיסִיס
אִיפֵּיתִיקָאן סְטוֹן קָזְמוֹן אִיטוּטוֹן. אִי פֵּינֵיסִיס אִיטוּטֵי
אֲנוֹטֵירָא אַפּוֹלְקְטוֹס: טִין פֵּינֵיסִין טִין פְּרוֹטִין טִן
אִיפֵּי אוֹ אָדָם סְטוֹן קֵירוֹן פּוּ סְטוֹחוֹרְיָת אִיס אַפְּטוֹן טוּ
פְטְקְסִימוֹ טוּ. אִלְתִּימֵירָא אַפּוֹ טוּ שַׁבָּת קֵי אַפֵּנְדְרֵסֵי
אִיפֵּנוּ טוּ, אִינְקְסֵי טוּ סָטוֹמָא טוּ קֵי אַפֵּן פְסַלְמוֹן.פֵּי
נֵיסִין דִּיאָה טִין אִימֵירָן טוּ שַׁבָּת:טִין פֵּינֵיסִין טִין
רֶפְטֵיָרן.טִין אִיפֵּין אוֹ מֹשֶׁה מֵי כּוּס אִיאוּס טוּ יִשְׂרָאֵל
אוֹטָן אֶסְחִיסֵין אִיסְפְּטוּס אוֹ אַפֵּנְדְּיס טוּ קָזְמוֹ,טִין תָלַסַן
טוּ סוּף.אִינְקְסָן אוֹלִיטוּס קֵי אַפּוֹן פֵּנֵיסִין אוֹס אִיס־
פּוּ אֵצֵינֵי גְרַמֹנוּן,טוֹטֵי אִיפֵּינֵיסֵי אוֹ מֹשֶׁה קֵי טָא פֵּרֵ'א
טוּ יִשְׂרָאֵל: טִין פֵּינֵיסִין טִין טְרִיטָן. טִין אַפּוֹן אִיאִי
טוּ יִשְׂרָאֵל. אוֹטָן אִיסְפְּטוּס פִּיגְדֵ' אַפּוֹ נִירוֹן. פּוּ אִיצֵינֵי

אֲרוֹתֵי

גְרַמֹנוּ.טוֹטֵי אֵפֵּינֵיסִין אוֹ יִשְׂרָאֵל:טִין פֵּינֵיסִין טִין טֵ'־
טֵרטִין.טִינֵיפֵּי אוֹ מֹשֶׁה אוֹ פְּרוֹפֵיטִיס.אוֹטָן אַלְתִּין אֹקֵרֵשׁ
טוּ דִּיאָנָה חוֹרֵסְתֵּי אַפּוֹ טוֹן קָזְמוֹן.קֵי אֶקְסִילֵּיסֵן מֵאֵסָן
טוֹן לָאוֹן בֵּית יִשְׂרָאֵל.פּוּ אֵצֵינֵי גְרַמֵּינוּן. אַקְרוֹאַסְתֵּיטֵי
יַאגְרֵנֵי קֵיתָא אוֹמֵילֵ'סוֹ: טִין פֵּינֵיסִין טִין פֵּמְטִין.טִינֵיפֵ
אוֹ יְהוֹשֻׁעַ יוֹס טוּ נוּן. אוֹטָן אֶקְרֵירְקָסֵי פוּלְמוֹן אִיס
גָּבְעוֹן.קֵי אֶסְטַאתִיקָן אִיס אַפְּטוֹן אוֹ אִילֵּאם קֵי טוּ פְנֵ'
גְרִי טְרִיאָנְדְרָא אֶקְסֵי אוֹרִיס.קֵי אַפַּפְסָן נָא אִיפָן פֵּנֵיסֵן
אִינְקְסֵי אַפְּטוֹס טוּ סָטוֹמָאטוּ קֵי אִיפֵּן פֵּמְסֵן. פּוּ אֵצֵינֵי
גְרַמֵּינוּן. טוֹטֵי אִיפֵּינֵיסֵי אוֹ יְהוֹשֻׁעַ אֶמְבְּרְסְתָּן טוֹן אַדֹנָי:
טִין פֵּינֵיסִין טִין אֶקְטִין.טִין אַפּוֹן טִין בָּרָק קֵי אִי דְּבוֹרָה.
אִיס

Shir ha-Shirim Rabba (a *midrash* on the biblical Song of Songs) in Judeo-Greek translation. The word אִיאִי *iii* 'the sons' appears at the end of line 15. Columbia University, Rare Book & Manuscript Library, ms. X893.1.BQ.J, fol. 1r.

The language of the poem includes some interesting dialectal vocabulary. For example, the villain Marcus is called *ksilothrimenos*, a wonderfully descriptive word that means something like 'grown up with spankings' (i.e., 'a naughty boy'!). And the word *piriklo* 'danger', which is derived from the Italian word *pericolo* 'danger', betrays the Sicilian origins of this particular Greek-speaking community.

Over time, Jews developed their own distinctive variety of spoken Greek, which included a significant number of words borrowed from Hebrew, some of which acquired meanings unknown in Hebrew. Many of these words were recorded by researchers in the 20th century. For example, in addition to the many direct and transparent borrowings of words from Hebrew, they used the word *chasicha* (< Hebrew חשיכה *ḥashekha* 'darkness') to mean 'a church' and *rimonim* (< Hebrew רימונים *rimmonim* 'pomegranates') as a euphemism for 'breasts'. Tragically, the majority of Greek Jews perished in the Holocaust or subsequently emigrated to Israel, with the result that there are very few remaining speakers of this Jewish variety of Greek today. A few very small communities still exist in Greece.

References and further study

For an overview of Judeo-Greek in all periods, see Krivoruchko (2017). Aitken and Paget (2014) is an introduction to ancient Jewish Greek culture and literature. Jobes and Silva (2000) is an introduction to the Septuagint. Bons and Joosten (2016) focuses specifically on the language of the Septuagint. The excerpt from the poem on Little Purim comes from Matsa (1971–81). Dalven (1990) is a history of the Jews of Ioannina, one of the last surviving Jewish communities in Greece, and one of the places where Little Purim was celebrated.

15 Hebrew, Inscriptional

Almost everything we know about ancient Hebrew comes from the Hebrew Bible, which was written over the course of roughly a thousand years, between about 1200 BCE and 165 BCE (see HEBREW, BIBLICAL). However, we don't actually have physical copies of the Bible from that period. The oldest biblical texts are found among the Dead Sea Scrolls, some of which may date to around 100 BCE, while the first complete Hebrew Bible is only from the year 1006 CE. We do have Hebrew texts from the biblical period, but they are not from the Bible. Rather, they are inscriptions written on stone or pottery.

Ancient Israel had nothing like the grand monuments that we find from ancient Egypt, Babylon, or Greece. The long hieroglyphic inscriptions in Egyptian tombs have no Israelite parallels. Likewise, nothing like the great royal archives of the Babylonian or Assyrian kings has ever been found from ancient Israel. The ancient Israelites did write, of course, but presumably most of what they produced was on perishable material like papyrus and wood and has long since disintegrated. They did sometimes write on stone or pottery, and some of this has survived. But there are no long historical narratives or literary texts, and nothing giving us any significant insight into the veracity of the Bible or the culture of ancient Israel; in fact, the surviving texts are in themselves quite short and unimpressive. But from a linguistic point of view, these are of great importance, because they constitute the oldest physical evidence that we have of the Hebrew language.

The oldest Hebrew inscription is believed to be a short text known as the Gezer Calendar. This text of only about twenty words appears to be a list of months and their associated agricultural activities, and is thought to have been written sometime around 900 BCE. One of the more interesting Hebrew inscriptions commemorates the construction of a tunnel in the eastern part of Jerusalem. This text, known as the Siloam Tunnel inscription, was carved on rock around 700 BCE, but lay hidden for many centuries until it was rediscovered in 1880. The complete text, which is one of the longest of the ancient Hebrew inscriptions, follows. The transcription in English letters does not include any vowels, since Hebrew writing in that period did not (see HEBREW, BIBLICAL). The letters and words shown in brackets are no longer legible on the rock, but we can infer their presence from the context.

וזה היה דבר הנקבה בעוד [החצבם מנפם את] הגרזן אש אל רעו ובעוד שלש אמת להנ]קב
נשמ]ע קל אש קרא אל רעו כי הית זדה בצר מימן ומ]שמ[אל ובים הנקבה הכו החצבם אש

לקרת רעו גרזן על [ג]רזן וילכו המים מן המוצא אל הברכה במאתי[ם ו]אלף אמה ומ[א]ת
אמה היה גבה הצר על ראש החצב[ם]

*wzh hyh dbr hnqbh b'wd [hhṣbm mnpm 't] hgrzn 'š 'l r'w wb'wd šlš 'mt
lhn[qb nšm]' ql 'š qr' 'l r'w ky hyt zdh bṣr mymn wm[śm] 'l wbym hnqbh hkw
hhṣbm 'š lqrt r'w grzn 'l [g]rzn wylkw hmym mn hmwṣ' 'l hbrkh bm'ty[m
w]'lp 'mh wm[']t 'mh hyh gbh hṣr 'l r'š hhṣb[m]*

'And this was the matter of the breakthrough. While the stonecutters were
swinging the axe towards one another, and while there were still three cubits
to be cut, the voice of a man calling to his fellow was heard, because there
was a crack in the rock from right to left. And on the day of its breakthrough
the stonecutters struck towards one another, axe against axe, and the waters
went from the outlet to the pool, (a distance of) a thousand and two hundred
cubits, and a hundred cubits was the height of the rock above the heads of
the stonecutters.'

Hebrew inscriptions from the biblical period were written in a form of the
Hebrew alphabet known as Paleo-Hebrew. (The image shows how the Siloam
Tunnel inscription looks in its original script; the version presented here is in
the modern Hebrew script.) The Paleo-Hebrew script can be traced back to the
earliest known alphabetic writing in history, the Proto-Sinaitic script. Proto-
Sinaitic was invented sometime around 1700 BCE by Canaanite workers in
the Sinai Peninsula, who were inspired by the Egyptian hieroglyphic writing
that they saw around them. Egyptian hieroglyphic writing is highly complex,
with thousands of symbols, some representing entire words, some representing
groups of two or three consonants, and some representing just individual consonants. The novelty of the proto-Sinaitic script was that it drastically simplified the concept of writing by using only a small number of symbols (around
twenty-five or thirty), each of which represented a single consonant. Each letter
is based on a picture of an object, and the sound of that letter is taken from the
initial sound of that object. For example, the word for 'house' was pronounced
something like *bet*, so the picture of a house stood for the sound *b*. Likewise,
a picture of a camel (*gimmel*) stood for *g*, and a picture of a door (*dalet*) stood
for *d*. The pictographic origins of these letters are obscured in later versions of
the alphabet, including Hebrew.

Only a small number of short rock graffiti survive in the proto-Sinaitic script,
but the script itself spawned a lasting legacy. It was borrowed by the Phoenicians,
an ancient sea-faring people who lived in the region of present-day Lebanon. It
is from the Phoenicians that the ancient Israelites got their alphabet. The Phoenicians had extensive trading contacts throughout the Mediterranean and gave their
alphabet also to the Greeks, who made their own modifications to it. The Greeks,
in turn, gave their alphabet to the Etruscans, who then gave it to the Romans. This
means that the ancient Hebrew script is related to the Greek and Latin alphabets.
This relationship can be seen in the order of the alphabets, in the names of the
letters, and in the similar shapes of some of the letters. For example, the first four
letters in the Hebrew alphabet are *alef*, *bet*, *gimmel*, and *dalet*, corresponding to

Siloam Tunnel Inscription (ca. 700 BCE), Istanbul Archaeology Museums. Photograph courtesy of Erich Lessing/Art Resource, NY.

Greek *alpha*, *beta*, *gamma*, and *delta*. As for the shapes of the letters, have a look at the following table:

Proto-Sinaitic	Phoenician/Paleo-Hebrew	Hebrew	Greek	Latin
𐤀	𐤀	א	A	A
𐤁	𐤁	ב	B	B
𐤂	𐤂	ג	Γ	C
𐤃	𐤃	ד	Δ	D

The similarities between the letters are not always immediately obvious, because each language has made its own modifications. For example, the Phoenician *alef* was turned ninety degrees clockwise by the Greeks to create their *alpha*, while the Phoenician *gimmel* is almost a mirror image of the Greek *gamma*.

After the Babylonian Exile in the 6th century BCE (see HEBREW, BIBLICAL), the Paleo-Hebrew script was replaced by the script that we associate with Hebrew today, and Hebrew inscriptions after this time used this later script. However, the Paleo-Hebrew script was not totally forgotten for another 500 years or more, as proven by the fact that it is used in some of the Dead Sea Scrolls (approximately 100 BCE–100 CE), as well as on coins from the period of the Bar Kokhba Revolt (132–135 CE). The choice to use the Paleo-Hebrew script in some of the Dead Sea Scrolls seems to have been a conscious choice to reassert its cultural significance as the "original" Hebrew alphabet. Likewise, the Bar Kokhba Revolt was an attempt to re-establish a Hebrew kingdom amid the Roman occupation, and the ancient Paleo-Hebrew script was a symbol of their national identity.

As Jews spread throughout the Middle East, North Africa, and Europe, they sometimes continued to produce inscriptions in Hebrew, particularly on tombstones. In some cases these inscriptions provide important historical information about lost Jewish communities, whether it be in 1st-century Rome (see LATIN) or 19th-century Warsaw. In fact, the Jewish tradition of carving Hebrew onto tombstones continues until the present day.

As for the ancient inscriptions, it is possible that some remain buried underground, waiting to be unearthed. Archaeologists continue to excavate ancient sites throughout Israel, and there is always the hope that they will discover unknown texts that will reveal new information about the earliest stages of the Hebrew language or life in ancient Israel.

References and further study

Aḥituv (2008) provides a comprehensive overview of ancient Hebrew inscriptions, including photographs, transcriptions into the modern Hebrew alphabet, translations, and commentary. Yardeni (2002) contains a discussion of the historical development of the Hebrew script.

16 Hebrew, Biblical

The Hebrew Bible (called the Old Testament by Christians) is often thought of as a single book, but in fact it is an anthology of many books covering a variety of different genres: historical narrative, legal instructions, poetry, proverbs, myth, prophecy, letters, and more. The books of the Bible were written at various times, spanning a period of more than a thousand years. The earliest portions of the Hebrew Bible are thought to have been composed perhaps as early as 1200 BCE, while the latest book, Daniel, is thought to have been written only around 160 BCE.

Because the texts making up the Hebrew Bible were composed over such a long period, their language is not uniform. We can see many differences between the earliest parts of the Bible and the latest ones. If we consider how much English has changed since the time of Shakespeare (roughly 400 years ago) or since the time of Chaucer (roughly 600 years ago), it should not come as a surprise to learn that the Hebrew language did not remain static over the course of the biblical era. To refer to the distinct types of Biblical Hebrew that we find from different times, scholars usually divide the language into three main periods, referred to as Archaic, Standard, and Late Biblical Hebrew.

Archaic Biblical Hebrew is the language of some of the poetic texts appearing in the Bible, most famously the Song of the Sea (Exodus 15) and the Song of Deborah (Judges 5). At least some Archaic Biblical Hebrew poems were probably composed and transmitted orally and only later incorporated into other biblical texts. In the archaic period, we find grammatical features and vocabulary that users of Standard or Late Biblical Hebrew would consider outmoded, similar to how a modern speaker of English would recognize 'thou' and 'doth' as archaic features of Shakespeare. At the same time, certain features typical of later phases of Hebrew had not yet become standard in the archaic period. For example, the Hebrew definite article -ה *ha-* 'the', such a seemingly fundamental feature of Hebrew, was not yet in common use in the archaic period, and so it is often missing where we might expect it, as in אֶרֶץ רָעָשָׁה גַּם־שָׁמַיִם נָטָפוּ *'erets ra'asha gam-shamayim naṭafu* 'the earth trembled and also the heavens dripped' (Judges 5:4), where we would expect הָאָרֶץ *ha-'arets* for 'the earth' and הַשָּׁמַיִם *ha-shamayim* for 'the heavens'.

Much of the Hebrew Bible is written in the variety that we call Standard Biblical Hebrew, which covers texts written between approximately the 10th and 6th centuries BCE—that is, during the period of the Israelite monarchy, from King Saul until the time of the Babylonian Exile. This is not to say that all Standard Biblical Hebrew texts are linguistically the same. Besides the expected stylistic differences between prose and poetry, we also find evidence of regional dialects within the Hebrew Bible. Generally speaking, written languages tend to mask difference in spoken dialects. For example, it is easy to identify a speaker of English from New York, London, or Sydney based on his or her speech, but these differences are much harder to detect in the written language. The Bible is no different in this regard.

Standard Biblical Hebrew is based on the dialect that was spoken in the Kingdom of Judah and its capital Jerusalem, but there is good evidence that other dialects of Hebrew existed in other parts of biblical Israel. One famous piece of evidence for the existence of regional dialects in Biblical Hebrew comes from Judges 12:6, in an exchange between two Israelite groups. A group of Gileadite men ask a stranger to pronounce the word שִׁבֹּלֶת *shibbolet* 'ear of grain'. Apparently, the Ephraimites, who were at war with the Gileadites, were unable to pronounce the first consonant of that word (*sh*, or perhaps *th*). Therefore, when the stranger in the story pronounces the word as *sibbolet*, they immediately understand that he is an Ephraimite and take appropriate action:

וַיֹּאמְרוּ לוֹ אֱמָר־נָא שִׁבֹּלֶת וַיֹּאמֶר סִבֹּלֶת וְלֹא יָכִין לְדַבֵּר כֵּן וַיֹּאחֲזוּ אוֹתוֹ וַיִּשְׁחָטוּהוּ

way-yomeru lo 'emor-na shibbolet way-yomer sibbolet we-lo yakhin le-dabber ken way-yoḥazu 'oto way-yishḥaṭuhu

'They said to him, "Please say Shibboleth," but he said, "Sibboleth," for he could not pronounce it right. And they seized him and killed him.'

(Judges 12:6)

This whole incident tells us of just one way that the dialects of these two groups differed. (It is also the source of the English word *shibboleth*.) Moreover, there was likely a marked difference between southern and northern dialects of Hebrew. Most biblical texts were composed in the South (Judah), but perhaps 10% or more of the texts in the Bible were composed in the North, and these northern texts are often identifiable by certain linguistic features. For example, in northern texts we find the words גֶּרֶם *gerem*, קֶרֶת *qeret*, and לָחַם *laham* in place of the standard (southern) words עֶצֶם *'etsem* 'bone', עִיר *'ir* 'city', and אָכַל *'akhal* 'eat', and there are many more examples like this. Very often these northern dialectal words have counterparts in the languages of Israel's northern neighbours, like Phoenician and Aramaic. This is equivalent to how the dialects of northern England share some similarities with Scottish English, or how we hear more words of Spanish origin in the southwestern United States.

In 586 BCE, much of the population of the Kingdom of Judah was exiled to Babylonia, and the capital city of Jerusalem was laid waste. (The Ten Tribes of the breakaway Northern Kingdom of Israel had been deported into exile by the Assyrians already in 722 BCE.) The Babylonian Exile had a major effect on the Hebrew language. In Babylonia, the Judean exiles learned Aramaic, which was the official language used for Babylonian administration and was widely spoken across the entire Near East. The Persians under King Cyrus conquered Babylonia in 539 BCE and granted the exiled Judeans permission to return to Judah and rebuild the Temple. When the exiles returned to Judah, they brought back the Aramaic language and a Hebrew evidently influenced by Aramaic. Books of the Hebrew Bible written after the Babylonian Exile—books like Esther, Ezra, and Chronicles, among others—use a slightly different form of Hebrew, which is usually called Late Biblical Hebrew. Late Biblical Hebrew is the result of both natural evolution of the language and the influence of Aramaic. It is not dramatically different from Standard Biblical Hebrew, but has a number of distinctive features. It is likely that the spoken language of the people in this period was even more different than in earlier periods, though we do not have direct evidence of this.

Late Biblical Hebrew is characterized by greater influence from Aramaic, some vocabulary borrowed from Persian (Persians ruled over the Land of Israel from 539 to 332 BCE), and a number of grammatical developments. Persian loanwords are especially common in the books of Esther and Daniel, in which we find, for example, the borrowings פַּרְדֵּס *pardes* 'orchard, grove' (the Persian word is also the source of English *paradise*) and דָּת *dat* 'decree, law' (in later Hebrew this came to mean 'religion').

One important fact about the Hebrew Bible is that we don't actually have any copies, or even fragments, from the biblical period itself. The only Hebrew texts that survive from the biblical period are inscriptions on stone and clay, none of which contain any biblical passages (see HEBREW, INSCRIPTIONAL). The earliest copies of biblical texts come from the Dead Sea Scrolls, which date from between the 2nd century BCE and the 1st century CE. But even among the Dead Sea Scrolls we have only pieces of the Bible (far less than half, in many fragments), not a complete copy. The oldest complete copy of the Bible dates only from about the year 1006 CE, more than a millennium after the last biblical book was composed!

Because copying of manuscripts was done by humans, who are prone to error, all known biblical manuscripts—even the oldest ones from among the Dead Sea Scrolls—contain copyist mistakes. Some mistakes are extremely minor, such as a slight change in the spelling of a word, with no effect on the meaning. In other cases, errors are more significant: the omission or addition of words, or even of entire lines of text, for example. One of the major pursuits of modern biblical scholars is to figure out the original form of the biblical texts, by comparing the most reliable ancient Hebrew manuscripts, as

Exodus 14:28–15:15, including the Song of the Sea, one of the oldest poems in the Hebrew Bible, in a 12th-century manuscript. Hebrew Union College, ms. 1. COURTESY OF THE KLAU LIBRARY, CINCINNATI, HEBREW UNION COLLEGE–JEWISH INSTITUTE OF RELIGION.

Numbers 14:45–15:2 in a book of weekly Torah portions, probably from Iran, written in 1106 or 1107. National Library of Israel 28°2238, fol. 23r. Courtesy of the National Library of Israel.

well as early translations like the Septuagint (see GREEK) and Targumim (see ARAMAIC, ANCIENT AND MEDIEVAL). Despite two centuries of such scholarship, we still don't know, and will likely never know, exactly how the biblical books originally looked.

Something else we don't know for sure is how Biblical Hebrew was pronounced in biblical times. This is because in that period the Hebrew alphabet did not normally indicate vowels. So, for example, the Hebrew consonants שמר *sh-m-r* could represent the past-tense verb *shamar* 'he guarded', the imperative *shemor* 'guard!', the noun *shomer* 'a guard', or the place name *shemer*. Usually context makes clear what word was intended, but the lack of vowels sometimes leaves room for ambiguity. The proper reading of the biblical texts was preserved by oral tradition, both during the biblical period and afterwards. Sometime between the 7th and 9th centuries CE, some Jewish scholars (known as Masoretes) decided that they needed a way to record their pronunciation tradition in writing. So they devised a system of points and other symbols (called the Masorah) that could be combined with the existing consonants in order to indicate the missing vowels. With this new system, they were now able to distinguish שָׁמַר *shamar*, שְׁמֹר *shemor*, שֹׁמֵר *shomer*, and שֶׁמֶר *shemer*. Torah scrolls used in the synagogue are still written without vowel points, but manuscripts intended for study include them, as do printed Bibles.

Scholars today still debate whether the system of vowels accurately reflects the intentions of the biblical authors, and some of these debates can have far-reaching implications. For example, three times in the Torah we find the commandment לֹא־תְבַשֵּׁל גְּדִי בַּחֲלֵב אִמּוֹ *lo-tevashel gedi ba-ḥalev 'immo* 'do not cook a (goat) kid in its mother's milk'. It has been suggested (though not widely accepted) that the word חֲלֵב *ḥalev* 'milk' was meant to be read as חֵלֶב *ḥelev* 'fat', since the two words would have looked identical in the original consonantal text. If correct, this revised reading would require a reconsideration of the laws of *kashrut* regarding the mixing of meat and milk.

Since the vowel points were added so long after the writing of the biblical books, it is likely that they are not actually accurate representations of biblical pronunciation; rather they reflect the pronunciation of the later Hebrew scholars who devised the system in the 7th to 9th centuries CE. That oral traditions are unreliable is further illustrated by the fact that Jewish communities around the world often have very different traditions of pronouncing vocalized Biblical Hebrew. For example, the word שַׁבָּת 'Sabbath' is traditionally pronounced *shabbat* in most Sephardic traditions, but *shabes* in the Ashkenazi tradition. The word עוֹלָם 'eternity' was traditionally pronounced *olam* in some Sephardic communities, *oylem* in Ashkenazi communities, and *ngolam* in some Italian Jewish communities. The pronunciation of Modern Hebrew is based mostly on the Sephardic reading tradition, and it is not identical with the pronunciation intended by either the Masoretes or the biblical authors.

Biblical Hebrew is still widely studied around the world in traditional Jewish and Christian schools and seminaries, as well as in secular university settings by large numbers of students of all ages. The importance of the Hebrew Bible within multiple faith groups ensures the continued relevance of this ancient variety of the Hebrew language.

References and further study

For the different phases of Biblical Hebrew, there are a number of relevant articles in Khan et al. (2013) and Garr and Fassberg (2016). Rendsburg (2003) is a detailed analysis of the northern dialect of Biblical Hebrew. Tov (2012) is a comprehensive introduction to how scholars analyse the textual history of the Hebrew Bible. Ulrich (2010) is an edition of the biblical Dead Sea Scrolls, while Abegg, Flint, and Ulrich (1999) is an English translation of the same.

17 Hebrew, Rabbinic and Medieval

Following the return from the Babylonian Exile in the late 6th century BCE, the use of Hebrew began to slowly decline as a spoken language in the Land of Israel, while Aramaic steadily gained popularity. Aramaic was by the 6th century BCE widely spoken throughout the entire Near East and was actually the official administrative language of the Persian Empire, which had dominion over the Land of Israel from about 538 BCE until the coming of Alexander the Great in 332 BCE (see ARAMAIC, ANCIENT AND MEDIEVAL). Even afterwards, when Israel and its neighbours were controlled by various Greek overlords, Aramaic remained the most widely used language throughout the Near East. It increasingly began to supplant Hebrew in the Land of Israel, so that by the time that the Romans took over in the 1st century BCE, Aramaic was probably spoken by most Jews in the region, either alongside or in place of Hebrew. (Jesus was an Aramaic-speaking Jew, for example.)

Though the Romans were welcomed by the Jews at first, their rule became more and more oppressive, culminating in a failed revolt in the years 66–73 CE, during which time Jerusalem was burnt and the Temple was destroyed. The surviving Jewish population mounted a second unsuccessful revolt led by Simeon Bar Kokhba in the years 132–136 CE, with further disastrous consequences. The decimation of the Jewish population that came as a result of these wars with Rome, and the subsequent resettlement of many of the survivors, dealt a serious blow to the existence of Hebrew as a spoken language.

Despite its waning use, Hebrew continued to be spoken in the Land of Israel until at least the 2nd century CE. By this time, the language had evolved somewhat from that of the Bible (see HEBREW, BIBLICAL), into a variety that scholars call Rabbinic Hebrew. Not only does Rabbinic Hebrew have a number of grammatical and lexical differences compared to Biblical Hebrew, but it shows much greater influence from Aramaic. In addition, Rabbinic Hebrew is actually not the direct heir to Biblical Hebrew. Instead, it is thought to descend from the dialect of Hebrew that was spoken in the northern areas of Israel (especially in the Galilee), whereas much of the Bible reflects the dialect of the South (i.e., Judah). One immediately recognizable feature of Rabbinic Hebrew is the common use of the masculine plural suffix ין- -in, instead of Biblical Hebrew ים- -im, e.g., מלכין melakhin 'kings' (cf. Biblical Hebrew מְלָכִים melakhim). Some basic vocabulary items and function words that are well known in Modern Hebrew are first attested only in Rabbinic Hebrew, for example, של *shel* 'of', איזה *'eze* 'which?', תלמיד *talmid* 'student', צריך *tsarikh* 'needs', and לחזור *la-ḥzor* 'to return'.

By the 3rd century CE, because of the long-standing pressure from Aramaic, the political turmoil of the previous two centuries, and the fact that most Jews now lived outside of the Land of Israel, Hebrew stopped being used as a spoken language. That is, Hebrew was no longer anyone's native tongue. However, this does not mean that Hebrew fell out of use. Hebrew was, of course, still used for reading and copying the Bible, as well as for prayer in the home and synagogue, but it also was widely used as a written language. Rabbinic scholars in communities in Palestine, Babylon, and elsewhere continued composing important works. The most well-known text in Rabbinic Hebrew is the Mishnah, a collection of discussions and commentary on the legal portions of the Torah, which was composed during the first two centuries CE (when Hebrew was still spoken) and took its final form around the year 200. Another important early text is the Tosefta, a compendium of discussions on Jewish law structured in the same way as the Mishnah. From throughout the first thousand years of the Common Era, there are numerous other rabbinic writings in Hebrew, including a large corpus of texts in the genre called Midrash, which, loosely defined, includes biblical interpretations in the form of explanations, retellings, or expansions of biblical stories.

By the 9th century CE, there were flourishing Jewish communities in Iraq, Egypt, Spain, and in many other places. All these diaspora communities, as well as communities still living in Palestine, continued composing written materials in Hebrew, even though they spoke other languages as their mother tongue. The era of the great rabbinic works had passed, but Jews began to compose texts on a much more varied range of subjects than had been the case in the rabbinic period. As the memory of Hebrew as an everyday language faded further and further into the past, writers began to compose Hebrew texts using a mixture of linguistic features from both Biblical and Rabbinic Hebrew, combined with influences from their own native languages (Arabic, Spanish, French, and others). This new form of Hebrew has come to be known as Medieval Hebrew, since it can be distinguished in linguistic and literary terms from both Biblical and Rabbinic Hebrew.

One of the characteristics of Medieval Hebrew was the extremely varied nature of the texts produced. There was a large body of biblical and Talmudic commentaries, including those of the famous scholars Rashi (see FRENCH) and Naḥmanides (see CATALAN), among many others. There were also numerous works on Jewish law, the most famous of which are probably the משנה תורה *Mishneh Torah*, written by the prominent 12th-century scholar and physician Moses Maimonides (see ARABIC, MEDIEVAL) and the שולחן ערוך *Shulḥan 'Arukh*, written by the Sephardic scholar Joseph Karo (1488–1575). Other Hebrew scholars produced works on a wide variety of topics, including, but not limited to, mathematics, astronomy, philosophy, medicine, grammar, history, and geography. We find Hebrew editions of fables and folktales, and even a Hebrew version of the legend of King Arthur. There was also a flourishing poetic tradition, which included liturgical compositions called *piyyuṭim* (singular *piyyuṭ*), as well as secular poetry.

Some of the most prolific Hebrew writers came from Muslim Spain in the 11th and 12th centuries. One of the most well known is Abraham ibn Ezra (1089–1164), who wrote in Hebrew on a variety of subjects. Though born in Spain, he travelled extensively, living at times in London, Rome, and Provence, as well as various other cities in France, Italy, and his native Spain. Among his Hebrew writings are commentaries on much of the Bible, and treatises on astronomy, astrology, mathematics, philosophy, and grammar; he even wrote secular poetry. His native language was Arabic, and he also produced Hebrew translations of some Arabic scientific works. Despite his fame and talents as a scholar, he seems to have remained poor. He laments his lack of financial success in one of his most moving poems:

galgal u-mazzalot be-maʿmadam	גלגל ומזלות במעמדם
naṭu be-mahalakham le-moladti	נטו במהלכם למולדתי
lu yihyu nerot seḥorati	לו יהיו נרות סחורתי
lo yeḥeshakh shemesh ʿade moti	לא יחשך שמש עדי מותי
ʾigaʿ le-hatsliaḥ we-lo ʾukhal	איגע להצליח ולא אוכל
ki ʾiwwetuni kokhve shamay	כי עותוני כוכבי שמי
lu ʾehye soḥer be-takhrikhin	לו אהיה סוחר בתכריכין
lo yigweʿun be-khol yamay	לא יגועון אישים בכל ימי
lu ʾemtseʾa ḥefets be-milḥama—ʾazay	לו אמצאה חפץ במלחמה—אזי
kol sonʾim shalmu we-lo nimtsa qerav	כל שונאים שלמו ולא נמצא קרב

'The stars and constellations / fell off their course at my birth.
If candles were my business / the sun would not set until my death.
I strive to succeed but am unable / for my heavenly stars have hexed me.
If I were a seller of shrouds / no one would die as long as I lived.
If I were to take delight in battle, then / all enemies would make peace and
there would be no war.'

Many of the familiar Jewish prayers and other liturgical texts still in use were composed in the medieval era. For example, the Passover Haggadah as we know it today was composed in the medieval period, though it includes within it earlier texts from the Bible and Mishnah. Well-known daily prayers like אדון עולם *ʾadon ʿolam* and the Sabbath prayer לכה דודי *lekha dodi* are also medieval compositions.

A large number of texts were also translated into Hebrew in the medieval period, from languages like Spanish, Italian, Latin, and, especially, Arabic. Jews were especially important as translators in the field of medicine. In the early Middle Ages, medicine was far more advanced in the Arab-speaking world than in Europe, and there were many important medical discourses written in Arabic. Because Jews living in Muslim Spain knew Arabic, they had access to the latest Arabic medical knowledge, and they made Hebrew translations of many of these works. These Hebrew translations allowed the knowledge to then be available to Jews all throughout Europe, making Jews sought after as physicians. The renowned English scholar Roger Bacon (ca. 1220–ca. 1292) remarked that Jewish physicians were far more capable than their Christian counterparts, because of their ability to

The *Sheheḥiyanu* blessing in a 14th-century prayer-book for Yom Kippur, written in Germany or Northern Italy. National Library of Israel 38°5214, fol. 2r. Courtesy of the National Library of Israel.

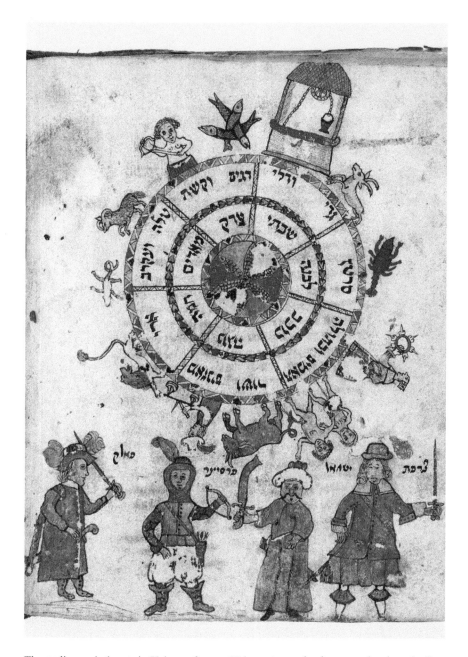

The zodiac and planets in Hebrew, from a 17th-century calendar manual written in Germany. Hebrew Union College, ms. 906, fol. 68v. COURTESY OF THE KLAU LIBRARY, CINCINNATI, HEBREW UNION COLLEGE–JEWISH INSTITUTE OF RELIGION.

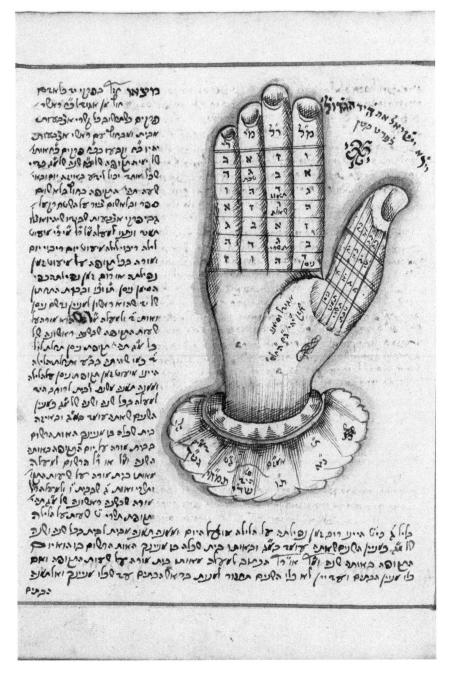

An illustration dealing with the calendar in a manuscript of ספר העברונות *Sefer ha-ʿEvronot*, written in Germany around 1779. Hebrew Union College, ms. 902, fol. 20r. Courtesy of the Klau Library, Cincinnati, Hebrew Union College–Jewish Institute of Religion.

read Hebrew and Arabic. The existence of Hebrew translations of major medical texts, along with original writings in Hebrew, is one of the main reasons that Jews have been associated with the medical profession for so long.

A significant amount of medieval Hebrew literature remains unpublished, in manuscripts hiding away in libraries around the world. Much medieval Hebrew writing has also surely been lost to history, as countless manuscripts deteriorated, got thrown away, or were burned during one of the many outbreaks of anti-Jewish violence throughout history. When the Cairo Genizah was discovered in the 19th century (see ARABIC, MEDIEVAL), hundreds of medieval Hebrew texts were redis-covered, and manuscripts continue to turn up in various places.

Because Hebrew stopped being spoken in the 3rd century CE, the written lan-guage did not continue to evolve naturally as a spoken language would have done. Moreover, medieval authors wrote in a variety of styles; some chose to write in imitation of Biblical Hebrew style, others in imitation of Rabbinic Hebrew, and still others in a combination of the two. Nevertheless, the Hebrew language did continue to change and grow, in particular as authors encountered the need to express new things. For example, new words were needed to convey abstract con-cepts borrowed from contemporary Arabic philosophy or grammar, or to explain advances in medicine, mathematics, and astronomy. Sometimes authors invented new words simply out of poetic creativity. Many of the words coined by medieval writers remain in use in Hebrew until the present day, e.g., איכות *'ekhut* 'quality', שטח *sheṭaḥ* 'area', חרוז *ḥaruz* 'rhyme', תליין *talyan* 'hangman', and זמיר *zamir* 'nightingale'. Therefore, medieval Hebrew is an essential link between the ancient and modern varieties of Hebrew.

References and further study

Sáenz-Badillos (2013) provides a brief overview of Medieval Hebrew and its lit-erature. Halper (1921) is an anthology of post-biblical Hebrew literature, including both original texts and English translations. Though originally published in the 19th century, Steinschneider (1967) is still a useful survey of the many genres of medieval Hebrew writing. Carmi (2006) and Cole (2007) are collections of medi-eval Hebrew poetry; both include the Abraham ibn Ezra poem cited in this chap-ter. Hoffman and Cole (2011) discuss the rediscovery of many medieval Hebrew works in the Cairo Genizah. The Hebrew version of the legend of King Arthur was published by Leviant (2003).

18 Hebrew, Enlightenment

When people think of Hebrew language and literature, what comes to mind is most likely the modern language of Israel, as well as earlier texts like the Bible, the Mishnah, and perhaps medieval works by famous Jewish scholars like Maimonides. Most people are unaware that there was a rich and thriving Hebrew literature produced throughout the 1800s in Central and Eastern Europe, well before Hebrew once again became a spoken language in Palestine in the late 19th century (see HEBREW, MODERN). This was the language of the Haskalah, or Jewish Enlightenment, a Jewish intellectual movement—modelled on the earlier European Enlightenment—that emerged in Berlin around the Jewish philosopher Moses Mendelssohn and a few likeminded visionaries in the late 1700s (see GERMAN). Over subsequent decades, the ideas of the Haskalah spread throughout the Jewish populations of Central and Eastern Europe, holding sway until the 1880s, when the Haskalah gave way to early political Zionism.

One of the key goals of the Maskilim (followers of the Haskalah) was to establish a modern Jewish literary canon modelled on the example of major European literatures, primarily French, German, English, and, later on, Russian. Even though Hebrew wasn't actually spoken in this period, the Maskilim generally believed that it was the natural choice for their new literature, because it had been the main and most prestigious language of Jewish composition since the biblical period. Thus, they began composing Hebrew texts in a wide variety of genres. The concept of using Hebrew for new literature was not an innovation on the part of the Maskilim, but rather (as discussed in the previous chapter), it was common practice already in the medieval period, when Jews used Hebrew as the language of all kinds of writings, from medical and scientific treatises to travelogues, and even for translations of epic tales from European languages and Arabic. However, the Maskilic era marks a new and exciting chapter in the history of Hebrew, because it was the first time when Jews began to produce literature that 21st-century readers would recognize as 'modern', i.e., novels, short stories, newspapers, satires, etc., as well as works of popular science, medicine, history, and other kinds of nonfiction. The first Maskilic Hebrew novel, called אהבת ציון *'ahavat tsiyyon* 'The Love of Zion', by Abraham Mapu (Vilna, 1853), was set in biblical Israel, but many other Maskilic novels and short stories were written about the contemporary Eastern European Jewish experience, and thus offer a vivid insight into life in this setting. For example, the short story שני ימים ולילה אחד בבית מלון אורחים *shne yamim we-layla ʾeḥad be-vet melon ʾorḥim* 'Two Days and One Night in a Guesthouse' (Odessa, 1868), by the prominent Maskilic writer Judah Leib Gordon, tells the story of a small-town Hasidic *rebbe* (see HUNGARIAN and YIDDISH, MODERN HASIDIC), who becomes embroiled in a scandal when it is discovered that his protégé is actually a girl disguised as a boy. This story not only gives us a detailed depiction of everyday life in a small Eastern European Jewish village in the mid-19th-century, but it also reflects an anti-Hasidic sentiment very commonly seen in Maskilic literature (as well as prefiguring the theme of the 1983 musical film *Yentl*!). A popular work of Maskilic nonfiction was the multivolume composition תולדות הטבע *toledot ha-ṭeva*ʿ 'Natural History' (Leipzig, Zhitomir, and Vilna, 1862–72) by the famous Hebrew and Yiddish author Mendele Moykher Sforim (see YIDDISH, MODERN STANDARD). This influential work consists of a detailed and fascinating compendium of zoology, including descriptions of exotic animals that were unknown in Eastern Europe at the time, such as monkeys, tigers, and elephants.

Maskilic writing in Hebrew included not only original compositions, but also translations of famous works from European languages, both fiction and nonfiction of all kinds. Maskilic writers and thinkers were keen to provide the Jewish population of Central and Eastern Europe with all the latest literature available in European languages, particularly German, which was their main literary and cultural model. While Yiddish might have been the more obvious choice of language for these translations, since it was the native tongue of most Jews in the region, Maskilim were generally adverse to using it, believing it to be a corrupt and inadequate language (though some authors in the period did use it; see YIDDISH, MODERN STANDARD). An example of a Hebrew translation from a German source is an adaptation of Goethe's *Faust* called בן אבויה *ben ʾavuya* 'Ben Abuya' (Vienna, 1865), named for an infamous heretical rabbi from the 1st century CE. During this period, Hebrew authors also translated other beloved European works into Hebrew, such as Daniel Dafoe's *Robinson Crusoe* (מעשה ראבינזאהן *maʿase robinzon* 'The Story of Robinson'; Warsaw, 1849), Jules Verne's *20,000 Leagues under the Sea* (במצלות ים *bi-mtsulot yam* 'In the Depths of the Sea'; Warsaw, 1876), and Miguel de Cervantes' *Don Quixote* (אבינועם הגלילי, או משיח האויל *ʾavino ʿam ha-galili, ʾo mashiaḥ ha-ʾevil* 'Abinoam the Galilean, or the Foolish Messiah'; Iaşi, 1871).

Among the translations of popular literature, we even find Hebrew versions of the most revered English author of all, William Shakespeare. Over the course of the Haskalah, and in the two decades immediately following, there were several attempts to translate Shakespeare into Hebrew, but until the 1870s these only consisted of short speeches and passages, rather than entire plays. Like many Maskilic Hebrew translations, these were all based on German versions of Shakespeare rather than on the English originals, as few Jews in Central and Eastern Europe were able to read English very well at the time.

The first complete Shakespearean plays were translated into Hebrew in the 1870s by a Lithuanian Jew called Isaac Salkinson (1820–1883). Salkinson's remarkable life story was the catalyst for his ability to carry out the unusual achievement of translating two full plays, *Othello* and *Romeo and Juliet*, directly from English into Hebrew. The product of a traditional Eastern European Jewish education, including advanced Talmudical studies in yeshiva, Salkinson eventually settled in London and converted to Christianity, becoming fluent in English. He was then posted by a missionary society to Vienna, which was a thriving hub of Maskilic literary activity at the time, and was commissioned by the prominent author and editor Peretz Smolenskin to translate Shakespeare into Hebrew. Salkinson produced a translation of *Othello*, which he called איתיאל הכושי מוינעצטא *ʾiti'el ha-kushi mi-vinetsia* 'Ithiel, the Cushite of Venice' (Vienna, 1874), and a translation of *Romeo and Juliet*, called רם ויעל *ram we-ya'el* 'Ram and Jael' (Vienna, 1878), but was unable to complete further translations before his death in 1883. However, his ground-breaking translations inspired other Eastern European Jewish writers to produce Hebrew versions of additional Shakespearean plays, with another four appearing before the turn of the 20th century. This small but significant group of early Hebrew Shakespeare translations includes a version of *Macbeth* (Isaac Barb; Drohobycz, 1882), *The Taming of the Shrew* (Judah Elkind; Berditchev, 1893), *King Lear* (Samuel Gordon; Warsaw, 1899), and *Hamlet* (Chaim Yechiel Bornstein; Warsaw, 1900–01).

Salkinson's translations, and the other Eastern European Hebrew Shakespeare translations that followed them, display a number of noteworthy linguistic features, which are also found in Maskilic Hebrew literature more widely. One of these is the use of rare biblical words to designate concepts unknown in earlier forms of Hebrew. For example, in his version of *Othello*, Salkinson translates the English word 'epilepsy' with the Hebrew שבץ *shavats*, which appears only once in the Bible (in 2 Samuel 1:9) and has been translated variously as 'death throes', 'agony', and 'convulsions'. This strategy for finding ways to express modern concepts was used also in the development of Modern Hebrew (see HEBREW, MODERN). However, the Maskilic creations were not always incorporated seamlessly into Modern Hebrew. For example, while the word שבץ *shavats* is still used in 21st-century Israel, it now means 'stroke' instead of 'epilepsy'. Other Maskilic neologisms were adopted into Modern Hebrew in abbreviated form. For example, the Maskilic term קנה רובה *qene rove* 'rifle', which literally means 'shooting stick' or 'archer's stick', and which appears in Salkinson's Shakespeare translations, has been replaced in Modern Hebrew by the shorter form רובה *rove*. And in many cases the Maskilic inventions simply did not survive in Modern Hebrew at all. An example is the term חלי רע *ḥoli ra'* 'cholera', literally 'bad illness', which appears frequently in Salkinson's translations. The Maskilic inspiration for this coinage was the fact that it sounds similar to the word for 'cholera' in many European languages while also meaning something relevant in Hebrew. In Modern Hebrew, this evocative Maskilic term has been replaced by the straightforward European loanword כולרה *kolera*.

In some cases the Maskilic coinages have continued to be used in Modern Hebrew until the present day. For example, in his Hebrew version of *King Lear*, Samuel Gordon translates Shakespeare's line of dialogue 'if it be nothing, I shall not need spectacles' as והיה אם אפס הוא, לא אצטרך למשקפים *we-haya ʾim ʾefes hu, lo ʾetstarekh le-mishkafayim* 'if it is nothing, I won't need spectacles'. This translation employs the recently minted term משקפים *mishkafayim* 'spectacles, glasses' to convey a concept for which there was no established Hebrew word before the late 19th century. The word is still the normal term for 'glasses' in Modern Hebrew.

Another interesting feature of the Shakespeare translations, as well as of the original Maskilic novels and plays, is the everyday speech appearing in dialogue portions of the texts. Since Hebrew was not a spoken language in 19th-century Eastern Europe, the composition of dialogue in it is actually quite remarkable. It's comparable to the idea of a modern writer creating everyday dialogue in Latin or Ancient Greek. Many common features of verbal exchanges in the English plays, even simple things like basic greetings, had no obvious contemporary Hebrew equivalents, and so the translators often relied on circumlocutions to convey these expressions. For example, near the beginning of his Hebrew version of *King Lear*, Gordon translates a short colloquial exchange between the characters Gloucester and Edmund. The English original reads 'How now! What news?' 'So please your lordship, none'. Gordon renders this into Hebrew as "מה-בפיך?" "אין כל חדש בפי, אדוני" *'ma-be-fikha?' 'ʾen kol ḥadash be-fi, ʾadoni'*, which literally means 'What is in your mouth?' 'There is nothing new in my mouth, my lord'. This type of expression, containing a reference to having something in one's mouth, was commonly used in Maskilic writing for colloquial questions such as 'how are you?' or 'what's new?' and their corresponding responses. This particular example would sound quite silly in Modern Hebrew, which uses completely different expressions for basic greetings like these.

A particularly striking characteristic of many Maskilic authors' Hebrew translations of Shakespeare's plays (and other works of European literature) is a strong tendency to change the non-Jewish cultural elements of the original works into Jewish ones. This can be seen in the titles of the translations, in which non-Jewish names of people and places are replaced with Jewish, usually biblical, ones. For example, Shakespeare's Juliet becomes Salkinson's Jael, a name with a similar sound but with a completely different origin and associations: Jael is a biblical heroine who occupies a respected position in Jewish tradition, and many Jewish girls have been named after her. Likewise, the Maskilic Hebrew translators typically transform references to Christianity present in the originals into Jewish equivalents. For example, Salkinson replaces Shakespeare's 'Easter' with the unambiguously Jewish חג המצות *ḥag ha-matsot* 'Passover' (literally 'holiday of matzah'), and substitutes 'church' with בית המקדש *bet ha-miqdash* 'the Temple', a reference to the Temple in Jerusalem. References to Greek and Roman mythological figures get the same treatment in the Hebrew translations. For example, Salkinson replaces Shakespeare's Venus with עשתרת *ʾashtoret* (Ashtoreth, also known as Astarte),

The cover of the first Hebrew translation of Shakespeare's *King Lear* (Warsaw, 1899).

the Canaanite goddess of love and war whom the Israelites are condemned for worshipping in the Bible, while Bornstein, in his Hebrew translation of *Hamlet*, replaces Shakespeare's Hercules with שמשון *shimshon* (Samson), the famous biblical strongman whose adventures and misadventures are recounted in the Book of Judges.

Maskilic writers of all genres also rely heavily on a literary technique known by the Hebrew term שיבוץ *shibbuts*, or the practice of inserting biblical verses and fragments of verses into original compositions. This technique is not unique to Maskilic authors, having been a common feature of many Hebrew texts since the medieval period, but it is strongly associated with the Maskilic period because of its particular prominence in that era. A nice example of *shibbuts*, from Salkinson's translation of *Romeo and Juliet*, can be found in the famous balcony scene: while Shakesepeare's Romeo says 'O, it is my love! O, that she knew she were!', Salkinson's Ram exclaims, זו היא שאהבה נפשי! מי יתן וגם היא תאמר, דודי לי ואני לו! *zu hi she-'ahava nafshi! mi yitten we-gam hi tomar, dodi li wa-'ani lo!* 'This is the one whom my soul loves! If only she would also say, my beloved is mine and I am his!'. Salkinson's version is not simply a translation of the English; instead, it is based closely on the biblical love poem Song of Songs. It contains a direct quote from verse 1:7 and an adaptation of the famous line from verse 6:3, אני לדודי ודודי לי *'ani le-dodi we-dodi li* 'I am my beloved and my beloved is mine', a passage which is often recited at Jewish wedding ceremonies.

While the Bible is the most common textual source for Maskilic authors, they also sometimes quoted rabbinic literature. For example, Salkinson's version of Othello's line 'One unperfectness shows me another' is עברה גוררת עברה *'avera goreret 'avera* 'one transgression brings another transgression', a well-known phrase from the ethical teachings in the Mishnah called *Pirke Avot*. Another fun aspect of these early translations is their treatment of languages other than English appearing in Shakespeare's work. For example, in Judah Elkind's Hebrew translation of *The Taming of the Shrew*, the snippets of Italian dialogue sprinkled throughout the English original appear in Aramaic! This makes sense considering that most Eastern European Jews reading the Hebrew translation are unlikely to have had any knowledge of Italian, but probably had at least basic familiarity with Aramaic through study in yeshiva and knowledge of traditional prayers and songs in that language.

From the early 1880s onwards, many followers of the Haskalah began to settle in Ottoman Palestine, and the centre of Hebrew literary activity gradually shifted to the burgeoning Jewish settlements there. However, the Haskalah was instrumental in the emergence of Modern Hebrew in Palestine, as its vibrant legacy of literary activity, including inventive ways of representing dialogue and describing modern concepts and items, paved the way for people to be able to conceptualize how the language could be rejuvenated, and it provided a template for its use in everyday speech. Further details on the revival of Hebrew as a spoken language, the remarkable outcome of the Maskilic project, appear in the next chapter (HEBREW, MODERN).

References and further study

See Slutsky and Baskin (2007) and Kahn (2013) for surveys of the Haskalah and Maskilic Hebrew language, respectively. Kahn (2017a) is a discussion of Elkind's Hebrew translation of *The Taming of the Shrew*, and Kahn (2017b) is a bilingual edition and commentary on Salkinson's Hebrew translations of *Othello* and *Romeo and Juliet*. The latter also includes many more details of the fascinating life of Salkinson. Shavit (1993) is a discussion of the role of Hebrew in the Berlin Haskalah. Patterson (1988) is an overview of Maskilic prose fiction, and Patterson (1964) is a study of the prominent Maskilic writer Abraham Mapu. Kahn and Yampolskaya (forthcoming) is a reference grammar of Maskilic Hebrew.

19 Hebrew, Modern

When Hebrew began to be used again as a spoken language in the late 19th century, one of the many challenges faced by its early advocates was finding ways to express modern concepts and inventions. Even though Hebrew had been used throughout the medieval and early modern periods for a wide range of literary activities (see the two previous chapters), it wasn't a real spoken language. It lacked a lot of everyday vocabulary, especially words for recent technological, cultural, and scientific innovations, such as electricity, newspapers, and anesthesia, as well as items that simply were not known in the ancient Near East, such as germs, turkeys, and tomatoes. The necessity of coining new words has continued until the present day, in order to meet the demands of an ever-changing world.

There are a variety of techniques for creating new Hebrew vocabulary. Often foreign words are simply borrowed into the language. For example, we find in Modern Hebrew words like טלפון *telefon* 'telephone', אנטיביוטיקה *'antibyotika* 'antibiotics', אינטרנט *'internet* 'Internet', אימייל *'imeyl* 'email', אבוקדו *'avokado* 'avocado', שוקולד *shokolad* 'chocolate', and זברה *zebra* 'zebra'. Such borrowings have tended to come mainly from English, Arabic, Yiddish, and a few other languages. However, the early Modern Hebrew speakers tried to avoid direct borrowings, preferring to keep the language somewhat "pure". Still today, the Hebrew Language Academy, the Jerusalem-based organization devoted to the promotion of the Hebrew language, generally eschews foreign words, though their recommendations are not always heeded by the public. For example, their suggestion of the word תקליטור *takliṭor* (from a Hebrew root) for 'compact disc' has never found acceptance, and Hebrew speakers instead use the loanword דיסק *disk*. Borrowings from foreign languages, especially English, are particularly common in colloquial Hebrew, in which one often hears words like לוזר *luzer* 'loser', דדליין *dedlayn* 'deadline', האשטאג *hashtag* 'hashtag', צ'ט *chet* '(online) chat', and דייט *deyt* 'date'.

Some foreign borrowings are incorporated more completely into the grammatical structure of Hebrew, especially when it comes to verbs. For example, we find Modern Hebrew verbs like לפסטר *le-faster* 'to pasteurize' (from the name 'Pasteur'), לסמס *le-sames* 'to text' (from 'SMS'—i.e., text message), לפלרטט *le-flartet* 'to flirt' (from English 'flirt'), לקנפג *le-kanfeg* 'to configure', and לגגל *le-gagel* 'to google' (from the name Google). These have been thoroughly Hebraized, so we can find regularly conjugated forms like גיגלתי *gigalti* 'I googled' and אגגל *'agagel*

'I will google', as well as derived forms like מפוסטר *mefustar* 'pasteurized' (adjective), להסתמס *le-histames* 'to text one another' (reciprocal verb), and גיגול *gigul* 'googling' (noun), following productive Hebrew word-forming patterns.

Sometimes, instead of loanwords, we find what linguists call 'calques' or 'loan translations'. Calques most often involve the literal translation of a foreign compound word. For example, the Hebrew word תפוח אדמה *tapuaḥ 'adama* 'potato' literally means 'earth apple'. It is made up of the elements תפוח *tapuaḥ* 'apple' and אדמה *'adama* 'earth', and is a direct translation of the German compound *Erdapfel* and the corresponding French term *pomme de terre*, both of which also literally mean 'earth apple'. Other such calques in Modern Hebrew include גן ילדים *gan yeladim* 'kindergarten' (literally 'children's garden', based on German *Kindergarten*), שולחן כתיבה *shulḥan ketiva* 'desk' (literally 'writing table', based on German *Schreibtisch*), סוס היאור *sus ha-ye'or* 'hippopotamus' (literally 'Nile horse', based on German *Nilpferd*), and חד-קרן *ḥad-keren* 'unicorn' (literally 'uni-horn', based on German *Einhorn* or similarly constructed words in other European languages). Examples of calques based on English include כדורסל *kadursal* 'basketball' (from כדור *kadur* 'ball' and סל *sal* 'basket'), עדשות מגע *'adashot maga'* 'contact lenses' (from עדשות *'adashot* 'lenses' and מגע *maga'* 'contact'), לוח אם *luaḥ 'em* 'motherboard (in a computer)' (from לוח *luaḥ* 'board' and אם *'em* 'mother'), and טלפון נייד *telefon nayad* 'mobile phone' (in speech usually shortened to נייד *nayad* 'mobile', just like its English equivalent). One of the most colourful examples of a Hebrew calque is פרת משה רבנו *parat moshe rabenu* 'ladybug', which literally means 'our teacher Moses' cow'. This is a direct translation of Yiddish משה רבנוס קיעלע *moyshe rabeynes kiele* 'our teacher Moses' little cow', which is itself a partial calque of Russian божья коровка *bozh'ya korovka* 'God's little cow'.

Not all calques are exact translations of compound words or phrases. Some are translations of part of a foreign word or its underlying root. For example, the Hebrew word עיתון *'iton* 'newspaper' is made up of the biblical word עת *'et* 'time' and the suffix ־ון *-on*. This coinage was based on the German word *Zeitung* 'newspaper', which appears to derive from the word *Zeit* 'time'. Other examples are חמצן *ḥamtsan* 'oxygen', from the Hebrew word חמוץ *ḥamuts* 'sour' (based on German *Sauerstoff* 'oxygen', literally 'sour material'), מימן *meman* 'hydrogen', from the Hebrew word מים *mayim* 'water' (based on German *Wasserstoff* 'hydrogen', literally 'water material'), and יומן *yoman* 'diary', from the Hebrew word יום *yom* 'day' (based on corresponding terms in many European languages, e.g., French *journal*, from *jour* 'day'; Latin *diārium*, from *diēs* 'day'; and Russian дневник *dnyevnik*, from день *dyen'* 'day').

Sometimes a pre-existing Hebrew word is given an additional meaning based on the fact that the corresponding word in another language has multiple meanings. For example, the original meaning of the Hebrew word גרעין *gar'in*, which is attested already in the Mishnah (ca. 200 CE), is 'kernel, pit', but in contemporary Hebrew it also has the scientific meaning 'nucleus', in imitation of the fact that the German word *Kern* and the French word *noyau* can mean both 'nucleus' and 'kernel, pit'. Other examples of this phenomenon are כוכב *kokhav*, which originally meant 'star (in the sky)' but now also means 'celebrity', under the influence of

English 'star', and אתר *'atar*, which originally meant 'site, location' but now also means 'website'.

Very often, new words are simply created from existing Hebrew words or roots, either by the addition of a prefix or suffix, or by changing the internal structure of a word. For example, Modern Hebrew כוכבית *kokhavit* 'asterisk' comes from the older כוכב *kokhav* 'star'; פותחן *pothan* 'can opener' comes from the verb פתח *patah* 'open'; חזאי *hazay* 'weather forecaster' comes from the verb חזה *haze* 'see, foresee'; לשדרג *le-shadreg* 'to upgrade' comes from דרגה *darga* 'grade, rank'; תרדמת *tardemet* 'coma' comes from the verbal root רדם *rdm* 'sleep'; מטוס *matos* 'airplane' comes from the verb טס *tas* 'fly'; and פרצופון *partsufon* 'emoji' comes from פרצוף *partsuf* 'face'. This type of creation is extremely common.

Some newly created Hebrew words are formed by blending two different words or parts of words. Examples are תפוז *tapuz* 'orange (the fruit)', which is a combination of the words תפוח *tapuah* 'apple' and זהב *zahav* 'gold'; מדרחוב *midrahov* 'pedestrian street', from מדרכה *midrakha* 'sidewalk, footpath' (itself a modern creation) and רחוב *rehov* 'street'; עדכני *'adkani* 'current, up-to-date', from עד *'ad* 'until' and כאן *kan* 'here'; קרנף *karnaf* 'rhinoceros', from קרן *keren* 'horn' and אף *'af* 'nose'; and חידק *haydak* 'germ, bacterium', from חי *hay* 'creature' and דק *dak* 'thin, fine'.

Another strategy that has been used to find new Modern Hebrew words has been to take obscure words from the Hebrew Bible, whose exact meanings are sometimes uncertain, and assign them a modern meaning. This was a particularly popular technique in the 19th and early 20th centuries. For example, the word מלצר *meltsar* occurs twice in the biblical book of Daniel, where it means something like 'steward'. In Modern Hebrew, it has become the regular word for 'waiter' and has even spawned a feminine form, מלצרית *meltsarit* 'waitress'. In the Bible, the words לויתן *livyatan* and תנין *tanin* usually refer to mythical sea creatures of uncertain description, but in Modern Hebrew they are the respective words for 'whale' and 'crocodile' (note also the calque דמעות תנין *dim'ot tanin* 'crocodile tears'). Another example is the word חשמל *hashmal*. In the Book of Ezekiel, where it occurs three times, it refers to some sort of shiny substance, perhaps amber or the metal alloy electrum. This word was conscripted by early speakers of Modern Hebrew and given the meaning 'electricity'. The word תרדמה *tardema* 'deep sleep' (not to be confused with תרדמת *tardemet* 'coma', mentioned earlier) occurs several times in the Bible, most notably in Genesis 2, when God casts a deep sleep over Adam before taking out his rib in order to make Eve; in Modern Hebrew it normally means 'hibernation'.

In some cases an existing Hebrew word or root was assigned a new meaning based on the fact that it sounded like a foreign (usually European) word with the desired meaning. For example, the word ספה *sapa* appears in 2 Samuel 17:28 (in the plural form סַפּוֹת *sappot*), where it seems to refer to some kind of basin or bowl. In Modern Hebrew, it was assigned the meaning 'sofa' because it sounds like the word *sofa*, which exists in several European languages, including German, French, and English. The word מכונה *mekhona* 'machine' occurs several times in the Bible with the meaning 'base (e.g., of a pillar)', but it was given the modern meaning 'machine' because it sounds similar to the Latin *machina* 'machine' and its derivatives in modern European languages. The modern word גלידה *glida* 'ice cream' was created from the obscure Hebrew verb גלד *galad* 'congeal, harden' on account of its similarity to the Italian word *gelato*.

New Hebrew words are still being created all the time, by means of the various strategies described earlier. The Academy of the Hebrew Language routinely publishes lists of newly coined words, though, as noted already, these are not always embraced by the general Hebrew-speaking population. Direct borrowings of foreign words are becoming more and more common, much to the chagrin of language purists, thanks in large part to the constant availability of foreign mass media. Still, the ability of Hebrew to create new words speaks to its vibrancy and adaptability moving forward after 3000 years of continuous use.

References and further study

The *Encyclopedia of Hebrew Language and Linguistics* (Khan et al. 2013) contains numerous articles on loanwords in Hebrew, as well as other articles dealing with neologisms. Among the most relevant are the articles of Yadin (2013) and Hoestermann (2013). The historical surveys of Hebrew by Kutscher (1982) and Sáenz-Badillos (1993) also treat the development of vocabulary in Modern Hebrew. Information on the Academy of the Hebrew Language can be found on their website.

20 Hungarian

Tombstones and other monuments with Jewish symbols testify to the presence of Jews in Hungary from as early as the 2nd or 3rd century CE. At that time, Hungary was part of the Roman Empire, and many of the Jews who settled there seem to have been soldiers or administrative officials. In the medieval period, Jews from Western Europe began to settle in Hungary in greater numbers. There was a particularly large influx during the Crusades, by Jews fleeing mass expulsions and massacres in Western Europe. In later centuries, Jews also settled in Hungary from other parts of Eastern Europe, and continued to arrive from areas to the west of Hungary, such as Austria.

Prior to the medieval period, it is unclear which language or languages the Jews who settled in Hungary spoke, but we know that their main language was Yiddish from at least the 15th century onwards. Their non-Jewish neighbours mainly spoke Hungarian. Yiddish, a Germanic language (see YIDDISH, OLD AND EARLY MODERN), is very different from Hungarian, which belongs to a completely separate language family called Uralic. The Uralic family includes Finnish and Estonian, as well as a number of minority languages spoken mostly in Russia. Hungarian is the most widely spoken member of the Uralic family, with around thirteen million speakers.

Beginning in the 19th century, substantial numbers of Hungarian Jews, particularly those in the more urbanized areas in the western part of the country, started to embrace the ideas of the Haskalah, or Jewish Enlightenment. The Haskalah was a movement that emerged in Berlin in the late 1700s and promoted rationalist philosophy, the study of science and mathematics, and the adoption of the German language among Jews. (See GERMAN and HEBREW, ENLIGHTENMENT for more detailed discussions of the Haskalah.) Many Hungarian Jews who were influenced by the ideas of the Haskalah began to abandon Yiddish in favour of German, which was the language of politics and high culture in Hungary at the time, as well as the main spoken language of some Hungarian cities, including Pest (part of the present-day capital Budapest). In the same period, some pro-Haskalah Jews began speaking Hungarian, either instead of or in addition to German. Over the course of the 19th century, Hungarian increasingly gained ground as the language of choice among urbanized pro-Haskalah Jews in Hungary, replacing both Yiddish and German in these circles by the end of the century. In the

20th century, Hungarian became even more common as a first language among Hungarian Jews more generally, though many of them still retained some passive knowledge of Yiddish or at least familiarity with some Yiddish vocabulary (as is common among, for example, English-speaking Jews whose grandparents or great-grandparents spoke Yiddish).

The widespread adoption of Hungarian by Jews had effects even outside of the Jewish community. As large numbers of Jews became acculturated into urban Hungarian society during the 19th century, they introduced their non-Jewish compatriots to numerous Yiddish words that they still used in their everyday Hungarian speech. Over the course of the following decades, many of these words were adopted by non-Jewish speakers of Hungarian and subsequently became established features of the language. Present-day Hungarian has dozens of Yiddish loanwords, and many non-Jewish Hungarian speakers use them regularly without being aware of their origins. This can be compared to the way that some Yiddish words, like *shlep* and *chutzpah*, have entered into mainstream English (particularly in North America) and are now widely used by Jews and non-Jews alike. Examples of commonly used Yiddish borrowings in colloquial Hungarian include *dafke* 'just because; just for spite', from Yiddish דווקא *dafke* 'precisely'; *majré* 'worry', from Yiddish מורא *moyre* 'fear'; *slepp* 'entourage', from Yiddish שלעפ *shlep* 'drag'; and *mázli* 'luck', from Yiddish מזל *mazl* 'luck'.

Around the same time that many Hungarian Jews were beginning to embrace the ideals of the Haskalah and were acculturating into mainstream Hungarian society, another Jewish movement was emerging in Eastern Europe, which would go on to shape the life of the Jews of the rural and eastern areas of Hungary in a very different way. This movement came to be known as Hasidism. Its founder, Eliezer Baal Shem Tov (died 1760), preached a mystical form of spirituality and encouraged worship through dance, spontaneous prayer, and communion with nature. This marked a radical departure from the previous established Jewish model, which stressed Talmudic education and the mastery of Jewish law. The Baal Shem Tov, as he became known, attracted a following among many Jews in Eastern Europe, and the movement grew over the following decades, developing a network of Hasidic leaders, called *rebbes*, whose followers were devoted to their teachings and would travel to hear them speak. Eventually these circles of followers evolved into different Hasidic courts based around a *rebbe*. The *rebbes* formed dynasties which were generally named after the location in which they were based. Today there are over a hundred Hasidic dynasties, some of the more well-known of which are Chabad-Lubavitch, Vizhnitz, Belz, Bobov, and Satmar. Each of these dynasties is based around a *rebbe* and his particular interpretation of Hasidism.

Although the Hasidic movement started in Ukraine, several of the Hasidic dynasties have their roots in eastern Hungary. The most well-known Hungarian Hasidic group is Satmar, which was founded around 1900 in the then-Hungarian town of Szatmárnémeti (present-day Satu Mare in Romania). Two other prominent Hasidic groups with strong Hungarian connections are Vizhnitz and Kaliv. The

Vizhnitz Hasidic dynasty originated in the town of Vizhnitz (present-day Vyzh-nytsia in Ukraine) but had many followers throughout Transylvania, whose Jews generally identified with Hungary. The Kaliv dynasty was founded in the town of Nagykalló in eastern Hungary. Like other Eastern European Jews, the Hungarian Hasidic population was decimated in the Holocaust, though many refugees were able to settle in newly established Hasidic centres in North America, Israel, and Western Europe (see YIDDISH, MODERN HASIDIC).

As mentioned already, the main language of Hungarian Jews, whether Hasidic or non-Hasidic, was traditionally Yiddish until the 19th century. But while non-Hasidic Jews began to abandon Yiddish in favour of German or Hungarian, the Hasidic Jews, who were not interested in integrating and urban-izing, retained Yiddish to a much greater extent. However, they too began to adopt Hungarian, and by World War II, many Hungarian Hasidic Jews spoke Hungarian as their main language and had little or no knowledge of Yiddish. Thus, the Hungarian language eventually became an element of Hasidic culture in Hungary.

An example of the use of Hungarian among Hasidic Jews can be seen in the existence of Sabbath songs in Hungarian written in the Hebrew alphabet. Among Hasidic and other Orthodox Jews, it has long been the custom to sing songs—called *zmires* in Yiddish—at Sabbath meals. The words of the *zmires* are printed in small books that are handed out to family members and guests at the Sabbath table so that they can be sung communally. Many of the *zmires* are medieval compositions with lyrics in Hebrew or Aramaic, while others are somewhat more recent and are sung in Yiddish. Other languages are much less commonly represented among the *zmires*. A number of *zmires* popular among Kaliv, Vizhnitz, and other Hungarian Hasidim are based on Hungarian folksongs and are sung in Hungarian.

Nearly all Hasidim of Hungarian backgrounds now live outside of Hungary, and most no longer speak Hungarian. Nevertheless, they know the words to these Hungarian *zmires* and sing them on a regular basis at the Sabbath table. One of the songs, known from multiple published versions, is called סול א קאקאש מאר *sol a kokosh mar* (*szól a kakas már* in standard Hungarian spelling), which means 'the rooster is already crowing'. *Szól a kakas már* was a Hungarian folksong—no longer very well known—about love and longing. In the 18th or 19th century, the first Kaliver Rebbe, Yitzchok Ayzik Taube (died 1821), composed a new version of the song with specifically Jewish-themed lyrics in Hungarian. Taube's lyrics became popular in the Jewish community and the song was adopted by many Hasidim. The Jewish version, rather than being a straightforward love song, is about the hope of rebuilding the Temple in Jerusalem; the lyrics tell of a bird who yearns to fly off to Jerusalem, but is implored by the narrator to wait until the Temple is restored.

In printed editions, the words of the song are provided in Hungarian in Hebrew script, as well as in the Latin alphabet using standard Hungarian spelling. The following excerpt of the song shows the Hungarian in Hebrew script, along-side the standard Hungarian in Latin script and an English translation. (In the

סול א קאקאש מאר (מהרה״ק מקאליב זי״ע)

קְרייֶען טוּט שוֹין דֶער הָאן,	סוּל אַה קַה–קַהש מַר,
דֶער טָאג טָאג'ט שוֹין אָן,	מוֹיד מֶגוִרד מַר,
אִי'ן אַ גרִינעם וֶועלְדְל,	זֶלד עֶר–דֶבֶן,
נֶעבְּן אַ פוֹסְטְן פֶעלְדְל,	שֶׁיק מֶ–זֶבֶן,
אַ פֿייגֶעלֶע שפַאצִירְט אַרום.	שֶׁיטַל עֶדִי מָהדר.
וַואס פַאר אַ פוֹיגֶל איז דאס,	דֶה מֶטְשָׁדַה מָהדר?
וַואס פַאר אַ פוֹיגֶל איז דאס,	דֶה מֶטְשָׁדַה מָהדר?
גֶעלֶע פִיסֶל, פֶּערְל פִיסְקֶל,	שָׁרְגֶה לַבֶּה ד'יִנְד'י אַה סַיֶּה,
קיין ירושָׁלַיִם וֶויל זי גֵיין.	אֵינְגֶם אַדַה וַר.
וַוארְט פֿייגֶעלֶע וַוארְט,	וַרְי מָהדר וַרְי,
וַוארְט פֿייגֶעלֶע וַוארְט,	וַרְי מָהדר וַרְי,
אַז גָאט וֶועט דִיר בַּאשֶׁערְן,	הַה אָהז אֵש–טֶן נֵקֶד רֶנְדֶל,
וֶועסְטוּ קיין ירושָׁלַיִם אום קֶערְן.	אַה טָאט לֶסֶג מַר.
אָבֶּער וֶוען וֶועט דאס זיין,	דֶה מִקְהר לֶס אָהז מַר,
אָבֶּער וֶוען וֶועט דאס זיין,	דֶה מִקְהר לֶס אָהז מַר,
יִבָּנֶה הַמִקְדָּשׁ עִיר צִיון תְּמַלָּא,	יִבָּנֶה הַמִקְדָּשׁ עִיר צִיון תְּמַלָּא,
דֶעמָאלְס וֶועט דאס זיין.	אָהקְהר לֶס אָהז מַר.

Szól a kakas már,	Várj madár várj,
Majd megvirrad már,	Várj madár várj,
Zöld erdőben	Ha az I-ten néked rendelt,
Sik mezőben	A tiéd leszek már.
Sétál egy madár.	
	De mikor lesz az már,
De micsoda madár?	De mikor lesz az már,
De micsoda madár?	Jibune Hamikdos ir
Sárga lába, gyöngy a szája,	Cijon tömále
Engem oda vár.	Akkor lesz az már.

The Judeo-Hungarian song called סול א קאקאש מאר *sol a kokosh mar*, with a Yiddish translation and standard Hungarian version. Published in זמירות לשבת קודש ויום טוב *zemirot le-shabbat qodesh we-yom ṭov* 'Songs for the Holy Sabbath and Festivals' (Bnei Brak, 2007).

published books of *zmires*, there is also a rhyming Yiddish translation of this song, but no English version.) An interesting feature of this Judeo-Hungarian text is the use of the Hebrew symbol הַ (the letter *he* with the central dot called *dagesh*) in combination with the vowel symbol *qamets* (ָ) to indicate (with a few exceptions) the Hungarian vowels *a* and *o* (which are pronounced similarly), while the Hebrew vowel symbol *pataḥ* (ַ) indicates the Hungarian vowel *á*. Note also that one line of the song (beginning with the word *Jibune*) is Hebrew, and so the Hungarian-letter version of that line is simply a phonetic rendering of the Hebrew. Finally, note that in the third line of the Latin-script version, the Hungarian word *Isten* 'God' is written *I-ten* in the printed edition; the replacement of the *s* (which stands for the sound *sh* in Hungarian) with a dash is a common Jewish convention designed to avoid spelling out the name of God in full. In the Judeo-Hungarian spelling, no letter is omitted, but a dash separates the word into two parts: אִשׁ–טֶן.

Várj madár várj,	וַרְי מָהֹדַר וַרְי,
Várj madár várj,	וַרְי מָהֹדַר וַרְי,
Ha az I-ten néked rendelt,	הָה אָהֹז אִשׁ–טֶן נֶקֶד רֶנְדֶל,
A tiéd leszek már.	אָה טִאֶט לֶסֶג מַר.
De mikor lesz az már,	דֶה מִקָהֹר לֶס אָהֹז מַר,
De mikor lesz az már,	דֶה מִקָהֹר לֶס אָהֹז מַר,
Jibune Hamikdos ir Cijon tömále,	יִבָּנֶה הַמִּקְדָּשׁ עִיר צִיּוֹן תְּמַלֵּא,
Akkor lesz az már.	אָהֹקָהֹר לֶס אָהֹז מַר.

'Wait, little bird, wait,
Wait, little bird, wait,
When God destines me for you,
I'll be yours.

But when will that be?
But when will that be?
The Temple will be built; You will fill the City of Zion.
It will be then.'

The adoption of non-Jewish Eastern European lyrics and melodies by Jews is not unique to the Hungarian-language *zmires*. In fact, the Jewish folk music tradition in Eastern Europe in general was strongly rooted in the local environment, and many melodies were shared between Jews and their non-Jewish neighbours. This musical heritage has left its mark on Jewish culture until the present day, even outside of Eastern Europe. For example, the melody of the Israeli national anthem התקווה *Ha-Tikva*, which was composed in Eastern Europe in the late 19th century and adopted by the fledgling Zionist movement, is based on a Romanian folksong called *Carul cu boi* 'Ox-Cart', which was popular in Romania and Moldova at the time.

References and further study

Rosenhouse (2017) provides an overview of Jewish Hungarian. Komoróczy (2018) is a discussion of the shift among Hungarian Jews from Yiddish to Hungarian in the 19th and 20th centuries. Biale et al. (2018) is a comprehensive study of the history of Hasidism, and Wodziński (2018) is a historical atlas of Hasidism with images and discussions of Hungarian Hasidic history. Mlotek (2010) is a survey of Eastern European Jewish folk songs.

21 Israeli Sign Language

Sign languages are too often forgotten in the study of human languages. We associate language with speech and writing, and most people assume that a language has to be either spoken, or written, or both. But in fact, sign languages are fully developed systems of communication that are no less complex and functional than their written and spoken counterparts. Moreover, sign languages are not simply signed versions of the languages spoken and written around them. Rather, they are completely independent. For example, ASL (American Sign Language) and BSL (British Sign Language) are not English. They have completely different grammatical structures.

In the same way, ISL (Israeli Sign Language) is not a form of Hebrew. For example, compare how one would say the sentence 'I broke my leg last week' in ISL and Israeli Hebrew (words in capital letters under the ISL heading represent different signs):

ISL	Hebrew
I LEG BREAK WEEK-AGO	שברתי את הרגל בשבוע שעבר
	shavarti ʾet ha-regel ba-shavuaʿ she-ʿavar
	(Literally: I broke the leg in the week that passed)

These two sentences are distinct in a number of ways. First, the word order is quite different. In ISL, the verb 'break' comes after its object 'leg', while in Hebrew, the verb (*shavarti*) comes before 'leg' (*regel*). In ISL, there is an independent word for 'I', whereas in Hebrew it is built into the past-tense verb (*shavarti*). In ISL, the verb 'break' has no indication of tense, whereas the Hebrew form can only be past tense. Hebrew requires a special particle (*ʾet*) to mark the object of the verb, while ISL has no such particle. Hebrew makes use of a definite article 'the' (*ha-*), while ISL does not. The phrase for 'last week' is also different in the two languages.

ISL also has grammatical structures that are absent from Hebrew. For example, Hebrew does not distinguish between a past tense and a present perfect tense, so the verb *shavarti*, cited earlier, can mean both 'I broke' and 'I have broken'. By contrast, ISL, like English, can distinguish between these two verb tenses.

<u>Hebrew</u>
שברתי את הרגל
shavarti ʾet ha-regel
'I broke my leg/I have broken my leg'

<u>ISL</u>

I LEG BREAK	I LEG ALREADY BREAK
'I broke my leg'	'I have broken my leg'

Like spoken languages, sign languages have histories and can be grouped into different families with a shared origin. For example, Hebrew and Arabic both belong to the Semitic family of languages, English and Dutch both belong to the Germanic family, and French and Spanish belong to the Romance family. The relationships between sign languages do not always correspond to the relationships between the spoken languages of their respective home countries. For example, ASL and BSL are not closely related to each other, despite the fact that American and British English are nearly identical forms of the same language. ASL is actually much more closely related to French Sign Language.

We know that there was a small Jewish (and Arab) deaf community in Palestine in the late 19th century, but little is known about the sign language that they used. ISL is believed to have emerged in the 1930s with the establishment of local communal groups for deaf adults and the foundation of a Jewish school for the deaf in Jerusalem. Although the school did not actually teach sign language—in fact, it banned its use until decades later—it provided a place where deaf Jewish children from various backgrounds could interact with one another for extended periods. Around this time, clubs were also established that gave deaf adults the same chance to meet and exchange ideas. Both the school and the clubs included immigrants as well as locals, all of whom brought with them different traditions of signing. The result of these various influences was a new and specifically Israeli sign language. The greatest influence on ISL seems to have been German Sign Language, most likely due to the fact that a number of the early influential figures in the community were German Jews. The 1930s were also a time when many German Jews immigrated to Israel. With the large-scale immigration of Jews from the Middle East and North Africa in the 1950s and 1960s, ISL was further enriched with input from new deaf immigrants from countries such as Algeria, Egypt, and Morocco.

Despite the fact that ISL and Hebrew are two distinct languages with completely different grammatical structures, there is some influence of Hebrew on ISL due to the fact that ISL users also know Hebrew, which they use as their normal medium of reading and writing, and for communication with hearing people. ISL often borrows words from Hebrew. A borrowed word may simply be finger-spelled; for example, an ISL user would finger-spell to refer to people's names or to express concepts for which no sign exists. We also see something called loan translations, where a Hebrew compound noun is translated literally into ISL using existing signs. For example, the word for 'slippers' in ISL is made up of the signs for 'shoe' and 'house', which is based on the Hebrew phrase נעלי בית *na'ale bayit*, literally meaning 'shoes (of) house'.

Today ISL is used by about 10,000 people. Although the language was initially developed by Jews, they are not the only ones to use it: deaf Israeli Arabs and other non-Jewish groups in the country also learn it in school and use it among themselves. This parallels Modern Hebrew, which emerged in a Jewish context but is also spoken fluently by non-Jewish minorities in Israel. With the arrival of over a million immigrants from the former Soviet Union in the 1990s came about a thousand users of RSL (Russian Sign Language). This means that a significant percentage of the deaf community in Israel uses RSL instead of or in addition to ISL, and it remains to be seen how ISL will be affected by this new immigrant community.

The fact that Israeli Sign Language is a very distinct communication system that grew out of an amalgamation of different Jewish sources, including vocabulary borrowed from Hebrew, makes it a true Jewish language. Just as the Israeli people comprise a fusion of Jews from all over the world and Israeli cuisine is a mixture of different Jewish traditions, so this uniquely Israeli sign language is also a blend of Jewish sign languages from Central and Eastern Europe, North Africa, and the Middle East.

References and further study

Meir and Sandler (2008) is a comprehensive survey of the history and structure of ISL, while Meir (2013) provides an accessible overview of the subject. Fox (2007) is an excellent introduction to the history of sign language, including a lot of information on ISL and other sign languages used in Israel.

22 Italian

Jews have been living in the Italian Peninsula since perhaps as early as the 2nd century BCE, during the time of the Roman Republic. The earliest Jewish settlers were probably Greek speaking, though with knowledge of Hebrew and Aramaic, as evidenced by surviving tombstones. Some Jewish communities, namely those in southern (Byzantine) territories, remained Greek speaking for many centuries, but most adopted Latin, which evolved into Italian (and its dialects) by the late 1st millennium CE (see LATIN).

The modern Italian language in its written form is the same all over Italy. This variety emerged as the literary standard in the 14th century, based on the local dialect of Florence. But just as spoken English dialects can sound very different from written English, as well as from one another, so spoken Italian dialects can differ considerably from the written language. In fact, many language varieties that are often referred to as Italian "dialects"—such as Piedmontese, Bolognese, Neopolitan, Venetian, and Sicilian—are actually different enough from standard Italian to be considered separate languages. Other spoken varieties (e.g., Roman and Livornese) are close enough to the standard language to safely be called dialects. Today, almost any Italian who still speaks a regional language variety is bilingual in standard Italian, which serves as the sole language of education and of the media, though this was a 20th-century development. In fact, in many areas the regional dialects have been or will soon be completely replaced by standard Italian.

Jews living in different regions of Italy likewise spoke various Italian dialects. As early as the 10th century, we find occasional Italian words (of various dialects) in Hebrew script—that is, Judeo-Italian—embedded within Hebrew texts. From the 13th to the 18th centuries, we find entire texts in Judeo-Italian, both translations and original compositions. The amount of extant literature in Judeo-Italian is greater than in the other Judeo-Romance dialects (see CATALAN, FRENCH, PORTUGUESE, and PROVENÇAL), with the exception of Judeo-Spanish (see LADINO). Judeo-Italian texts exist in a variety of genres, and they range in length from a few words to entire volumes. We find translations of biblical and liturgical texts, glossaries and other types of word-lists, sermons, letters, grammars, medical recipes, and more. We even find a handful of Judeo-Italian printed books (as opposed to hand-copied manuscripts), mainly from the 16th and 17th centuries. The language of some

קָאיסטוֹ אֵי לִיבְּרוֹפֵּיטִיסִימוֹ רִי שִיר הַשִׁירִי־ם

קָאנְטוֹ

דִי לִיקָאנְטִי קִ אִי אֵשֵׁלְפֵה בָּאשֵׁרַהפִּי
רִי לִיבָּאשַׁאפֵּטִי דִי לַאבּוֹקָה סוּאָה רֵי
בּוֹנִ לַאמוֹרִי טוֹאִ פֵּלוּ קִי לוֹמֵירוֹ שֶׁ
אַלוֹסִימוֹ רִי לוֹלִי טוֹאִ בּוֹנ אוֹלִיוּ שֶׁ
וֵיטָאטוֹ לוֹנוֹמִי טוֹאוֹ פֵּרְצֶ צֵיטִילִ אַפָא רוֹ
טִי סְטִירַה קִי דִירִיטוֹ טִי אֵיקוֹרִירִמוֹ
פֵיצֵ וֵיכֵרִי קִי לוֹרִי כָלִיקָאמוֹרִי סוּאָה
אַלְצֵרָארְפּוֹצֵ אִי אַלְגֵרָארְפּוֹצֵ אִינְפֵ
אֵרִיקוֹרְדָארְפִי לַאמוֹרִי טוֹאִ פֵּלוּ רֵק

The opening of a Judeo-Italian translation of the Song of Songs (15th century). Bibliothèque nationale de France, ms. hébr. 1342, fol. 45v.

The first three stanzas of a Hebrew–Judeo-Italian poem, written in 1553 by Samuel di Castiglione. The excerpt reproduced in the chapter is the third stanza. Archiginnasio Municipal Library of Bologna, ms. Cod A. 1281, fol. 13r.

Judeo-Italian texts is identical (or nearly so) to standard literary Italian, while other texts, including a number of *siddurim* (prayer-books) and some biblical translations, reflect a uniquely Jewish dialect of Italian, which makes them particularly interesting from a linguistic perspective.

Among the many genres of Judeo-Italian texts are biblical and other types of glossaries that provide Judeo-Italian translations of Hebrew words. The oldest biblical glossary ever published is a work entitled מִקְרֵי דַרְדְקֵי *Maqre Dardeqe*, written in the early 15th century by a French-Catalonian immigrant to Italy named Perets Trabot and first published in Naples in 1488. It is actually a trilingual glossary: each Hebrew root is followed by a gloss (translation or explanation) in both Judeo-Italian and Judeo-Arabic (see ARABIC, MEDIEVAL). Besides being of linguistic interest, this glossary highlights the cultural connections between the Jews of Southern Europe and the Arabic-speaking Jews of Spain, Malta (see MALTESE), and North Africa.

As with Judeo-French (see FRENCH) and a number of other Jewish languages, Judeo-Italian glossaries can provide examples of rare or unknown words, as well as early attestations of words. One fun example comes from a 14th-century glossary of difficult words in Maimonides' *Mishneh Torah*. Included in this glossary is the term חררה *ḥarara*, a Rabbinic Hebrew word that refers to a kind of cake or baked dough. The Judeo-Italian gloss provided is פיצא *pitsa*, or, in modern Italian spelling, *pizza*. The first attestation of the word *pizza* in a non-Jewish Italian text is only from the mid-1500s, which is nearly 200 years later than this glossary. To put it another way, this means that the earliest attestation of the word *pizza* in Italian comes from a Jewish text in Hebrew characters!

One of the most famous Judeo-Italian texts is an elegaic poem of 120 lines known as *La ienti de Zion* 'People of Zion', which was intended for use during the holiday of Tisha B'Av. Though the text itself was probably composed in the 12th or 13th century, it survives only in two 14th-century manuscripts of *maḥzorim* (holiday prayer-books). The opening lines are as follows:

la gente de-tsion plange e-lutta	לַאֵינְטֵי דְּצִיוֹן פְּלַנְיֵי אלוּטָא
dice taupina male so condutta	דִיצֵי טָאוּפִּינָא מָלֵי סוֹ קוֹנדוּטָא
em-manu de-lo-nemicu ke m'ao strutta	אמָאנוּ דְלוֹנְימִיקוּ קֵי מָאוֹשְׁטְרוּטָא

'People of Zion, weep and mourn
Say: Woe is me, I have been handed over cruelly
into the hand of the enemy who has destroyed me.'

The elegy is full of dialectal grammar and vocabulary, including forms like *so* for standard Italian *sono* 'I am', *lo nemicu* for standard *il nemico* 'the enemy', and *ao* for standard *ha* 'has'.

A number of later Judeo-Italian poems are what scholars call "macaronic", featuring a mixture of Judeo-Italian and Hebrew or, in at least one case, a mixture of Judeo-Italian and Yiddish. Perhaps the most inventive is a poem written by the Venetian rabbi Leon Modena (1571–1648) when he was just thirteen years old. His poem can be read either in Hebrew or in Italian, with nearly identical sounds but totally different meanings. Here is the second line of both the Hebrew and Judeo-Italian versions, according to Modena's original spelling and use of vowel points:

	Judeo-Italian	Hebrew
Original	קוֹלְטוֹ וְיֵין לְ אוּמְ קוֹסִי אוֹרְדִינָה לְ צְיֵילוֹ	כָּל טוֹב עֵילוֹם : כּוֹסִי : אוֹר דִין אֶל צִלוֹ
Transliteration	*Colto vien l'uom, così ordin'il Cielo*	*kol ṭov 'elum kosi 'or din 'el tsillo*
Meaning	'Learned comes the man, thus ordains Heaven'	'All good is hidden, my cup, the light of justice to its shadow'

We also find other types of macaronic poems, in which Hebrew and Judeo-Italian lines alternate in regular patterns. For example, one such poem by the Mantuan Jewish physician Samuel di Castiglione, written in 1553, includes stanzas with eight half-lines; numbers 1, 3, 6, and 7 are in Hebrew, while numbers 2, 4, 5, and 8 are in Judeo-Italian. Following is a sample stanza from this poem, which focuses on the dangers of women. Numbers have been added for easier reference, and the Judeo-Italian is transliterated using standard Italian spelling:

2. קיאי אונה גראן אינפריסה	1. ואל תקח אשה
4. סינון פואי פארי לאספיסה	3. קלון חרפה בושה
6. פסוק טוב לשבת	5. מיסורא בין אי פיסא
8. די קוויסטא פימינאריאה	7. ומוצא מר ממות

1. *we-'al tiqaḥ 'isha*
3. *qalon ḥerpa busha*
5. *misura ben e pesa*
7. *u-motse mar mim-mawet*

2. *che è una gran'inpresa*
4. *se non puoi fare la spesa*
6. *pasuq ṭov la-shevet*
8. *di questa femminarìa*

'1. Don't take a wife,
3. Dishonour, disgrace, shame,
5. Consider well and weigh
7. and "I find more bitter than death"

2. which is a big undertaking.
4. if you can't sustain the cost.
6. the verse "it's better to dwell"
8. about this kind of woman.'

The two biblical verses referred to in this poem are Proverbs 21:9 ("it's better to dwell in the corner of a rooftop than in a house shared with a contentious wife") and Ecclesiastes 7:26 ("I find more bitter than death the woman who is a snare, whose heart is a trap, and whose hands are fetters").

A much more cheerful Judeo-Italian poem is the Purim song known as *Fate onore al bel Purim* ('Honour the beautiful Purim'), which goes back to at least the

17th century (when it was first published), and was still known to Italian Jews in the 20th century. Much of the poem focuses on food and drink, and we find in it good-humoured lines like נוֹן אַבְּיָיטֵי אַלְקוּן סוֹסְפִּיטוֹ \ דִי אֵיסִיר טֵינוּטִי שֵׁכּוֹרִים *non abbiate alcun sospeto / di eser tenuti shikorim* 'you shouldn't have any misgiving about being considered drunk!'.

After the 18th century—following a trend that had begun already in the 16th century—Jews wrote Italian almost exclusively in the Italian alphabet, and their written language was identical to that of non-Jews in Italy. Still, Jews continued to speak their own local dialects. There is no single spoken Judeo-Italian dialect, but rather there existed regional varieties like Judeo-Roman, Judeo-Florentine, Judeo-Piedmontese, Judeo-Venetian, Judeo-Mantuan, and more. These correspond geographically to the many regional dialects of Italian described earlier, though in some cases the Judeo-Italian spoken dialects differed markedly from those of their non-Jewish neighbours, including differences in pronunciation, grammar, and vocabulary. So, for example, the spoken dialect of the Jews of Rome is quite different from the non-Jewish spoken dialect, both of which differ from standard written Italian. The same was true of the Jewish dialects of Mantua, Livorno, and a number of other places. (For a nice parallel, see ARABIC, MODERN).

Spoken Judeo-Italian dialects, typical of Jewish languages, incorporated numerous words from Hebrew. Many of these words are connected with Judaism in some way, as we would expect, including words like *caser* (or *cascer*) 'kosher' (from Hebrew כשר *kasher* 'fit, proper') and *tefilà* 'prayer' (from Hebrew תפילה *tefilla* 'prayer'). But we also find many Hebrew words with no overt Jewish connection that have been incorporated into the grammatical system of Italian. For example, we find verbs like *achlare* (or *ahlare*) 'to eat' (from Hebrew אכל *'akhal* 'eat') and *dabberare* (or *dabrare*) 'to speak' (from Hebrew דבר *dabber* 'speak'). We also find derived adjectives and nouns like *malmazallo* 'unlucky' (from Italian *mal-* 'bad' + Hebrew מזל *mazzal* 'luck') and *scigazzello* 'little boy' (< Hebrew שקץ *sheqets* 'abomination; non-Jewish man' + the Italian suffix *-ello*). Sometimes borrowed Hebrew words are used in Judeo-Italian dialects with a meaning not found in Hebrew. For example, the word *macom* (< Hebrew מקום *maqom* 'place') is used in several Judeo-Italian dialects as a euphemism for 'toilet', and the word *tafus* (< Hebrew תפוס *tafus* 'captured') is used in nearly all the dialects to mean 'prison'.

Some spoken Judeo-Italian dialects have also been influenced by other Jewish languages. The various waves of Ashkenazi immigrants that came to Italy beginning in the late 15th century contributed some Yiddish words to Judeo-Italian dialects, especially those in northern Italy, most notably the word *orsài* 'anniversary of a death' (from Yiddish יאָרצײַט *yortsayt*). In Livorno, which had a large community of Sephardic Jews who came after the Spanish Expulsion of 1492, the local Judeo-Italian dialect incorporated many Ladino words (see LADINO), such as *agora* 'now' and *cabezza* 'head' (from Ladino

אגורה *agora* and קאביסה *kavesa*). We also find words of Ladino origin in other dialects, for example, Judeo-Piedmontese *calavassa* 'fool', borrowed from Ladino קאלאבאסה *kalavasa*, a word that originally meant 'pumpkin'. One word of Ladino origin that is found in all Judeo-Italian dialects—in fact, still used by Italian Jews—is *negro*, meaning 'miserable', 'ugly', or 'good for nothing'. This word means 'black' in Spanish, but in Ladino it means 'bad' (and פריטו *preto* means 'black').

On rare occasions, mostly in the early 20th century, Jews wrote down their spoken dialects (using Italian script, not Hebrew), especially to record things like poetry or theatrical plays. Sadly, because of the political, demographic, and social changes of the 19th and 20th centuries, nearly all spoken Judeo-Italian varieties have become extinct. Judeo-Roman is perhaps the only dialect of Judeo-Italian that is still spoken, albeit by a mostly elderly group.

References and further study

For a comprehensive survey of Judeo-Italian, with extensive bibliography and text samples, see Rubin (2017). For a general history of the Jews in Italy, Roth (1946) is still the most comprehensive work in English. A digital scan of *Maqre Dardeqe* is available online via the Münchener DigitalisierungsZentrum

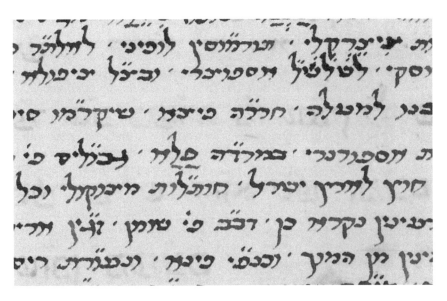

A Hebrew–Judeo-Italian glossary of Maimonides' *Mishneh Torah* from the 14th century. In the middle of line 3, we find the gloss פיצא *pitsa*, seemingly the oldest known example of the word *pizza* in Italian. Bibliothèque nationale de France, ms. hébr. 1311, fol. 5v.

(www.digitale-sammlungen.de). The appearance of *pizza* in the glossary of *Mishneh Torah* was first noticed by Debenedetti Stow (1983). One manuscript of *La ienti de Zion* is in the Biblioteca Palatina in Parma (Parm. 2736) and the other (Valmadonna ms. 10) is privately owned; digital images of both manuscripts are available via the National Library of Israel's Ktiv website. The text has been published by several scholars, including Cassuto (1929) and Natale (2017), though in the latter the text of the poem is printed only in transliteration. The poem of Leon de Modena is reproduced in Rubin (2017), with further references. The poem of Samuel di Castiglione was published by Debenedetti Stow (1980). On the macaronic poem in Judeo-Italian and Yiddish, see Rosenzweig (2020). Dictionaries of spoken Judeo-Italian dialects include Fortis (2006) and Aprile (2012).

23 Karaim (and Krymchak)

The Karaites are a distinct sect within Judaism, with a history going back more than 1200 years. Unlike mainstream (so-called Rabbanite) Jews, Karaites accept only the Hebrew Bible as an authoritative text, and they do not follow the teachings laid down by the rabbis of the Mishnah and the Talmud. As a result, Karaites have their own interpretations of many of the Jewish laws regulating everyday life, and so their religious and cultural practices sometimes differ from those of Rabbanite Jews. The sect originated in 8th-century Iraq and then quickly spread to Jewish settlements throughout the Middle East. The Karaite and Rabbanite communities were often at odds due to their differing interpretations of Judaism, but there were still close ties between them.

Much of what we know about the Karaites in the first few centuries of their existence comes from the documents found in the Cairo Genizah (see ARABIC, MEDIEVAL), since Cairo was home to vibrant Karaite and Rabbanite populations throughout the Middle Ages. Documents found in the Genizah testify to the close business and personal relationships between the two communities, including inter-marriage, despite their sectarian differences. The Karaites also made significant contributions to Jewish scholarship. Because their primary focus was on the Bible as opposed to rabbinic literature, Karaite scholars in this period produced important biblical commentaries and grammatical analyses of Biblical Hebrew, many of which were preserved in the Cairo Genizah, despite the fact that the Genizah itself was housed in a Rabbanite synagogue.

In medieval Egypt and Palestine, both Karaite and Rabbanite Jews spoke Arabic and often wrote in Hebrew, but the Karaites did distinguish themselves linguistically in one interesting way. When copying biblical manuscripts, Karaites sometimes used Arabic letters instead of Hebrew ones, even though the language of the texts was still Hebrew. This phenomenon, which we might call Karaeo-Hebrew, is the opposite of Judeo-Arabic, which is the term for the Arabic language written in Hebrew characters. The Karaites were writing the Hebrew language in Arabic script! Even more bizarre, perhaps, is that they combined the Arabic letters with the traditional Hebrew vowel points. A number of these Karaeo-Hebrew biblical manuscripts were found in the Cairo Genizah.

Around the 11th century CE, Karaism began to spread westward into Europe, and northward into places like Turkey (at that time part of the Byzantine Empire).

Karaite Hebrew Bible in Arabic script (Exodus 8:1–8:3), with Arabic translation, written in the 12th century. British Library, ms. Or. 2544, fol. 157v. © The British Library Board.

בה עזרת שמא

בְּשֵׁם הַנִמְצָא בְּצָרוֹת עֶזְרָה ה׳ וּבוֹרֵא עוֹלָם

בַּאֲמִירָה ה׳ אַתְחִיל לִכְתּוֹב תַּרְגּוּם הַתּוֹרָה

בְּרֵאשִׁית בָּרָא אֱלֹהִים אֵת הַשָּׁמַיִם וְאֵת
הָאָרֶץ

אַוְול בַּשְׁטָא   ...

...

וְיֹאמֶר   ...

...

וְיֹאמֶר   ...

...

The first page of the Bible (Genesis 1) in Karaim, probably from the late 18th century. Cambridge University Library, BSMS 288, vol. 1, fol. 1r. Courtesy of the British and Foreign Bible Society.

By the 17th century, large numbers of Karaites had become concentrated in Crimea, on the northern coast of the Black Sea. That region was inhabited predominantly by peoples who spoke a Turkic dialect that is related to the more well-known Turkish language spoken in Turkey. The Crimean Karaites adopted this local Turkic dialect, and it is possible that some of the area's Turkic-speaking population even converted to Karaite Judaism. From Crimea, many Karaites migrated northwards into Poland, Ukraine, and Lithuania, bringing with them their Turkic dialect, which developed into a unique language called Karaim. The Karaim used by the speakers who settled in Poland and Lithuania, which were cut off from speakers of other Turkic languages, evolved into a different variety from the one used by those who had stayed in Crimea. Crimean Karaim died out in the 19th century, so most of what we know about Karaim comes from the Polish and Lithuanian varieties.

Karaim can be distinguished from other Turkic languages in a number of ways. Because Karaim speakers in Poland and Lithuania were surrounded by speakers of Polish, Ukrainian, and Russian, Karaim has been influenced by these Slavic languages. Moreover, like other Jewish languages, Karaim has traditionally been written in the Hebrew script (see the sample poem) and contains vocabulary borrowed from Hebrew. For example, we find Karaim words like *kahal* 'community' (from Hebrew קהל *qahal*), *tsaddik* 'righteous man' (from Hebrew צדיק *tsaddiq*), and *ganeden* 'paradise' (from Hebrew גן עדן *gan 'eden* 'Garden of Eden'). Written Karaim also shows some grammatical influence from Hebrew. For example, Turkic languages do not normally have a word like the English definite article 'the'. Thus, the Turkish word *yer* can mean 'earth' or 'the earth', depending on the context. By contrast, written Karaim can sometimes use the word *ol* (which also means 'that') as a definite article, in imitation of the Hebrew definite article ה- *ha-*, e.g., יֵיר *yer* 'earth' but אוֹל יֵיר *ol yer* 'the earth' (compare Hebrew ארץ *'erets* 'earth' vs. הארץ *ha-'arets* 'the earth').

The oldest surviving texts in the Karaim language are poems from the 16th and 17th centuries. In the following centuries, Karaim speakers produced translations of biblical texts and prayer-books, as well as a small amount of original literature, mostly poetry. While the poems are more reflective of spoken Karaim, the Bible translations are somewhat artificial, as they usually follow the original Hebrew text word for word. The following is an excerpt from a poem by Isaac ben Abraham Troki (1533–1594), the most well-known Lithuanian Karaite scholar in Europe. Note the heavy use of alliteration in the poem: every word (more than 150 in total!) starts with the letter י *y*.

Yigit yigit yüvrüklär yaḥšï yolġa	יִיגִּיט יִיגִּיט יוּבְּרוּכְלַר יַחְשִׁי יוֹלְגָּא
Yarlïġašïna yoġarġïnïn yetärlär	יַרְלִיגָּשִׁינָא יוֹגַּרְגִּינִין יֵיטַרְלַר
Yazïqlardan yolduzlay yarïrlar	יַזִיקְלַרְדַן יוֹלְדוּזְלַאיְ יַירִירְלַר
Yuvuz yüräklilär yapraqlay yašarïrlar	יוּבּוּז יוּרַכְלִילַר יַפְּרַקְלַאיְ יַשַׁרִירְלַר

'Young man, young man, the fast runners will reach the good path
And attain the blessing of the Sublime.
[Those who are washed] from sin will sparkle like the stars.
The upright will blossom like leaves.'

Already in the 19th century, Karaite Jews in the Russian Empire sought to disassociate themselves from Rabbanite Jews—mainly to avoid the oppressive laws that affected the Jewish community—and eventually they ceased to consider themselves Jews at all. During World War II, the Nazis classed the Karaites as non-Jews, and thus they were spared annihilation. This perceived separation between Karaites and Jews persists among present-day Eastern European Karaites, who consider themselves to be of Turkic heritage and want to have nothing to do with the Jewish community. (By contrast, the Karaites in the Middle East have always identified as Jews, maintaining good relations with the Rabbanite community. There are some 30,000 descendants of these Middle Eastern Karaites today, mainly living in Israel.)

The Karaim language remained relatively vibrant into the 20th century. In the 1920s, some Karaim speakers began to write their language in the Latin alphabet under the influence of Polish and Lithuanian, and also in an effort to distance themselves from Rabbanite Jews. The oppressive policies of the Soviet government in the mid-20th century led to a decline in many Karaite communities in Eastern Europe, and now only about a thousand remain in Crimea, while fewer than three hundred are left in Lithuania and Poland. Another few thousand descendants of Eastern European Karaites are scattered worldwide. Most Karaim speakers have lost their language, and there are now only a handful who still use it, mostly in Lithuania. Interestingly, while Karaim is most commonly associated with traditional literature such as Bible translations, the language is still being used creatively despite its severely endangered status. For example, a Karaim version of Saint-Exupéry's famous novella *The Little Prince* was published in 2018 under the title *Kiçi Bijçiek*.

The Karaites were not the only Jewish group in Eastern Europe to speak a Turkic language. In Crimea there was also a Rabbanite Jewish community called the Krymchaks, who adopted the local Turkic dialect, Crimean Tatar. The variety of Crimean Tatar used by the Krymchaks is usually called Krymchak as well, though it is sometimes referred to as Judeo-Crimean Tatar. The Krymchaks used their own Jewish language variety among themselves, and non-Jewish Crimean Tatar with their Muslim neighbours. Many Krymchaks were also familiar with Russian, which was commonly used for communication between the different ethnic groups in multicultural Crimea, and which was considered a language of prestige.

Krymchak is historically related to Karaim, and, like the Karaites, the Krymchaks wrote their language in Hebrew script. The first known Krymchak text comes from the late 16th century. There are also some surviving texts from the 18th century, consisting of legal and community records. The first printed book in the language was a bilingual Hebrew–Krymchak book of hymns, published in Jerusalem in 1902. A few more Krymchak books were published in the first decade of the 20th century, all bilingual Hebrew–Krymchak editions of religious texts. After this, all publication in Krymchak ceased.

Crimea became a part of the Soviet Union in 1920. Despite the small size of the Krymchak community, which numbered only in the thousands, the Soviet authorities recognized the Krymchak language as distinct from Crimean Tatar, and a network of Jewish schools was established, with Krymchak serving alongside Russian as the language of instruction. Despite this official recognition of their language, during the 1920s and 1930s the Krymchaks began to shift to Russian in ever increasing numbers, and knowledge of Krymchak dwindled. As there was no Krymchak publishing activity in this period (other than some Krymchak textbooks used in schools), most cultural expression in the language is likely to have been oral, but very little of this has survived. One of the few documented pieces of Krymchak verbal art from this time is a thirty-two-line poem about the Russian famine of 1921–1922, in which roughly 10% of the Krymchak population perished. The poem, which survives in a manuscript, is based on the style and conventions of traditional Turkic oral verse. It contains fascinating descriptions of specifically Krymchak cultural practices, such as the custom of kindling lights in the synagogue after a burial.

In 1928, the Soviets issued a policy requiring Krymchak to be written in the Latin script instead of the traditional Hebrew alphabet. Crimean Tatar, which had previously been written in a version of the Arabic alphabet, was also Latinized, but there were some differences between the new Krymchak and Crimean Tatar Latin scripts. (This Latinization policy affected other Jewish language varieties in the Soviet Union in the late 1920s and early 1930s; see Tajik and Tat.) In 1938, the Soviets altered this policy, demoting Krymchak to the status of an oral language without its own alphabet. This sudden change in status led rapidly to the complete cessation of educational, literary, and cultural activities in Krymchak.

The small Krymchak community, which numbered 8000 in 1941, was decimated by the Nazis in World War II, and those who survived largely abandoned their language in favour of Russian. Most of the documentary evidence pertaining to the community was also destroyed in the war. However, two original Krymchak poems have survived from this period. Both poems are anonymous and address the horrors of the Holocaust from a Krymchak perspective. Like the earlier poem about the Russian famine, they were based on the model of traditional Turkic oral poetry. One describes how the Jews were killed 'like sheep', while the other includes the moving lines 'On these Crimean fields, we have been victimized . . . Do not forget us, my people'.

In 1955, members of the surviving Krymchak community in Crimea petitioned the Soviet authorities for their official status to be changed from Jewish to that of an independent nationality. The petition was accepted, and the Krymchaks officially ceased to be considered Jews under Soviet law. Following their change in status, the Krymchaks assimilated relatively quickly into the surrounding (mainly Russian) population and largely lost their distinctive linguistic and cultural identity. The only remnant of their former Jewish status was a Holocaust remembrance ceremony, which was conducted annually until at least the 1990s and which included a recitation of the *kaddish*, the traditional Jewish prayer for the dead. At least 2000 Krymchaks remain, some still in Russia and the Ukraine, and others in the United States and Israel.

References and further study

See Jankowski (2017) for an overview of both Karaim and Krymchak language and literature. Polliack (2003) is a thorough guide to Karaite history and culture. The excerpt of Isaac ben Abraham Troki's poem comes from Jankowski (2014); another edition, with a slightly different translation, can be found in Kizilov (2007). The poem itself is attested in two 17th-century manuscripts, both held by the National Library of Russia in St. Peterburg (ms. Evr. IIA 161/9, folios 5r–5v, and ms. Evr. I 699, folios 15v–16r). Zand (1991) has an overview of Krymchak history and literature. Firkavičiūtė and Kobeckaitė (2018) is the Karaim translation of *The Little Prince*. On the Karaite Bible manuscripts in Arabic script, see Khan (1990). On 20th-century Karaite communities, see Kizilov (2015).

24 Ladino (and Spanish)

There is evidence of Jews living in Spain since the 3rd century CE, when it was still part of the Roman Empire. Jews were present during the period of Visigothic rule (5th–8th centuries) and for the subsequent Muslim conquest in the 8th century. During the time that the Muslims ruled Spain, especially during the 10th–13th centuries CE, the Jewish community in the country experienced something of a golden age. This was the time of famous Hebrew scholars, philosophers, and poets like Shmuel HaNagid, Abraham ibn Ezra, and Judah HaLevi. Jews in Muslim Spain typically spoke Arabic and wrote in Judeo-Arabic (see Arabic, Medieval) or Hebrew.

As the Catholic monarchs began to reconquer Spain from the control of Muslim rulers, Arabic was gradually replaced by Spanish within Jewish communities. By the 1400s, Jews were thoroughly Hispanized, though traces of their Arabic linguistic past remained. For example, the Spanish word for Sunday is *domingo*, which is related to the Latin word *dominus* 'Lord'. But to avoid using a word associated with the Christian Sabbath, Spanish Jews instead used the Arabic-derived word אלחאד *alhad*, which means something like 'the first', since Sunday is the first day of the week in the Jewish tradition.

Along with the Christian reconquest of Spain came a worsening of conditions for Jews, including a massacre of thousands of Jews in 1391, and culminating with the institution of the Inquisition and the Expulsion of all Jews from Spain in 1492. The majority of Jews who left Spain settled primarily in areas corresponding to present-day Morocco, Greece, Turkey, Serbia, Bosnia, and Bulgaria. These Jews, who are referred to as Sephardim (from the Hebrew word for Spain, ספרד *Sefarad*), took the Spanish language with them to these new places, where they continued to use it into the 20th century and in some cases even until today. In addition, some Jews fleeing Spain found temporary refuge in Portugal (see Portuguese), while others settled in Amsterdam, Italy, North America, and elsewhere. (Some of these Jews, such as those who settled in Amsterdam, continued speaking Spanish, while others abandoned it in favour of other languages, such as Portuguese, Italian, English, etc.)

At the time of the Expulsion, the Spanish dialects spoken by Jews, which varied by location, were very similar to those of their Christian neighbours. There were some minor differences in vocabulary, such as the use of אלחאד *alhad* mentioned earlier. There is also evidence that Jews sometimes used the word דייו *Dio* for 'God' (as they continued to do post-Expulsion) instead of the standard Spanish *Dios*, because they perceived the latter as a plural form and therefore incompatible with their monotheistic worldview. In addition, Spanish Jews would have used some Hebrew and Aramaic vocabulary, especially for words pertaining to religious and cultural practices.

The Jews who left Spain continued to speak Spanish, mixing the various regional dialects they had brought with them. They also began to incorporate elements from the languages of their new neighbours, most importantly Turkish and Greek. At the same time, the Spanish of Christian Spain continued to evolve separately. As a result, the language of the exiled community developed into a unique blend that in part preserved elements of different Spanish dialects as they were spoken in the 15th century, and in part innovated in ways unknown in Spain. Native speakers have referred to the language by various names, including Ladino, Judezmo, Eshpanyol, and (in North Africa) Ḥaketía, but today it is best known to the world as Ladino.

One of the more striking aspects of Ladino is its preservation of archaic features that have disappeared from modern forms of Spanish. These features include differences in pronunciation, grammar, and vocabulary. For example, Ladino sometimes preserves the sound *f* at the beginning of a word when it has been lost in Spanish, as in the verb פֿאזיר *fazer* 'to do' vs. Spanish *hacer* (derived from the Latin verb *facere*). The Ladino word for 'I am' is still סו *so*, which was the form used in Medieval Spanish, while modern Spanish uses the newer form *soy*. Likewise, Ladino אגורה *agora* 'now' is older than Spanish *ahora*. Another example of an archaic word in Ladino is ביירבו *biervo* 'word' (from Latin *verbum*); in Spanish, the cognate word *verbo* has taken on the restricted technical meaning of 'verb', while *palabra* has replaced it in the more general sense of 'word'.

Another distinctive characteristic of Ladino is the presence of a large number of words that have been taken from Turkish and Greek. (An exception is the North African variety, which instead has taken in many words from Arabic.) While some of these borrowings denote things that were unknown in 15th-century Spain, such as the Turkish-derived words בוריקה *borreka* 'stuffed pastry' and טולומבאג'י *tulumbadjí* 'fireman', many of them have simply replaced or are used alongside older Spanish terms. For example, some everyday words, like אמה *amá* 'but', בוז *buz* 'ice', and פינגאן *findjan* (or פילגאן *fildjan*) 'cup', come from Turkish. Others, like מאנה *maná* 'mom', פאפו *papú* 'grandfather', and פירון *pirón* 'fork', come from Greek. There are also borrowed words from French, Italian, and Slavic languages like Serbian and Bulgarian.

Like other Jewish languages, Ladino has also borrowed many words from Hebrew. Unsurprisingly, many of these are connected with Jewish life, such as תפילה *tefila* 'prayer' (from Hebrew תפילה *tefilla* 'prayer'), קהל *kal* 'synagogue' (from Hebrew קהל *qahal* 'community'), and חכם *hahám* 'rabbi' (from Hebrew חכם *ḥakham* 'wise man'). However, some Hebrew borrowings have no specifically Jewish associations, like גרון *garón* 'neck' and עני *aní* 'poor'. Sometimes a

Hebrew borrowing is combined with a Ladino ending, creating new adjectives and verbs, such as מאזאלוזו *mazalozo* 'lucky' (from Hebrew מזל *mazzal* 'luck') and קאסיינטו *kasiento* 'quick to anger' (from Hebrew כעס *kaʿas* 'anger'), or דיסחינאדו *deshenado* 'unkempt' and אחינאר *ahenar* 'to beautify, adorn' (both from Hebrew חן *ḥen* 'favour, charm').

The following Ladino proverbs illustrate the similarity of Ladino to Spanish, as well as some of its distinctive features:

קין אל באנייו אינטרה, סין סודור נו סאלי.
Ken al banyo entra, sin sudor no sale.
(Spanish: *Quien al baño entra, sin sudor no sale.*)
'Whoever enters the bath(house) doesn't leave without a sweat.'

די איל דייו אי דיל ויזינו נו סי פואידי אינקובריר.
De el Dió i del vezino no se puede encuvrir.
(Spanish: *De Dios y del vecino no se puede encubrir.*)
'From God and from the neighbour one cannot hide.'

אל ריקו איל גאייו לי מיטי גואיבוס, אל פרובّי ני לה גאיינה.
Al rico el gayo le mete guevos; al prove ni la gayina.
(Spanish: *Al rico el gallo le mete huevos; al pobre ni la gallina.*)
'For the rich man the rooster lays eggs; for the poor man not even the hen.'

איל טיימפו איס אונה איסקאלירה: איל אונו סובّי אי איל אוטרו באשה.
El tiempo es una escalera: el uno suve i el otro basha.
(Spanish: *El tiempo es una escalera: el uno sube y el otro baja.*)
'Life is a staircase: the one goes up, and the other goes down.'

אמור די מאדרי, ני לה נייבّי לו פאזי אינפֿריאר.
Amor de madre, ni la nieve lo faze enfriar.
(Spanish: *Amor de madre, ni la nieve lo hace enfriar.*)
'A mother's love, not even snow can make it cold.'

Like many other Jewish communities, including ones speaking other Romance languages (see Catalan, French, Italian, Portuguese, and Provençal), the Jews of medieval Spain wrote their language in a form of the Hebrew alphabet, at least much of the time. However, only a small number of pre-Expulsion Judeo-Spanish manuscripts have survived. After the Expulsion, as their language developed into Ladino, Jews continued to write in the Hebrew script, with some notable exceptions (like the Ferrara Bible of 1553, written in the Latin script), and we have abundant documentation of this from the 16th century up until the mid-20th century. In Turkey in 1929, the Arabic script used for Turkish was replaced by the Latin one, as part of President Kemal Atatürk's programme of secularization and modern cultural reform. The local Ladino-speaking community followed suit, giving up the Hebrew alphabet that they had used for so long. This change soon spread to Ladino-speaking communities outside of Turkey, and the Latin alphabet has remained the norm for writing Ladino ever since.

Judeo-Spanish instructions in a Passover Haggadah (ca. 1300). Line 7 begins *i bebran kada unu su vasu* 'and each one will drink his glass'. One of the few surviving examples of a Judeo-Spanish text from Spain, and maybe the oldest. Bibliothèque nationale de France, ms. hébr. 591, fol. 126r.

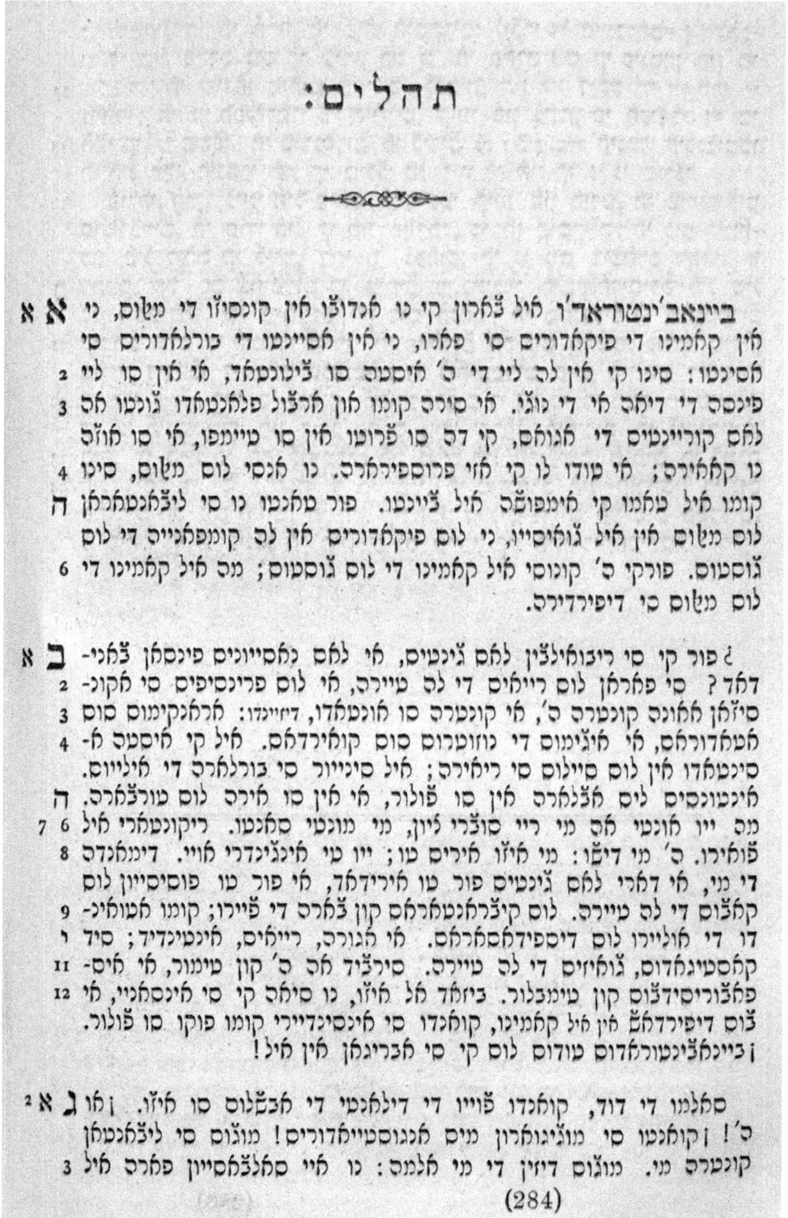

תהלים:

⟨decorative ornament⟩

א **א** כי מַצַּוֹם, די קוֹנסִיזוֹ אִין אַגְדוֹזוֹ כִּי כּוֹ בָּאדְרוֹן אִיל בֵּיינָאבֶנְטוּרָאדְ'וֹ
אִין קָאמִינוֹ דִי פִיקָאדוֹרִיס סִי פָּארוֹ, כִּי אִין אַסֵיינְטוֹ דִי בּוּרְלָאדוֹרִיס סִי
2 אָסֵינְטוֹ: סִינוֹ כִּי אִין לַה לֵיי דִי ה' מִיסְטֶה סוּ גִּ'ילוּנְטָאד, אִי אִין סוּ לֵיי
3 פִּינְסָה דִי דִיאָה אִי דִי נוֹגֶ'י. אִי סִירָה קוֹמוֹ אוּן אַרְבּוֹל פְּלָאנְטָאדוֹ גֹ'ונְטוֹ אַה
לָאס קוֹרְרִיינְטִיס דִי אַגְּוּאָה, קִי דַה סוּ פְ'רוּטוֹ אִין סוּ טְיֵיימְפּוֹ, אִי סוּ אוֹזָ'ה
4 כּוֹ קָאאֵירָה; אִי טוֹדוֹ לוֹ כִּי אָזִי פְּרוֹסְפֵּירָארָה. כּוֹ אַנְסִי לוֹס מַצַּוֹם, סִינוֹ
ה קוֹמוֹ אִיל טָאמוֹ קִי אִימְפּוּזָ'ה אִיל בֵּיינְטוֹ. פּוֹר טָאנְטוֹ כּוֹ סִי לֵיבָ'אנְטָארָאן
לוֹס מַצַּוֹם אִין אֵיל גִּ'וּאִיסְיָיו, כִּי לוֹס פִּיקָאדוֹרִיס אִין לָה קוֹמְפָּאנְיֵיאָה דִי לוֹס
6 גֹ'וסְטוֹס. פּוֹרְקִי ה' קוֹנוֹסִי אֵיל קָאמִינוֹ דִי לוֹס גֹ'וסְטוֹס; מַה אֵיל קָאמִינוֹ דִי
לוֹס מַצַּוֹם סִי דִיפֵּירְדֵירָה.

ב א פּוֹר כִּי סִי רִיבּוּאֵילְצָ'ן לָאס גֵּ'ינְטִיס, אִי לָאס נָאסְיָיוּנִיס פִּינְסָאן צָ'אנִי-
2 דָאד? סִי פָּארָאן לוֹס רֵייאִים דִי לָה טְיֵירָה, אִי לוֹס פְּרִינְסִיפִּיס סִי אָקוֹנְ-
3 סיֹזָ'אן אָאוּנָה קוֹנְטְרָה ה', אִי קוֹנְטְרָה סוּ אוּנְגָ'אדוֹ, דִיזְ'יינְדוֹ: אַרְאָנְקֵימוֹס סוּס
4 אָטָאדוּרָאס, אִי אֵיצָ'ימוֹס דִי נוֹזוֹטְרוֹס סוּס קוֹאֵירְדָאס. אֵיל קִי מִיסְטֶה אַ-
סִינְטָאדוֹ אִין לוֹס סִיֵילוֹס סִי רִיאִירָה; אֵיל סִינְיוֹר סִי בּוּרְלָארָה דִי אֵילְיַיוּם.
ה אֵינְטוֹנְסִיס לוֹס אַבְלָארָה אִין סוּ פֹ'ולוֹר, אִי אִין סוּ אִירָה לוֹס טוּרְבָּארָה.
6 7 מַה יוֹ אוּנְגִ'י אַה מִי רֵיי סוֹבְּרֵי לִיוֹן, מִי מוֹנְטֶי סָאנְטוֹ. רֵיקוֹנְטָארֵי אֵיל
8 פֹ'ואֵירוֹ. ה' מִי דִיזֹ': מִי אִיזֹ'וֹ אֵירִים טוּ; יוֹ טֶי אִינְגֵ'נְדְרִי אוֹיי'. דִימָאנְדַה
דִי מִי, אִי דָארֵי לָאס גֵ'ינְטִיס פּוֹר טוּ אִירֵידָאד, אִי פּוֹר טוּ פּוֹסִיסְיָיון לוֹס
9 קָאבוֹס דִי לָה טְיֵירָה. לוֹס קִיבְּרָאנְטָארָאס קוֹן בָּארָה דִי פְ'יֵירוֹ; קוֹמוֹ אַטוּאֵיל-
י דוּ דִי אוֹלְיֵירוֹ לוֹס דִיסְפִּידָאסָארָאס. אִי אַגוֹרָה, רֵייאִים, אִינְטֵינְגִידִיד; סֵיד
11 קָאסְטִינְגָּאדוֹס, גֹ'וּאֵיזִ'יס דִי לָה טְיֵירָה. סֵירְבִּיד אַה ה' קוֹן טִימוֹר, אִי אִיס-
12 פָּאבוֹרֵיסִידְצָ'וֹם קוֹן טֵימְבְּלוֹר. בֵּיזָ'אד אָל אִיזֹ'וֹ, כּוֹ סִימָה כִּי סִי אִינְסָאנְיֵיי, אִי
לוֹס דִיפֵּירְדָאשׁ אִין אֵיל קָאמִינוֹ, כְּוָאנְדוֹ סִי אִינְסֵינְדְיֵירֵי קוֹמוֹ פּוֹקוֹ סוּ פֹ'ולוֹר.
בֵּיינְאָבֵּינְטוּרָאדוֹס טוֹדוֹם לוֹס כִּי סִי אַבְּרִיגָאן אִין אֵיל!

2 **ג** א אוֹ, ! מִיזֹוֹ. סוּ אַבְּשָׁלוֹם דִי דִילָאנְטֵי דִי פֹ'ואִיי קוֹאַנְדוֹ דִי דוּד, סַאלְמוֹ
ה'! קוּאָנְטוֹ סִי מוּלְטִּיגוּאָדְרוֹן מִיס אַנְגוּסְטִייאָדוֹרִים! מוּג'וֹם סִי לִיבָּ'אנְטָאן
3 קוֹנְטְרָה מִי. מוּג'וֹם דִיזֵ'ין דִי מִי אַלְמָה: כּוֹ אִיי סַאלְבָּ'אסְיָיון פָּארָה אֵיל

(284)

Psalms 1:1–3:3, from a Ladino Bible published in Constantinople, 1873. Note the upside-down question mark at the beginning of Psalm 2, and the upside-down exclamation mark in the last line of Psalm 2.

Haketia

Haketia   חכיתיה

Haketia (tambien yamada **Hakitía**, **Haquetia**, **Haketiya**, **Jaketia**) es una variedad del djudeo-espanyol. Es el nombre del idioma djudeo-espanyol del Marroko avlado por los djudios arrondjados de Espanya enel anyo 1492. Alkunos estudiosos yaman a la Haketia el lashon *Oksidental* del Djudeo-espanyol. Este dialekto prezenta influensias del arabo i tamazight. El biervo *haketia* sale de del biervo *hak'a*, حكى, en arabo ke kere dizir *kontar* o *avlar* [1].

Los Haketia-avlantes son orijinalos de las sivdades ke se topan al nord de Marroko, komo Tetuan, Tanjer, Seuta, Meliya, Alkazarkivir, Larache, i de la rejion de Oran en Arjelia, ande alkunas personas lo yamavan Tetuani.

Contènidos [esconder]

1 Orijín

2 Enfluensia del Kastilyano modérno

3 Lingua en perikolo?

4 Evenementos relasionados kon la Haketia

5 Ver endemas

6 Referensias

7 Atamientos eksternos

Orijín   [trocar | trocar el manadero]

Este lashon tiene un triple fundamento: el kastizo (kastilyano antiko del syéklo XV), los ebrayizmos i los arabizmos uzados en Espanya i Portugal. Egzisten referensias ke el kastilyano avlado por los djudios antes de ser arrondjados de Espanya, era diferente al ke avlavan los kristyanos. Los arrondjados de la Peninsula Iberika enel anyo 1492 se asentaron, ubikaron i konformaron komunitas en munchas sivdades grandes i chikas del Nord de Marroko: Kasablanka, Tanjer, Tetuan, Xauen, Arzila, Alkazarkivir, Larache, Seuta i Meliya, i ansina se ivan agregando biervos arabos a la baza ispano-ebrea de ese lashón, más los arabizmos ke ya egzistian en Espanya por modre de Al-Andalus. Ma antes del arrondjamiento de los djudios de Espanya ya egzistia en Marroko una komunita diudia: los **toshavim** (rosidontos), los kualos tonían komo lingua el arabo o

An article from the Ladino version of Wikipedia (2019).

There exists a large body of literature in Ladino dating back to the 16th century. Ladino literature includes religious writings, such as Bible translations, prayer-books, and commentaries, as well as numerous works on philosophy, science, medicine, history, and other secular topics. In the 19th century a thriving Ladino press developed, especially in Thessalonika, Istanbul, and Izmir. In Thessalonika, which had 80,000 Jews in 1900—nearly half the population of the city at the time—there were two daily Ladino newspapers up until World War II. The contents of Ladino periodicals extended beyond reporting the news, often including a wide range of social and cultural material, such as serialized novels and poetry.

The Holocaust decimated the Ladino-speaking population of Europe. In Thessalonika, for example, some 98% of its prewar Jewish inhabitants died at the hands of the Nazis. Most Ladino speakers who survived the war emigrated to Israel or the United States, where the language has seldom been passed on to the younger generations. However, Ladino still lives on. There are currently at least two Ladino periodicals in existence; Radio Israel has a daily Ladino news broadcast; and Ladino is taught at a number of universities in Israel and abroad. There is even some new Ladino literature being produced, as well as translations of works from other languages. For example, a Ladino translation of Homer's *Odyssey*, made by a Holocaust survivor born in Thessalonika, was recently published in Israel. And organizations like the National Ladino Authority in Israel and the Sephardic Studies Program at the University of Washington are helping to preserve Ladino for future generations. Ladino has also developed quite a respectable online presence in recent years—there is even a version of Wikipedia in the language!

In recent years, another type of Jewish Spanish has emerged in Latin America, particularly in Mexico and Argentina, which have large Jewish communities that were established primarily in the 20th century. The Jews who settled in these communities came from various places, particularly Eastern Europe, Syria, and Lebanon. The languages that these Jewish immigrants brought with them, namely Yiddish, Judeo-Arabic, and Ladino, have all left their mark on this modern Jewish variety of Latin American Spanish and have helped to make it distinct from other local forms of Spanish.

References and further study

Bunis (2017, 2018), Schwarzwald (2018), and Lehmann (2018) provide historical introductions to Ladino; the chapters by Bunis and Schwarzwald include many linguistic details as well. Harris (1994) is a book-length overview of the history of the language with particular attention devoted to its status in the late 20th century, including interviews with native speakers in Israel and the United States. Díaz Mas (1992) is a comprehensive survey of the history of the Sephardim. Sola-Solé, Armistead, and Silverman (1980–84) is a three-volume compendium on Sephardic history, language, and literature. Lazar (1999) is a reader of Ladino literature from the 15th to the early 20th centuries. Borovaya (2012) is a discussion of Ladino literature, periodicals, and theatre in the Ottoman Empire. Lévy (1989) is a bilingual anthology of Ladino poetry of the Holocaust. The Ladino translation of Homer's *Odyssey* was published by Ha-Elion and Perez (2011–14). The online forum Ladinokomunita (www.sephardicstudies.org/komunita.html) contains a wealth of Ladino resources. Ladino Wikipedia, with entries in both Hebrew and Latin letters, can be accessed at lad.wikipedia.org. Dean-Olmsted and Skura (2017) is an overview of contemporary Jewish Latin American Spanish.

25 Latin

In a lot of ways, Latin has historically been to Roman Catholics what Hebrew has been to Jews. Hebrew died out as a spoken language by around the 3rd century CE, but remained in use as the primary written and liturgical language of the Jewish people. Jews read the Bible and other important religious texts in Hebrew; new literature and all manner of scholarly works were written in Hebrew; Hebrew continued to be used in some written correspondence; and new words were created to express new ideas and new things, so that the Hebrew vocabulary continued to grow (see further in HEBREW, RABBINIC AND MEDIEVAL). A very similar story can be told for Latin.

Latin—a member of the Indo-European language family, which also includes Greek, the Germanic languages, the Slavic languages, Armenian, and many of the languages of India—started as the language of the inhabitants of Rome and its surroundings. Beginning in about the 5th century BCE, as Rome expanded its borders and grew into the powerful Roman Empire, the domain of the Latin language grew also. Latin spread first across the Italian Peninsula, then into Spain and Portugal, France, the Balkans, and elsewhere. As Latin was adopted by the various native inhabitants of these new regions, it began to take on influences from the languages that it either replaced or existed alongside. Like any language, Latin also continued to evolve and change; however, it evolved differently in different regions. By the end of the first millennium CE, the written Latin language—the language that had been used by the famed classical Roman authors—was no longer what the people were speaking. In Italy, Latin had evolved into something that looked more like modern Italian; in France, into Old French (see FRENCH); in Spain and Portugal, into Spanish and Portuguese, respectively; and so on. These new languages, which descend from a common Latin ancestor, make up what linguists call the Romance family of languages.

Despite the fact that various peoples were speaking these newer Romance languages and not Latin, Latin continued to be the primary vehicle for writing throughout the Middle Ages. The great majority of medieval Western and Central European texts, especially scholarly texts, were written in Latin, and not in the languages that the authors were actually speaking. The Catholic Church adopted the Latin Bible translation of Jerome (ca. 347–420 CE), the so-called Vulgate, as its official Bible, and almost all other religious activity was conducted in Latin. And so Catholics, who made up the vast majority of the European population in the Middle Ages, read the Bible and prayed in Latin. In fact, translation of the Bible into local languages was at times considered heretical and forbidden. For example, the scholar William Tyndale (ca. 1494–1536), who made a highly influential English translation of much of the Bible, was charged with heresy and burned at the stake.

In addition to being the ancestral heartland of Latin, Rome is also home to one of world's oldest continuously present Jewish communities. Jews have been living in Rome since at least the 2nd century BCE, perhaps even earlier, and many other Jewish communities—including the entirety of the Land of Israel—came under Roman control in the 1st century BCE. In the Land of Israel, the relationship between the Jews and the Roman authorities was ultimately a contentious one, culminating in the Great Revolt (66–73 CE), during which the Temple in Jerusalem was destroyed and many thousands of Jews were killed or exiled. A second revolt (132–136 CE) was equally disastrous, and many Jewish survivors of the war were deported. The Jews in Rome remained, however, and were joined by some of the Jewish refugees from the two Roman wars.

The early Jewish community of Rome was mostly Greek speaking, as evident from tombstones and other written evidence, though surely they would have also been familiar with Latin. The most famous Jewish author from the period of the Roman Empire is no doubt Josephus, who lived in the 1st century CE, first in the Land of Israel and then later in Rome. Josephus wrote an important account of the Great Revolt, to which he was an eyewitness, as well as a general history of the Jewish people. Despite the fact that he wrote while living in Rome, his works were all written in Greek, which remained the primary working language of the Roman Empire in the East. From the following centuries, many Jewish inscriptions— mostly tombstones—are known from Italy and the surrounding Roman territories like Spain and France. Many of these are in Greek, Hebrew, or Aramaic, but a significant number are in Latin, which gradually became more widely spoken among the Jewish communities of the western Roman Empire. Following are four sample Latin tombstone inscriptions. We know that they are Jewish—despite the fact that some contain only Latin names rather than Hebrew ones—either because they contain Jewish imagery (like images of menorahs or shofars) or because they were found in a Jewish catacomb. All four come from around Rome and date to the 3rd or 4th century CE.

> *Iulius Iuda fecit Iulie Mariae coiugi bene merenti cun qua bixit annis XXV*
> 'Julius Juda made (the tombstone) for Julia Maria, his well-deserving wife,
> 　with whom he lived for 25 years.'

> *amici ego vos hic exspecto Leo nomine et signo Leontius*
> 'Friends, I wait for you here. My name is Leo, and my signum Leontius.'

> *Polla fecit Iuliae filiae que vixit ann(os) XXXIIII*
> 'Polla (had this) made for Julia (her) daughter, who lived 34 years.'

Alexander butularus de macello qui vixit annis XXX, anima bona, omniorum amicus. dormitio tua inter dicaeis

'Alexander the sausage maker from the market, who lived 30 years. Good soul, friend of all. (May) your sleep (be) among the just!'

There is no evidence that Jews in the Roman Empire ever wrote Latin in Hebrew characters (not counting some borrowed words that appear in Hebrew or Aramaic texts, like the Talmud). This is the case also for ancient Greek Jewish texts (see GREEK). As Latin evolved into Italian, French, Spanish, etc., Jews came to speak these languages and, eventually, to write them in Hebrew script. Educated Christians, especially clergy, studied Latin as an academic language, just as Jews studied Hebrew. But as a general rule, Jews did not study Latin, since Latin education was so closely associated with the Church, and since there were no secular schools until relatively recent times.

Nevertheless, some exceptional Jewish scholars did learn Latin, enabling them to study the latest works on science and philosophy, as well as the Christian Bible. For example, the anonymous polemical work ספר הנצחון *Sefer ha-Nitsaḥon* (also known to scholars as *Nitsaḥon Vetus*), written by a German Jew around the year 1300, contains numerous passages from the Latin New Testament transcribed into Hebrew letters. The Yiddish author and Hebrew scholar Elijah Levita (1469–1549; see YIDDISH, OLD AND EARLY MODERN) studied Latin, and he worked with prominent Christian scholars to translate some of his writings into Latin. The 16th-century Italian Jewish scholar Azariah de' Rossi (ca. 1511–1577) was highly proficient in Latin, and made use of Latin works in his famous Hebrew book מאור עניים *Me'or 'Enayim* (published 1573). Still, there are only a relatively small number of examples of Latin written in Hebrew script, most of which are short. Some texts are word-lists or glossaries, while others are transcriptions of Latin scientific texts into Hebrew characters. One text is a 15th-century Hebrew–Judeo-Latin glossary of about seventy-five scientific terms, found on just a single page of a manuscript (the back of page 91, to be exact). Following are a few sample entries from this glossary:

Hebrew	חום חזק *ḥom ḥazaq*	צורה *tsura*	שכל *sekhel*	רחוק *raḥoq*
Judeo-Latin	קַלִידִיטַשׁ אִינְטֶנְשָׂא *caliditas intensa*	פֿוֹרְמָא *forma*	אִינְטִילִיקְטוּשׁ *intellectus*	רֵימוֹטוֹם *remotom*
English	'intense heat'	'form'	'understanding'	'remote'

The Latin is transcribed according to the Italian style of pronunciation (also called Ecclesiastical pronunciation) rather than classical pronunciation or spelling. So, for example, the Latin word spelled *āctiō* 'action' is written אָקְשִׂיאוֹ, indicating a pronunciation *acsio* rather than classical *actio*.

A number of medical glossaries exist, with the names of plants and other ingredients used for medicine in Judeo-Latin, usually also with glosses in Judeo-Arabic and even other languages, like Judeo-Provençal (see PROVENÇAL). In one

15th-century manuscript from Italy, we find a list of the zodiac signs in Judeo-Latin, along with the name of some planets and stars. The zodiac signs are as follows:

אֵירִיאֵיש טַבְרוּש גֵימִינִיש קַנְסִיר שַׁגִּיטַרִיאֵוּש קַפִּיקוּרְנוּש אַקַרִיאוּש פִּיצֵש לִיאוֹנִיש וִירְגוֹ לִיבְרָא אֵשְׁקוֹרְפִּיאוֹ

Aries, Taurus, Geminis, Cancer, Sagittarius, Cap(r)icornus, Aq(u)arius, Pisces, Leonis, Virgo, Libra, Escorpio

One example of a Judeo-Latin transcription of a Latin text is a short poem of sorts called *Barbara Celarent*, which was once a popular mnemonic device used as an aid for the study of syllogistic logic in medieval times. The Judeo-Latin text itself is unremarkable, but, like the glossary, it attests to the study of medieval Christian scholarship by Jews (as does the Hebrew text that accompanies it). Another manuscript of Judeo-Latin texts, owned by the Vatican library and mostly

The Jewish Latin tombstone of Alexander the sausage-maker, found in Vigna Randanini, Rome (3rd or 4th century CE). Oxford, Ashmolean Museum, AN2007.51.

Some details of the Hebrew pointing system, described in Judeo-Latin. British Library, ms. Arundel Or. 50, fol. 19v. © THE BRITISH LIBRARY BOARD.

pertaining to the antiquated subject of geomancy (a method of fortune-telling using earth, sand, or rocks), runs to more than 100 pages.

The most unusual Latin text in Hebrew characters, probably from the 18th century, is a detailed description of Hebrew spelling and pronunciation, written with Yiddish-style spelling (most notably, with the letter א standing for the vowel *o* and the letter ע standing for the vowel *e*). Despite the fact that this text appears to meet the broad definition of a Judeo-language—that is, a language written in the Hebrew alphabet—we cannot really call it Judeo-Latin. This is because the text was actually written by a Christian, who knew Latin and was apparently using the Hebrew alphabet simply as an exercise. Towards the end of the text, which is only about twenty pages in total, the author made a fairly mangled attempt to translate the Lord's Prayer into Hebrew, making it clear that he was both a Christian and a novice in Hebrew. Another Christian student of Hebrew wrote the so-called Inscription on the Cross ("Jesus the Nazarene, King of the Jews") in Latin in Hebrew script at the back of a 14th-century volume of Hebrew psalms; the text was later erased, and is now scarcely visible.

While this phenomenon of Christians writing in Hebrew script is very rare, it is not limited to Latin. The cases discussed here are reminiscent of a long text in Lithuanian written in Hebrew characters by a Catholic bishop named Jan Chrizostom Gintyłło (1788–1857), though in that case the Christian author used the Hebrew alphabet because he was trying to reach (and convert) a Jewish audience.

References and further study

For a general history of the Jews in Italy, Roth (1946) is still the most comprehensive work in English. The tombstone inscriptions all come from Noy (1993 [#11] and 1995 [#104, #343, and #370]), which is a comprehensive collection of such texts. Photographs of the manuscripts discussed in this chapter are available online. On the *Nitsaḥon Vetus*, see the edition of Berger (1979). The scientific glossary, published as an appendix to Sermoneta (1969), is in the Biblioteca Palatina in Parma, Italy (ms. 2425, fol. 91v), as is the *Barbara Celarent* (ms. 2445, fol. 39v) and the list of zodiac signs (ms. 2269, fol. 92r). On the medical glossaries, see Bos and Mensching (2005). The grammatical text written by a Christian is in the British Library (ms. Arundel Or. 50), and the psalter with the erased line at the back is owned by the Bodleian Library in Oxford (ms. Bodley Or. 3, fol. 69v). For general studies of Hebrew translations and transcriptions of Latin texts, see the articles in Fontaine and Freudenthal (2013). The Lithuanian text in Hebrew characters was published by Verbickienė (2009).

26 Malay

Malay (not to be confused with MALAYALAM, the subject of the next chapter) is the official language of Malaysia, where it is spoken by at least twenty million people. It is very closely related to Indonesian, so much so that most linguists consider them dialects of the same language; the primary reason to regard Malay and Indonesian as separate languages is because of the political boundary between Malaysia and Indonesia, which is largely the result of old colonial borders imposed by Europeans. Indonesian has 200 or so million speakers in Indonesia, making Malay/Indonesian one of the top ten most widely spoken languages in the world. Malay belongs to a language family known as Austronesian, which comprises some 1200 different languages, almost all of which are spoken on islands in the Pacific. Other well-known members of the Austronesian family are Hawaiian, Samoan, Tahitian, Fijian, Maori (in New Zealand), Tagalog (in the Philippines), and Malagasy (in Madagascar).

The earliest Malay writing, beginning in the 7th century, used various Southeast Asian scripts that derive from the writing systems of India. After Islam came to the region in the 14th century, Malay began to be written in the Arabic alphabet. But when the region came under British and Dutch control in the 17th century, the Arabic script was gradually replaced by the Latin alphabet, and this alphabet is still in use today for both the Malay and Indonesian varieties of the language.

Though Malay has historically been written in a variety of different scripts, the Hebrew alphabet has not been one of them. Nevertheless, there is one known text in which Malay is written in Hebrew characters. This text is found in what is best described as a pocket-sized notepad, made up of forty-eight sheets of paper (with writing on both sides) that are bound at the top, rather than on the side. The whole notepad is just 14 centimetres (5.5 inches) tall, and dates to around the year 1900. It is now owned by the British Library in London. This remarkable little notepad contains writing in five different languages: Hebrew, Judeo-Persian (see PERSIAN), English, Gujarati (including Judeo-Gujarati; see URDU), and Judeo-Malay. The owner of the notepad was apparently a Persian-speaking Jew named either Rahamim Jacob Cohen or Ephraim Cohen (both names appear within the text). An address for a clothing shop in the northwestern Indian city of Ahmedabad, appearing several times in the notepad, may have been that of the owner.

A big part of the notepad—the first thirty-two sheets—contains Judeo-Persian poems. Much of the last fifteen sheets is taken up by a sort of glossary, in which we find words and phrases in Judeo-Persian, each with an equivalent in Malay written in Hebrew characters, i.e., Judeo-Malay. The words and phrases relate to everyday life. We find, for example, the following:

Judeo-Persian	אסמון *asmun*	זן *zan*	אדם *adam*	זֶנְדַה *zenda*	אוּן גָא *un ja*
Judeo-Malay	לַנְגִית *langit*	בַתִינַה *batina*	אוֹרַנְג *orang*	הִידוֹב *hidob*	סַנָא *sana*
English	'sky'	'woman'	'man'	'alive'	'there'

Judeo-Persian	מן נמיכם *man namikham*	תו גופתי *to gofti*	ג׳ סאעת *3 sa'at*	סאעת צ׳ן הסת *sa'at chan hast*
Judeo-Malay	סָאיַיה תִידַה מָאהוֹ *saya tida maho*	לוֹ צ׳כוֹב *lo chakob*	פוֹכוֹל תִיגַה *pokol tiga*	פוֹכוֹל בֵירַרבָה *pokol beraba*
English	'I don't want'	'you said'	'3 o'clock'	'what time is it?'

The words and phrases in the glossary are mainly ones that would be useful in basic conversation. Much of the glossary, however, is actually just numbers; over a hundred numbers are included. The numbers were written using the Hebrew numerical system (that is, with the Hebrew letters standing for numbers), each with a Judeo-Malay equivalent. The glossary includes the numbers 1–100 (counting by one), 100–1000 (counting by hundreds), and 1000–10,000 (counting by thousands). No doubt these numbers were essential for business dealings. So we find, for example, the following:

Hebrew	ד 4	ג 3	ב 2	א 1
Judeo-Malay	המפה *hempa*	תיגה *tiga*	דואה *dua*	סאתו *satu*

Hebrew	זא 7000	תר 600	נ 50
Judeo-Malay	תוגו ריבו *tuju ribu*	הנם רתוש *henam ratush*	נימה פולו *nima pulu*

As is typical for Jewish languages, the spellings of both Judeo-Persian and Judeo-Malay words in this notepad reflect actual colloquial pronunciation, rather than the standard spellings in the non-Jewish varieties. So, for example, the Judeo-Malay spelling תִידַה *tida* records the common pronunciation of this word (which means 'not'), even though it is spelled *tidak* in written Malay. Likewise, we find *pokol, beraba, chekob,* and *hidob* in place of standard Malay *pukul, berapa, cakap* (pronounced *chakap*), and *hidop*. The numbers *hempa* '3' and *nima* '5', instead of standard Malay *empat* and *lima*, could reflect variant pronunciations or simply errors. The Malay pronoun *lo* 'you' (more often pronounced *lu*) is a very colloquial form, which is actually borrowed from the dialect of the local Chinese community, called Hokkien Chinese. As for the colloquial forms in the Judeo-Persian words in the glossary, we find, for example, *un ja, chan,* and *namikham,* in place of standard Persian آنجا *anja,* چند *chand,* and نمیخواهم *namikhaham.*

A Judeo-Persian–Judeo-Malay word-list from circa 1900. British Library, ms. Or. 13914, fol. 34r. © THE BRITISH LIBRARY BOARD.

Since the owner of the notepad appears to have worked in the clothing business, it is possible that he was engaged in trade of some sort with garment merchants from Malay-speaking areas. The phrasebook-like nature of the Malay word-list in the notebook may indicate that its owner needed to learn some of the language in order to communicate with these merchants, or even that he was planning to travel to Malaysia himself. We know that medieval Middle Eastern Jewish traders travelled to India (see ARABIC, MEDIEVAL), as well as to China (see CHINESE), and there is some evidence that they may have traded in areas corresponding to modern-day Malaysia and Indonesia. In the 19th century, small Jewish communities were established in Penang (Malaysia) and in Singapore. These communities were founded by Baghdadi Jews from India (see URDU), who settled in Southeast Asia following the expansion of British colonial power in the region. At the same time, Baghdadi Jews also established communities in British-ruled Burma, Hong Kong, and Shanghai, as well as in Indonesia and Japan.

The Baghdadi Jews in India typically spoke Judeo-Arabic or Judeo-Persian amongst themselves, but those living in Penang and Singapore acquired at least basic familiarity with Malay, which was the language used for business. It may have been through contact with some of these Jews that the aforementioned Mr Cohen—whose primary language seems to have been Judeo-Persian—obtained the Malay vocabulary for the word-list that he wrote in his notebook. Or perhaps he had dealings with non-Jewish Malay merchants in India or during his own travels.

The Jewish communities of Southeast Asia suffered very badly during the Japanese occupation in World War II, and the Jews of Penang and Singapore were interred in Japanese prisoner of war camps. After the war, most of the Jews of Penang and Singapore moved away. The Penang community gradually ceased to exist, but the Singapore community persisted, and thanks to the country's rapid economic growth, many Jews have settled there in recent decades, mostly from Western countries. There are currently about 10,000 Jews in Singapore, but only a small fraction of them are descendants of the original 19th-century community.

References and further study

See Nathan (1986) and Bieder (2007) for the history of the Jews of Malaysia and Singapore. Goldstein (2015) also discusses these Jewish communities, as well as those from elsewhere in East and Southeast Asia. The fact that Mr Cohen's notebook contains five languages, including Judeo-Malay, is mentioned briefly in a footnote in Moreen (1995). The notebook itself (manuscript Or. 13914) can be viewed online through the British Library's archive of digitized manuscripts.

27 Malayalam

India has a long and well-established Jewish presence, with Jewish communities on the Indian subcontinent dating back at least 1200 years, and perhaps far longer. There are actually three different Jewish communities in India. The oldest of these are thought to be the so-called Bene Israel (literally 'children of Israel'), speakers of the Marathi language who historically have lived in western India. The second community is made up of Arabic- and Persian-speaking Middle Eastern Jews known as Baghdadis, who settled mainly in Kolkata and Mumbai (previously known as Calcutta and Bombay, respectively) in the late 18th and 19th centuries. These two communities are discussed elsewhere in this book (see URDU).

There is a third Jewish community, whose traditional home is on the western coast of southern India, in the modern state of Kerala. The Jews of Kerala are most often called Cochin Jews, in reference to the port of Kochi (formerly called Cochin), the city in which most of the region's Jews lived. Though the Cochin Jewish community has always been small, it can be divided into two discrete subgroups. The first is the Malabari Jews, named after the Malabar Coast of southwestern India. According to one local legend, the Malabari Jews arrived in India as merchants of the biblical King Solomon nearly 3000 years ago, though there is no evidence whatsoever for the veracity of this story. Another unsubstantiated legend tells of Jews arriving in the area after the destruction of the Temple in Jerusalem in around 70 CE. We know for certain that at least some members of the Malabari Jewish community came to India from the Middle East only in medieval times. The earliest written evidence of a Jewish presence in southwestern India comes from a copperplate tablet from 849 CE, inscribed with a royal grant in the Old Malayalam language. The grant was given by a local Hindu ruler to a group of Middle Eastern merchants settling in Kerala. Though the text itself makes no reference to Jews, it includes a few lines in Judeo-Persian, including the signatures of several Jewish merchants. Another early reference comes from the 12th-century Jewish traveller Benjamin of Tudela, who describes a community of several thousand Jews in Kollam (formerly called Quilon), a town on the Malabar Coast about 140 kilometres south of Kochi. He reports that the local Jews had black skin like their neighbours and were educated in the Torah. The Malabari Jews built synagogues in Kerala, with some archaeological remains dating back as far as the 12th century, around when Benjamin of Tudela was visiting the region. At that time, the Malabar coast was an important trading route, and documents found in the Cairo Genizah (see ARABIC, MEDIEVAL) provide ample evidence that there was a considerable amount of business exchange between Jews in southern India and the Middle East in the medieval period. In fact, David Maimonides, the younger brother of the famous medieval Jewish Torah scholar and philosopher Moses Maimonides, was lost at sea on his way to do business in Malabar.

The second group of Cochin Jews is called the Paradesis. In contrast to the Malabari Jews, the Paradesi Jews are the descendants of Sephardic Jews who came to the southwestern coast of India from Southern Europe, the Netherlands, and the Middle East in the 16th and 17th centuries. Traditionally, there was no intermarriage between the Malabari and Paradesi Jews, and the two communities remained quite distinct.

Unusually among Jewish communities worldwide, the Cochin Jews are believed to have had a completely harmonious relationship with their non-Jewish neighbours, without any experience of antisemitism throughout their long history in India. The only exception to this occurred during the period of Portuguese rule over Kochi and other parts of southern India in the late 15th and 16th centuries, when an Office of the Inquisition was established and the local Jews were subjected to persecution, including the burning of Torah scrolls and prayer-books.

The first local written document making specific reference to the Cochin Jews comes in the form of a series of copperplate tablets, again written in Old Malayalam, dating to the beginning of the 11th century CE. The tablets detail 72 privileges granted by the local king to a merchant called Joseph Rabban, the leader of the Jewish community in Kodungallur (formerly called Cranganore), a town about 45 kilometres north of Kochi. Joseph, who had come to India from the Middle East, was granted the privileges of the local aristocracy, such as the right to use elephants and to display parasols, as well as the authority to charge duties and tolls. These privileges, which were extended also to Joseph's descendants, were a great source of pride and prestige for the entire Malabari Jewish community, and were later commemorated in numerous songs sung by the Jewish women of Kerala.

The Cochin Jews, both Malabari and Paradesi, have traditionally spoken Malayalam, which is the language of their non-Jewish neighbours. The Paradesi Jews would have originally spoken Ladino (see LADINO), and may have known other languages, such as Portuguese, Arabic, Spanish, and Dutch, but all were given up as they adapted to the local culture. Malayalam is a member of the Dravidian language family, which is confined almost totally to southern India. Other important members of the family include Tamil, Telugu, and Kannada. Malayalam today has about thirty-five million speakers, mainly in Kerala, where it is the primary official language.

Jewish Malayalam, like other Jewish language varieties, has some unique elements that set it apart from the Malayalam spoken by non-Jews. One of its most distinctive markers is the use of Hebrew vocabulary, such as *shalom* 'peace' (from Hebrew שלום *shalom*), *khabburə* 'grave' (from Hebrew קבורה *qevura* 'burial'), and *sara* 'trouble' (from Hebrew צרה *tsara*). Like many other Jewish languages, Jewish Malayalam also has some differences in pronunciation and grammar from non-Jewish varieties of Malayalam.

In contrast to most other Jewish communities around the world, the Jews of Kerala apparently never wrote Malayalam in the Hebrew alphabet. When Jews have written Malayalam, they have used the Malayalam script, which is a relative of those used to write most other languages of India, including Tamil, Sanskrit, Hindi, and Marathi. However, Jewish Malayalam literature is primarily oral rather than written. One of the most prominent genres of Jewish Malayalam oral literature consists of songs sung by women on special occasions, such as weddings and Jewish holidays. The women's songs reflect a fascinating mix of central Jewish texts such as the Bible, Talmud, and Midrash, and local Cochin Jewish traditions. There are also other types of Jewish Malayalam songs, including songs about the different synagogues in Kerala, and songs celebrating the renowned copperplate tablets, with references to Joseph Rabban and the privileges granted to the Cochin Jews in the 11th century. There is even a category of songs featuring lyrics addressed to or narrated by parrots! The parrot is a known literary motif in classical Malayalam literature, but the Jewish Malayalam 'Parrot Songs' often feature distinctively Jewish elements.

Other Jewish Malayalam texts include a translation of *Pirke Avot*, the famous collection of aphorisms from the Mishnah, which would have been recited and discussed in the synagogue alongside the original Hebrew version. A rare example of Jewish Malayalam written in Hebrew script comes from a Hebrew book of prayers for weddings and other festivals, which was published in Amsterdam in 1757. In the introductions to some of the prayers we find three Judeo-Malayalam words, which are the local names for three types of songs performed in wedding rituals. However, since the prayer-book was published in Amsterdam by a European editor, these words do not reflect any South Indian tradition of writing Malayalam in Hebrew characters. Much more recently, Cochin Jews living in Israel have put together some Malayalam song booklets using the Hebrew alphabet, for the practical reason that the community has adopted Hebrew and many of its members are no longer as familiar with the Malayalam script.

The following extract from one of the Jewish Malayalam 'Parrot Songs', written down in the 19th century, offers us a fascinating glimpse into the cultural world of the Cochin Jews, with its fusion of South Indian and Jewish elements. The extract is a verse appearing at the end of a wedding song called 'The Noble Bridegroom'.

ആന്താളി പാടും കിളിയെ കേളു
ആന്നെരം എന്തൊരു വർത്തെ ഒള്ളും
ചുണ്ടും ചുകന്നും തലയിൽ പട്ടും
ചൂതകവത്തിലെ രണ്ടു വന്നം
പന്തെലിൽ പാലും പഴവും തെനും
കണ്ടതിൽ ഏറം തരുവാൻ തത്തെ
നല്ല തരം ചെല്ലി നെന്ന കണ്ടാൽ
നല്ല തരം ചെല്ലി തത്തപെണ്ണെ

antaḷi paṭuṃ kiḷiye keḷu/anneraṃ ent' oru vartte oḷḷuṃ
cuṇṭuṃ cukannuṃ talayil paṭṭuṃ / cutakavattile raṇṭu vannaṃ

pantelil palum paḷavuṃ tenuṃ / kaṇṭatil eṟaṃ taruvan tatte
nalla taraṃ celli nenna kaṇṭal/nalla taraṃ celli tattapeṇṇe

'Listen, bird singing [in a swing]! What happened that time?
Lips are reddened, silk on the head,
There are two groves in the Jewish [quarters].
In the wedding shed, there are milk, banana, and honey,
I shall give you more than is seen, parrot!
Wish me good luck if we meet, wish me good luck, she-parrot!'

As mentioned already, the Jewish community of Kerala has always been small, probably never numbering much more than 3000 people. Around the time of the establishment of the State of Israel in 1948, the Cochin Jews became interested in Zionist ideas, and the bulk of the community emigrated to Israel in 1954. Only a few dozen stayed in India, some of whom joined their relatives in Israel in the 1970s. There are currently around 8000 Cochin Jews in Israel (the community has grown due to intermarriage), and a small number also in the United States. Fewer than fifty remain in southern India. As a result of the dislocation of the community and subsequent assimilation, Jewish Malayalam is now almost extinct.

References and further study

Weil (2011) is a short sketch of the history and culture of the Cochin Jews, and Segal (1993) is a longer work on the same topic. Gamliel (2013, 2017) are overviews of Jewish Malayalam, including a discussion of the 18th-century Hebrew book containing Jewish Malayalam words in Hebrew script. N. Katz (2000) is a history of the Jews of India, with a chapter on the Cochin Jews. The excerpt from the 'Parrot Song' comes from the unpublished dissertation of Gamliel (2009), which is a thorough study of the Jewish Malayalam women's songs. The prayer-book from 1757 (titled סדר תפלות . . . . כפי מנהגי אנשי שינגלי . . . . וקהל קדוש בקוגין *seder tefillot . . . kefi minhage 'anshe shingli . . . we-qahal qadosh be-qochin* 'Book of Prayers . . . according to the Rites of the People of Shingli [= Kodungallur] . . . and the Community of Cochin [= Kochi]') has been digitized and can be found on Google Books; the three Judeo-Malayalam words appear on pages 38v, 43r, and 66r. The interior of the 16th-century Kadavumbagam Synagogue of Cochin was relocated to Israel, where it now makes up a whole room of the Israel Museum in Jerusalem.

28 Maltese

The tiny island-nation of Malta—actually, an archipelago of three inhabited islands: Malta, Gozo, and Comino—is located in the Mediterranean ocean, with Sicily to the north, Tunisia to the west, and Libya to the south. Its strategic maritime location and its proximity to both Italy and North Africa have made it attractive to successive waves of invaders, including the Phoenicians (who arrived in Malta not long after they arrived on the coast of biblical Israel), Romans (later supplanted by the Byzantines), Arabs, Norman Sicilians, and the French, not to mention a famous failed invasion by the Ottoman Turks in 1565. From 1800 until becoming independent in 1964, Malta was a British protectorate, and it remains part of the Commonwealth of Nations.

In the year 870, shortly after conquering most of Sicily, Muslim Arabs from North Africa, based in Tunisia, seized Malta from the ruling Byzantines. They governed there until they were defeated by the Normans in 1090–1091, after which Malta was incorporated into the Norman Kingdom of Sicily. Arab rule in Malta was relatively short—only around 200 years—but it had a lasting effect on Malta's linguistic makeup. Islam, the religion of the Arabs, survived in Malta for only a couple of centuries after its recapture by the Christian Normans, but the Arabic language, in a modified form called Maltese, remains in use to this day.

As discussed in an earlier chapter (see ARABIC, MODERN), spoken Arabic varies wildly across the Arab world, and some of the most divergent dialects (as compared with the classical written language) are those of North Africa. The invading Arabs from Tunisia brought to Malta (and Sicily) their local dialect, which remained widely used by locals even after the Norman takeover. However, when Islam ceased to exist in Malta, replaced by Roman Catholicism, Maltese speakers no longer had any connection to the written Arabic language. This is in stark contrast to the rest of the Arabic-speaking world, in which the written language connects Arabs to their religious texts, the most important of which is the Quran. Moreover, the standard Arabic language is part of a pan-Arab identity, and is used for education and mass media. In Malta, conversely, for the last 900 years, the cultural connection has been with Europe rather than with the Arab world. The Maltese language has continued to evolve under the influence of these European connections, and, as a result, has incorporated large numbers of words from Sicilian, Italian, and, more recently, English. In addition, the tradition of writing

Maltese is in the Latin alphabet rather than the Arabic one. In short, Maltese is an Arabic dialect that is written in Latin script, with a lot of vocabulary borrowed from European languages.

Jews were present in Malta already in Roman times, though surely only in small numbers. There were almost certainly Jews living there during the period of Arab rule, as there were also in Arab Sicily, and there are records of Jews living there under Norman rule since at least as early as the 1240s. It was during this period that the Maltese Jewish community reached its peak, though the total population of Jews probably never exceeded about a thousand. The most notable Jewish resident of Malta was the Kabbalistic scholar Abraham Abulafia (born 1240), who is said to have lived on the island of Comino for a short time in the 1280s.

In the archives of the Cathedral Museum in Mdina, the ancient capital city of Malta, there are at least nine documents in a sort of Judeo-Arabic—i.e., Arabic in Hebrew script (see ARABIC, MEDIEVAL)—with particular linguistic features that identify them as an early form of Maltese. Thus, we may reasonably call the language of these documents Judeo-Maltese. They are all legal or financial documents and are all very short; they range from about two to twenty-five lines of text each. The contents of the texts are not especially remarkable, but they are of great interest to those who study the history of Maltese. The oldest text known in Maltese (in Latin script) is a poem from the 1470s called *Il-Kantilena*, and Maltese writing of any kind was extremely rare before the 17th century. Yet the Judeo-Maltese documents date from the 1470s and 1480s. It is possible that the Jews had a dialect that differed from that of their Christian neighbours, and so we do not know for sure that their language reflects the ancestor of the modern Maltese language. Still, the documents show many undeniably Maltese features. Therefore, as with several other Jewish languages (see, for example, FRENCH, PAPIAMENTU, and PERSIAN), some of the earliest evidence of Maltese comes from a source in the Hebrew script.

There may also be another text in Judeo-Maltese. In the Vatican Library, there is (or was) a 15th- or 16th-century manuscript containing about forty pages of secular poems in a variety of Judeo-Arabic. The language of the poems has many features that suggest an origin either in Malta or Sicily; the Arabic dialect of the latter was very close to Maltese, though it died out in the 13th century. If these poems did indeed come from Malta, or from Maltese Jews who were expelled in 1492 (see later in the chapter), it would be yet another important witness to the history of the Maltese language, as well as to Maltese Jewish culture. Here is an excerpt from one of the poems, in which the personified characters of wine and water argue with one another about who is better:

qāl el-nəbīḏ ʾana hū el-wāli	קָאל אֶל נְבִיץ אַנָא הוּא אֶל וָאלִי
we-ʾanti yā mā ul-ši mā tiswā-li	וְאַנְתִּי יָא מָא וּלְשִׁי מָה תִסְוַאלִי
we-ʾeda nun ʿamel fi el kisān	וְאֶדַ' נוּנְעַמֶל פֵּי אֶל כִּיסָאן
u-nlahhi le-kol ʾansān	וּנְלָאהִי לְכֹל אָנְסָאן
rād el-mā yitkallem wi-ybayyan	רָאד אֶל מָא יִתְכַלֶם וִיבָיָין
qāl li-l-nabīḏ ʾanti hū el-khayyān	קָאל לִלְנָבִיד אָנְתִּי הוּא אֶל כַּאיָין

we-ʾda namṭor fi el-dunyā
u-min fuqrā naʾmel ghunyā

וְאְדָ' נַמְטוֹר פִּי אֶל דּוּנְיָא
וּמְן פוּקְרָא נָעְמֶל גוּנְיָא

'The wine said, "I am the master,
and you, O water, are worth nothing to me.
And when I am poured into the cups,
I give everyone delight."
The water wanted to speak and make clear,
It said to the wine, "You are the false one.
And when I bring rain into the world,
I make rich from the poor".'

Thanks to the shifting inheritances of the various European royal dynasties, the Kingdom of Sicily, including Malta, passed to the Spanish House of Aragon in the 1280s. Malta was still subject to Spanish rule in 1492, and so all Jews were expelled from Malta in that year, just as they were expelled from Spain (see LADINO). From 1530 to 1798, the islands were ruled by the Order of Knights of the Hospital of Saint John of Jerusalem, a Catholic order dating back to the Crusades. During this time, the Knights not infrequently attacked or captured Ottoman ships and other merchant vessels in the Mediterranean, and there are records of the Knights taking Jewish prisoners during these skirmishes. Some of these prisoners were made slaves, while others were ransomed and redeemed, mainly by Venetian Jews. The Jewish historian Joseph ha-Cohen (1496–1578), in his well-known work עמק הבכה *ʿemeq ha-bakha* ('Vale of Tears'), describes how, in the year 1552, some Maltese men 'set out to take booty, as was their custom, and found a ship coming from Salonika on which was about seventy Jews aboard. They captured it and returned to Malta. Those poor Jews had to send for the ransom money'. Of course, capturing Jews (or other prisoners) for ransom was by no means limited to Malta in the medieval period.

We have another account of captive Jews in Malta, from an English traveller named Philp Skippon (1641–1691), who wrote an account of his journeys throughout Europe. He informs us that

> Jews, Moors, and Turks are made slaves here, and are publickly sold in the market. A stout fellow may be bought (if he be an inferior person) for 120 or 160 *scudi* of Malta. The Jews are distinguish'd from the rest by a little piece of yellow cloth on their hats or caps.

A small Jewish community was established in Malta again around 1800, though it has never grown substantially. Today the community numbers only around 200. In short, the Jewish community of Malta was never large or important, and Maltese plays only a tiny role in the linguistic history of the Jews. Perhaps the greatest claim to fame by the community comes not from history, but from fiction, namely, Christopher Marlowe's play *The Jew of Malta*, first performed around 1590 with great success, and first published in 1633. It has remained a classic of English literature, famous especially for its antisemitic themes, and was performed by the Royal Shakespeare Company in England as recently as 2015.

References and further study

Roth (1928–31) provides a history of the Jews of Malta, including citations of numerous primary sources. Wettinger (1985) also includes a historical overview, as well as editions of the extant Judeo-Maltese texts with photographs. The account of Joseph ha-Cohen can be read in the English translation of May (1971: 86). The eyewitness account of Skippon appears on p. 621 of the 1746 edition of his travelogue. The poems from the Vatican manuscript (ms. ebr. 411) were published by Mainz (1949), and Wettinger (1985) also includes important commentary. Note that the manuscript was lost some time during the last forty years, but a legible microfilm exists in the National Library of Israel (now available online).

29 Papiamentu (and other creoles)

Papiamentu (also spelled Papiamento) is a creole language spoken by about 200,000 people on the Caribbean islands of Aruba, Bonaire, and Curaçao (the so-called ABC islands), and by another 100,000 or so speakers from those islands who have emigrated, mainly to the Netherlands. Inhabited by indigenous peoples for millennia, the ABC islands were first visited by the Spanish in 1499. The Spanish began to settle there in the following decades, though the lack of precious metals on the islands kept them from being considered of any great importance. In 1515, the Spanish deported the entire native population to Hispaniola (present-day Haiti and the Dominican Republic), and only a very small number ever returned. The sparsely populated islands were then seized by the Dutch between 1634 and 1636. Beginning in 1648, Curaçao become a major hub for the trade in African slaves, whom the Dutch sold mainly to the neighbouring Spanish colonies. Many African slaves also remained on the islands to work on local plantations, and it was not long before they made up the majority of the island's population. The slave trade was finally outlawed in 1814, though slavery itself was not abolished on the islands until 1863.

Sephardic Jews played a significant role in the early history of the ABC islands, especially in Curaçao. The first Jewish settlers came to Curaçao around 1650. They came mainly from Amsterdam, though some came from Mauritsstad (now the Brazilian city of Recife), the capital of the Dutch colony of New Holland, which existed from 1630 until it was lost to the Portuguese in 1654 (see PORTUGUESE). (At one point, there were perhaps as many as 1400 Jews in Mauritsstad, where in 1636 they established the first synagogue in the New World.) Jews quickly became an important part of the population of Curaçao; at some points in the 18th century, they made up as much as half of the islands' European inhabitants. According to a 1789 census, there were nearly 1500 Jews in Curaçao, out of a total European population of slightly less than 4000, and an overall population (European and African) of about 19,500. Jewish settlement in Aruba and Bonaire came later than in Curaçao, and mostly from Curaçao. Neither Aruba nor Bonaire ever had significant Jewish populations; in Bonaire it has never included more than a handful of people. The Aruban Jewish population never numbered more than a few dozen in the 19th century; in the 1820s there were thirty-two Jews there, a small number, but still a significant percentage of the 170 European residents. Today there are around a hundred Jews in Aruba (out of a total population of well over 100,000), but it is composed mainly of 20th-century immigrants from the Netherlands or elsewhere. Since achieving autonomous status from the Netherlands in 1986, two of Aruba's four prime ministers have been Jewish.

The early Sephardic Jewish community in Amsterdam and in the Caribbean spoke both Spanish and Portuguese, languages that they had retained since the mass expulsions from Spain and Portugal at the end of the 15th century. The Dutch settlers spoke Dutch, of course, though for all the European inhabitants, Spanish was the most useful language for business, since trade from the colony was mainly with Spanish territories in the Americas, especially Venezuela. The African slaves—who outnumbered the Europeans already by the end of the 17th century— would have originally spoken a number of different West African languages. They also brought to the Caribbean different African Portuguese creole dialects, the ancestors of what are today known as Cape Verdean Creole and Guinea-Bissau Creole, both still spoken in West Africa. (Incidentally, there were also Sephardic Jews in Portugal's West African colonies; see PORTUGUESE.)

A creole, like a pidgin (see ZULU), is a language that has developed from extended contact between two or more groups of people that do not share a common language. But while a pidgin is by definition no one's native tongue, a creole is spoken natively by an entire community. All creoles likely began as pidgins, but increased in complexity as they evolved. Still, creoles are, as a general rule, less grammatically and lexically complex than the languages from which they derive.

In most cases, a creole-speaking community has been displaced physically or culturally from its original language or languages, often as a result of colonization and/or slavery. In West Africa, Portuguese colonization that began in the 15th century resulted in the development of a Portuguese creole (or creoles) in the region. The subsequent establishment of the Atlantic slave-trade brought this creole (or creoles) to the New World. In Curaçao, the Portuguese-based creoles of the African majority blended to form the basis of a new creole that came to be called Papiamentu. This creole was heavily influenced by the Spanish spoken by the many Jews who lived on Curaçao. This means that while the underlying structure of Papiamentu is based on Portuguese, the majority of the vocabulary is actually derived from Spanish, in no small part thanks to the importance of the Sephardic Jewish population of Curaçao in the 17th and 18th centuries. Papiamentu also has numerous vocabulary items taken from Dutch, which was for centuries the language of the colonial administration. By the late 18th century, Papiamentu had become the native language of most of the inhabitants of Curaçao, including the Jews.

Not only did the Jewish population of Curaçao comprise a significant percentage of the first Papiamentu speakers, but the earliest surviving record of Papiamentu comes from a Jewish source, namely a love letter written in 1775 by a Curaçaoan Sephardic Jew to his pregnant Jewish mistress. This letter—the existence of which proves that Jews were using the language for intimate communication— now appears to have been lost, but a photograph of one page survives. The next oldest Papiamentu text comes from another Curaçaoan Jew, who repeated a short

Papiamentu conversation between two female slaves, as part of a court testimony pertaining to the author of the aforementioned love letter.

As an illustration of how Papiamentu compares to its source language, Portuguese, as well as an illustration of the influence of Spanish and Dutch, compare the following sentences.

Papiamentu:	*Mi tin dos maleta i un tas.*
Portuguese:	*Eu tenho duas malas e uma bolsa.*
Spanish:	*Yo tengo dos maletas y una bolsa.*
English:	'I have two suitcases and one bag'.

In Papiamentu, the word for 'I' is *mi*, which goes back to the Portuguese object pronoun *me* (e.g., Portuguese *ele me vê* 'he sees me'). Papiamentu makes no distinction between 'I', 'me', and 'my' (e.g., Papiamentu *mi tin* 'I have', *cu mi* 'with me', *mi cas* 'my house'), unlike Spanish and Portuguese, in which these would all be different. And whereas the verb 'to have' conjugates for person and number in Spanish and Portuguese (e.g., Portuguese *eu tenho* 'I have', *ele tem* 'he has', *nós temos* 'we have'), the verb has only one form in Papiamentu (e.g., *mi tin* 'I have', *e tin* 'he/she has', *nos tin* 'we have'). Plurals of nouns are often not used in Papiamentu when the context makes it clear that a plural is intended. Here 'two suitcases' is *dos maleta*; the number *dos* 'two' makes clear that there is more than one suitcase, and so the singular form *maleta* is used. Both the words *dos* and *maleta* come from Spanish. Papiamentu also has no grammatical gender: there is just one form *un* for 'a', where Spanish and Portuguese have masculine and feminine forms (e.g., Spanish *un* and *una*). The noun *tas* 'bag' is borrowed from Dutch *tas*. In short, as is typical for a creole, many aspects of Papiamentu grammar are much simpler than the equivalents in Portuguese and Spanish.

A number of Hebrew loanwords entered Papiamentu, at least among Jewish speakers. Among the many examples, we can cite *beshimantov* 'good omen' (< Hebrew בסימן טוב *be-siman ṭov* 'with a good sign'), *gadol* 'boss' (< Hebrew גדול *gadol* 'big'), *ganap* or *ganaf* 'thief' (< Hebrew גנב *ganav* 'thief'), and *zona* 'prostitute' (< Hebrew זונה *zona* 'prostitute'). However, these words do not seem to be widely known by non-Jews and do not appear in Papiamentu dictionaries. A few words of Hebrew origin that do appear in some standard dictionaries are *baké* or *bakiano* 'expert' (< Hebrew בקי *baqi* 'expert'), *hadrei* 'a sitting-room (in an old-style Antillean home)' (< Hebrew חדרי *ḥadre* 'rooms (of)'), and *kavot* 'respect' (< Hebrew כבוד *kavod*). Of all the Hebrew words cited thus far, only *baké* seems to be widely known. Of course, there are also many Hebrew words in Papiamentu that refer to Jewish life (e.g., *tora* 'Torah', *askenazi*, *sefardi*, *mikvá* 'ritual bath', and *rabino* or *rabi* 'rabbi'), as well as a few words from Spanish or Portuguese that ultimately derive from Hebrew (e.g., *amen* and *sabat* 'Sabbath').

The Jewish community of Curaçao today numbers only a few hundred, out of a total island population of about 160,000. Their Temple Mikvé Israel-Emanuelo is the oldest continually used synagogue in the Americas and the oldest Jewish cemetery still in use. It is perhaps a stretch to call Papiamentu a Jewish language, despite the fact that Jews speaking Papiamentu continue to use uniquely Jewish vocabulary items, at least when discussing Jewish topics. Still, there is no denying that the Jews played an important role in the formation of this creole, even though the Jewish influence on Papiamentu is hardly noticeable today. And because Jewish speakers helped create this language—today one of the most thriving creoles in the Americas—and because a Jewish text provides the earliest written evidence for this language, Papiamentu has earned its place in Jewish linguistic history.

Incidentally, Sephardic Jews left their mark on other creoles in the Americas. In Sranan, the English-based creole that serves as the lingua franca of Suriname (and is the native language of much of the population), there are two clear loanwords from Hebrew. The first is *kaseri* (< Hebrew כשר *kasher* 'kosher'), which means '(ritually) clean'. Interestingly, this word is so closely associated with the Afro-Surinamese Winti religion that local Christian churches reportedly prefer to use the word *krin* (< English *clean*) instead of *kaseri*. The second word is *trefu* (< Hebrew טריפה *ṭerefa* 'non-kosher food' or טרף *ṭaref* 'not kosher'), sometimes spelled *trefoe* (according to the Dutch-style spelling), which refers to a taboo food that is particular to each individual. Note that *kaseri* and *trefu* are not opposites, as their source words can be in Hebrew, and as the corresponding loanwords are in English. The word *trefu* is attested in Sranan already in the 1790s, in connection with indigenous food taboos and with no connection whatsoever to Judaism. These Hebrew loanwords in Sranan are a testament to the relatively large proportion of Jews among the European population of Suriname (as high as 75%) during the creole's formative years in the mid- to late-17th century. Much of the Portuguese vocabulary in Sranan comes from these Jews as well. Suriname was settled mainly by the English and Dutch, but the Jews among them were largely Portuguese speaking.

Saramaccan is another English-based creole of Suriname, spoken by the descendants of escaped slaves (called maroons), many of whom came from Jewish plantations. (One 18th-century dictionary of Sranan, compiled by a European missionary, referred to Saramaccan as *Dju-tongo* 'Jew language'!) The Saramaccan days of the week include *pikí sabá* 'Wednesday' and *gaán sabá* 'Thursday', which in the 18th century are attested in the forms *pikin sabba* and *grang sabba*. The words *pikí* (older *pikin*) and *gaán* (older *grang*) mean 'small' and 'big', respectively, and are derived from Portuguese *pequeno* 'small' and *grande* 'big'. The word *saba* (older *sabba*) comes from Portuguese *sábado* 'Sabbath, Saturday', which ultimately derives from Hebrew שבת *shabbat* 'Sabbath'. The word (or one of the words) for 'Friday' in Saramaccan is *dimíngo*, from Portuguese *domingo* 'Sunday', which shows that the Saramaccan names for the days of the week have shifted by two days from their original meanings. This means that the 'little Sabbath' and 'big Sabbath' originally fell on Friday and Saturday, illustrating Jewish influence in the naming of the days. There is also evidence from the 18th century that the Saramaccan New Year was once celebrated around October, perhaps in imitation of the Jewish New Year.

In short, while the Jewish presence in the Caribbean (including the northern coast of South America) is today very small, and in some places has totally disappeared, Jews played an important part in the early colonial history of the region, and they left their linguistic mark on several languages.

References and further study

For a history of Jews in the Caribbean, see Arbell (2002), and for Jews in the ABC islands specifically, see Emmanuel and Emmanuel (1970). On Portuguese Jews in the West African colonies, see Mark and da Silva Horta (2011). B. Jacobs (2012) is a thorough history of Papiamentu, with discussion of the Jewish population of Curaçao, while Maurer (2013) gives a much shorter overview of the history of Papiamentu, with a sketch of the language itself. Henriquez (1988) discusses Jewish features of Papiamentu and includes numerous words of Hebrew origin used by the Jewish community; Emmanuel and Emmanuel (1970: I.482–483) includes a few other words of Hebrew origin. On the earliest Papiamentu document, see Salomon (1982) and Maurer (1998); a legible photograph of one page of the letter appears in Emmanuel and Emmanuel (1970: 1.257). The 1776 court testimony is also transcribed in Maurer (1998). The cases of Sranan and Saramaccan are discussed in Rubin (2013), with further references therein.

30 Persian

Jews have been living in Persia (that is, the region corresponding to modern Iran) since biblical times. After the Jews were exiled from their homeland by the Babylonians in the 6th century BCE, it was the Persian King Cyrus who conquered the Babylonians and freed the Jews, allowing them to return to Jerusalem and rebuild the Temple. Because of the relative tolerance of the Persians, however, many Jews chose to remain in Persian lands. In the Bible, the story of Esther and parts of the book of Nehemiah take place in Susa (modern Shush), one of the capital cities of the Persian Empire, and part of the apocryphal story of Tobit takes place in the Persian town of Ecbatana (near modern Hamadan). During the Babylonian Exile, Jews would have spoken Hebrew and Aramaic, since Aramaic was the official language of administration under the Babylonian and Persian Empires (see ARA-MAIC, ANCIENT AND MEDIEVAL). But the Jews who remained in Persian territories eventually learned Persian as well, and over time most Persian Jewish communities adopted Persian as their first language.

The language of the Persian Empire in biblical times is known by scholars today as Old Persian. It is the ancestor of the modern Persian language, which is sometimes referred to by scholars as New Persian. Old and New Persian are quite different from one another, just as Modern English is extremely different from Old English, and French is very different from its ancestor Latin. New Persian is written in a form of the Arabic alphabet, and witnesses of the language in that script date back to the 9th century CE. These are not the earliest records of New Persian, however. New Persian is, in fact, first attested in texts written by Jews in the Hebrew script, in what we call Judeo-Persian.

The earliest Judeo-Persian (and therefore New Persian) text is believed to be a letter that was found in Dandan-Uiliq, an isolated site located in the far western part of China, in the province of Xinjiang. This letter, which deals with the trade of goods (sheep and clothing) and which was found in the ruins of a Buddhist temple, has been dated to the second half of the 8th century CE. Another early Judeo-Persian text, dating from the early 9th century CE, is a short inscription on a copper plate from the southwest of India, in the state of Kerala. The Indian text is quite fascinating, because the Judeo-Persian portion follows a long inscription in Old Malayalam (see MALAYALAM) and a short inscription in Arabic and another (non-Jewish) form of Persian called Pahlavi or Middle Persian. The early texts, especially the one from India, bear witness to the multicultural world of Persian-speaking Jews. They are also perfect examples of how Judeo-Persian texts can come from a wide range of locations throughout Asia, reflecting the fact that many Persian Jews were merchants who travelled widely, particularly along the Silk Road and Indian Sea trade routes (see also CHINESE).

In later centuries, a flourishing Judeo-Persian literature developed, especially in populous towns like Shiraz, Isfahan, Kashan, and Hamadan. Jews produced Bible translations and commentaries, as well as translations of other important religious texts; composed historical, philosophical, and mystical writings; and of course used Judeo-Persian for more mundane purposes connected with everyday life. Especially noteworthy from a literary perspective are the many Judeo-Persian poetic texts, particularly the biblical epics composed by authors like Shahin (14th century) and Emrani (1454–1530s). These Jewish poets lived at a time when Muslim Persian poetry was at its height, and their Judeo-Persian works were certainly inspired and influenced by this literary tradition. A prime example of a Judeo-Persian biblical epic is the *Musā-nāma* by Shahin, a retelling of the life of Moses with much added detail. This massive poem, composed in 1327, consists of roughly ten thousand rhyming couplets. The following is a short extract of seven couplets, which partially describes the time that Moses first saw the Burning Bush:

shabē mūsā qażā-rā būd dar dasht	שבי מוסא קצֿא רא בוד דר דשת
ba gird-i gūspandān gird mē-gasht	בגרד גוספנדאן גרד מי גשת
girifta rōy-i 'ālam-rā siyāhī	גרפתה רוי עלם רא סיאהי
zi haybat mē-shudē dil-rā tabāhī	זהייבת מי שודי דל רא תבאהי
siyāh dēvē zi har sū īstāda	סייה דיוי זהר סו אסתאדה
kamīn bar khitta-i daurān nihāda	כמין בר כוטה דוראן נהאדה
jahān chun zāgh dar mātam nishasta	גהאן גון זאג דר מאתם נשסתה
xurōs-i subh-rā gardan shikasta	כֿרוסי צובח רא גרדן שכסתה
. . .	. . .
bidīdash k'ātashē bar shud zi nāgāh	בדידש כה אתשי בר שוד זנאגאה
farāz-i yak dirakhtē hamchu khargāh	פֿראזי יך דרכֿתי המגֿה כֿרגאה
v'az ānjā bar dirakhtē chand dīgar	וזאן גֿא בר דרכֿתי גֿנד דיגר
ravān mēraft īn ātash barābar	רוֿאן מי רפֿת אין אתש בראבר
kalīm-i haqq chu dīdash ātash az dūr	כלימי חק גֿה דידש אתש אז דור
nadānistash haqīqat k'ān buvad nūr	נדאנסתש הקיקת כאן בוד נור

'One night, when Moses happened to roam the desert,
Walking round and round his sheep,
Night's face was veiled in darkness,
A sense of dread stirred discord in the heart.
Black demons were lurking everywhere; it seemed
That turning time itself was plotting ambush.
The world plunged into crow-black mourning,
And morning's neck was broken.

. . .

A manuscript (ca. 1700) of the Judeo-Persian *Fatḥ-nāma*, which includes a retelling of the biblical story of Joshua. The illustration shows Joshua fighting at the walls of Jericho. British Library, ms. Or. 13704, fol. 32r. © THE BRITISH LIBRARY BOARD.

> He saw all of a sudden
> Flames enveloping a tree, like a tent,
> Leaping from there to diverse other trees.
> From far away, God's interlocutor
> Was unable to see that the fire was,
> In truth, nothing but light.'

The language of Judeo-Persian texts is essentially the same as the written language used by contemporary Muslim authors, except for the use of the Hebrew alphabet and the occasional appearance of words from Hebrew and Aramaic (mostly proper names and words connected with Jewish practices). Early Judeo-Persian texts do, however, retain some archaic grammatical and lexical features not found in Muslim texts, thus making them important for linguists studying the history of the Persian language.

Written Judeo-Persian remained in use until the middle of the 20th century. With the advent of modern education and the increased integration of Jews into the surrounding culture, the traditional use of the Hebrew alphabet was discarded, and Jews began to write in the same form of the Arabic alphabet used for standard Persian. In 1948, there were between 100,000 and 120,000 Jews living in Iran, and still more than half that number into the 1970s. The exact number of Jews still living in Iran today is unknown, but there may be more than 10,000, far more than in any other Middle Eastern country besides Israel and Turkey. The language of contemporary Persian-speaking Jews, most of whom are now to be found in the United States or Israel, is identical to that of Muslim speakers.

Until the 20th century, some Persian Jews also made use of a secret language (or jargon) called Lotera'i. This language, which varied somewhat by region, uses mainly Iranian grammar but has a very heavy Hebrew/Aramaic lexical component. It was used when Jews wanted to converse without being understood by non-Jews; this would have come in handy in business dealings, for example. Lotera'i is of linguistic interest for a variety of reasons, one of which is that the Hebrew/Aramaic elements are sometimes used in novel ways. For example, the Lotera'i first-person singular pronoun 'I' is *ani*, a clear borrowing of Hebrew אני *'ani*, but 'we' is *ani-ā*, which is the singular *ani* plus the Iranian plural suffix -ā (cf. Hebrew אנחנו *'anaḥnu*). The Lotera'i singular 'you' is *atā* (< Hebrew אתה *'atta*), but the plural 'you' is the novel *kullam atem* (< Hebrew כולם *kullam* 'everyone' + אתם *'attem* 'you [pl.]'), a phrase which is grammatically impossible in Hebrew. A similarly constructed secret language was in use by the Tat-speaking Mountain Jews (see TAT).

In some regions of Iran (e.g., in Shiraz and Hamadan), Jews spoke other (unwritten) Iranian languages, and some from the northwestern part of Iran also spoke dialects of Aramaic (see ARAMAIC, MODERN). Jews also spoke Persian and other Iranian languages in historically Persian territories that now fall outside of the borders of modern Iran (see TAJIK and TAT).

References and further study

Borjian (2017) is a thorough survey of Judeo-Persian, as well as Jewish varieties of other Iranian languages. A very nice collection of Judeo-Persian texts in English translation can be found in Moreen (2000). The excerpt from the *Musā-nāma* comes from manuscript Or. 4742 (fol. 191v) in the British Library (which is available online in digital format), and the translation is a slightly modified version of the one found in Moreen (2000). On Lotera'i, see Yarshater (1977), Schwartz (2014), and Borjian (2017).

31 Polish (and Czech)

Jews began settling in the Kingdom of Poland around a thousand years ago. From its establishment in 1025 CE, the kingdom was a welcoming refuge for Jews fleeing persecution elsewhere in Europe, and by the 16th century Poland had become a thriving centre of Jewish life and culture. In 1569, Poland and Lithuania were united into a commonwealth called the Kingdom of Poland and the Grand Duchy of Lithuania, ruled by a single king. The Polish-Lithuanian Commonwealth was an important European nation, with a large, multi-ethnic population, and it lasted until 1795, when its territories were absorbed by Russia, Prussia, and Austria. In the early Commonwealth period, Jews continued to enjoy the good conditions and privileges that they had experienced in the preceding centuries, but this era came to an end in the mid-17th century with a series of rebellions and massacres that badly affected the Jewish population. Among these was the infamous Chmielnicki Uprising of 1648, which saw the massacre of tens of thousands of Jews. However, the Jewish population of Poland remained large and vibrant over the following centuries; in fact, Poland (including once-Polish territories that are today part of Ukraine, Lithuania, and Russia) was for a long time home to the largest Jewish community in the world. Jews made up a substantial percentage of the overall population in many Polish towns and cities until the Holocaust; for example, on the eve of World War II Jews made up roughly a third of the population of Warsaw, Poland's capital, and around a quarter of the population of Kraków, its second-largest city.

Jews living in Poland generally spoke Yiddish. They did not adopt Polish on a large scale until the 20th century (more on this later), so a distinctive Jewish variety of Polish never really developed. However, because the Yiddish-speaking Jews of Poland lived in such close contact with Polish speakers for many centuries, their Yiddish grew to be strongly influenced by Polish, and the language is replete with vocabulary of Polish origin. Common Yiddish words deriving from Polish (some of which are used mainly or exclusively in Polish Yiddish, but others of which came to be used by Yiddish speakers in other parts of Eastern Europe too) include ספּודניצע *spudnitse* 'skirt' (from Polish *spódnica*), טרושקאַװוקע *trushkavke* 'strawberry' (from Polish *truskawka*), טאָרבע *torbe* 'bag' (from Polish *torba*), שנורעװואָדלע *shnurevadle* 'shoelace' (from Polish *sznurowadło*), שפּיטאָל *shpitol* 'hospital' (from Polish *szpital*), פּאָליציאַנט *politsy-ant* 'police officer' (from Polish *policjant*), צי *tsi*, a word used to introduce a yes/no question (from Polish *czy*), and many more (see also YIDDISH, MODERN STANDARD).

Because Polish was not commonly used by Jews in the medieval or early modern periods, no tradition of writing the language in the Hebrew script ever really developed. However, we do find some occasional examples of Polish written in Hebrew letters. Some of the earliest evidence of any kind for Jews living in Poland comes from numerous 12th-century coins that have short, Hebrew-letter inscriptions. Most of these contain Hebrew names or words, but some contain Polish names or words. For example, several coins bear the inscription משקא קרל פולסקי, which corresponds to Modern Polish *Mieszko Król Polski* 'Mieszko, King of Poland'; this refers to Mieszko III, who was High Duke of Poland from 1182 to 1202. The existence of these coins is due to the fact that Jews were very active in the minting industry, both in Poland and elsewhere in medieval Eastern Europe.

We also have a fascinating document written in Polish in Hebrew script from the late 17th century, which is perhaps the only Judeo-Polish text of any consequence. The document is a copy of a charter detailing the royal privileges granted to the Jews of the town of Wiłkowyszki by King Jan Kazimierz of Poland (1609–1672) on 7 April, 1679. Wiłkowyszki, now known by the Lithuanian name Vilkaviškis, is a town located in southwestern Lithuania that was part of the Polish-Lithuanian Commonwealth (1569–1795). There were many such royal charters issued to Jewish communities in Poland in the 16th, 17th, and 18th centuries, but they were all written in either Latin or (standard) Polish. The reason that this particular document was written in the Hebrew script could be the fact it that was copied in a *pinkas*, or Jewish community record book. *Pinkasim* are handwritten volumes that were kept by European Jewish communities and regional councils between the 16th and 19th centuries. They were used to keep track of various kinds of information about the communities' organization and everyday functioning, including family and communal life, with details of the local religious, social, and economic structures. The *pinkasim* give us an invaluable perspective on what daily life was like for Jews in Europe in the early modern period. They were typically written in a mixture of Hebrew and Yiddish, but sometimes contain elements in other languages, as in this case.

The Judeo-Polish charter (shown in the image) was entered into the Wiłkowyszki *pinkas* in around 1792. It granted the Jews the right to settle in Wiłkowyszki and included a number of specific details of what they were allowed to do there. For example, it stipulated that the Jews were allowed to slaughter cattle and to sell alcoholic beverages, as well as to engage in specific types of crafts. It also gave them permission to build houses next to the market square and along the streets of the town, and authorized them to build a *mikveh* (ritual bath) and a Jewish cemetery. The following extract illustrates the language of the charter. Note that the spelling of the Polish in Hebrew script follows the orthographic conventions commonly used to write Yiddish—for example, the use of the Hebrew letter ע to indicate the vowel *e*.

A Judeo-Polish charter from 1679, in the *pinkas* (community record book) of the Jewish community of Wiłkowyszki. Central Archives for the History of the Jewish People, Jerusalem, ms. LI-27, fol. 101v. The text excerpt begins on the sixth line from the bottom.

A Judeo-Czech inscription on a Torah mantle. The text reads וִיְנֶנַ אָד רָדִנ גָּלְדשְׁטֵיְנֶ ז״ רֶנֶע *věnováno od rodiny Goldsteinové z Ronova* 'dedicated by the Goldstein family from Ronov'. Jewish Museum in Prague, inv. no. 37.161.

דעקלאָרויאנץ אי מי פּאזוואלאאיאנץ פּרזיקלאדעם מייאסט אינשיך, זע אים וואלנא וו דאמך
סוואיך וולאסניך אי נאייעמניך וושעלקיך פּאזיטקאוו זאזיווא'ץ, נאפּאיע שינקאוואץ, קראמי
אי סיעמיערזי אטוואָרזיסטע מוועץ אי וו ניך וושעלקין[ע] טאוואַרי מניישא אי וויענקשא,
דראָשא אי פּאדלײשא האנדלאוואַץ

*Deklarując i my pozwalając przykładem miast inszych, że im wolno w
domach swoich własnych i najemnych wszelkich pożytków zażywać, napoje
szynkować, kramy i siemierzy otworzyste mieć i w nich wszelkie towary
mniejszą i większą, droższą i podlejszą handlować*

'In the example of other cities, we declare and allow them to take any benefit of their own and of rented houses: to sell beverages, to run open stalls
and grain storages and sell in them all merchandise small and large, both
expensive and of lesser value.'

In addition to this legal document, there are other, shorter examples of Polish in
Hebrew script appearing in various Jewish texts written in Hebrew or Yiddish. For
example, the large body of tales about the Hasidic *rebbes*, or spiritual leaders (see
HUNGARIAN), composed in Hebrew in 19th- and early 20th-century Eastern Europe, is
sprinkled with citations of non-Jewish characters speaking in Polish, and these utter-
ances are printed in Hebrew script. The writers and readers of the tales would have
been most familiar with the Hebrew script, and so it was natural for them to reproduce
Polish dialogue in this format. The following extract from a Hebrew-language Hasidic
tale published in the early 20th century illustrates this. The first part of the sentence
is in Hebrew, while the second half (the quotation) is in Polish in Hebrew letters.

ויאמר להם, בלשון פּויליש, "מאזיעש אליע נעכטשעש".

wa-yomer lahem, bi-lshon poylish, "możesz ale nie chcesz".

'And he said to them, in the Polish language, "You can, but you don't want to".'

In the early 20th century, the Jewish population in Poland, particularly in urban
centres like Warsaw and Kraków, began to become more acculturated and integrated into non-Jewish society, and some Jews adopted the Polish language. A
number of Jewish newspapers in Polish (in the standard Latin-script Polish alphabet) were published in this period, and novels, poetry, and works of nonfiction on
Jewish themes were written in Polish as well.

The Holocaust decimated the Jewish population of Poland, and most Jewish
Polish-language cultural activity ceased. Most Polish Jewish Holocaust survivors
sought refuge in other countries after the war, though some Jews remained in Poland.
After the fall of communism in the late 1980s and early 1990s, Poland began to see a
Jewish cultural resurgence, and in the 21st century, the country is home to an active
Jewish community that hosts regular activities, such as an annual cultural festival
and a Yiddish summer school. In 2013, the POLIN Museum of the History of Polish Jews—a large-scale exhibition space and educational establishment dedicated
to the thousand-year story of the Jews of Poland—opened on the site of the Warsaw

Ghetto. Contemporary Polish Jews typically speak Polish and write the language in the Latin script, just as their non-Jewish counterparts do, and it remains to be seen whether a markedly Jewish variety of Polish will develop in time.

Polish is not the only Slavic language that is part of Jewish history. Although most Jews in the Slavic-speaking regions of Central Europe traditionally lived in Polish territories, Jews lived in other Slavic areas as well, including Russia (see RUSSIAN), Ukraine, the Czech Republic, Bulgaria, Bosnia, and elsewhere. And the earliest evidence of Jews speaking a Slavic language is probably not Polish, but rather its close linguistic relative Czech. This evidence comes from some individual words, phrases, and even whole sentences in the Hebrew writings of medieval European Jewish biblical and Talmudic commentators. Because Slavic languages like Czech, Polish, and a couple of others were very similar at that time, it is not always possible to identify the intended Slavic language with certainty, but most of the Judeo-Slavic words in these Hebrew texts can safely be identified as an early form of Czech. Among the most important sources for Judeo-Czech are the works ערוגת הבושם *'Arugat ha-Bosem* (a commentary on the *maḥzor*, or holiday prayer-book) by Abraham ben Azriel (active in the early 13th century) and אור זרוע *'Or Zarua'* (a work on Jewish law) by Isaac ben Moses (ca. 1180–1250). Both of these authors were born in Bohemia, in what is now the Czech Republic.

Interestingly, texts with Judeo-Czech glosses come not only from Czech-speaking areas, but also from further afield. For example, the commentaries of Rashi (see FRENCH) contain at least a dozen Slavic glosses, and even more can be found in the commentaries of his younger contemporary and compatriot Joseph Qara (ca. 1060–1125). This suggests that there was ongoing contact between Bohemian and Western European Jews. Here are two excerpts from *'Or Zarua'* that contain Judeo-Czech words:

ר' שמ' א' אדם רימה בחייו תולע במותו ואיזהו רימה בחייו אילו כנים שבראש דהיינו וֵיש שאין דרכו של בִילְחִי להיות בראש.

R(av) Shim('on) 'a(mar) 'adam rimma be-ḥayyav tolea' be-moto. we-'ezehu rimma be-ḥayyav 'illu kinnim she-ba-rosh. de-haynu vesh she-'en darko shel bilḥi lihyot ba-rosh.

'Rabbi Simeon said, "The one who cheats in his life will be like a worm in his death. He who cheats in his life is like fleas on the head". That is, like a louse (*veš*), since it is not the custom of a flea (*bilchy*) to be on the head.'

פתילות לשבת מצמר גפן שקורין קוטון בלע' ובלשונינו בלש' כנע' במוילנא.

petilot le-shabbat mi-tsemer gefen she-qorin qoton be-la'(az) u-vi-lshonenu bi-lsh(on) kena'(an) bamvilna

'The wicks of Shabbat (candles) are cotton, which is called *coton* in French, and in our language, in Slavic, *bamvilna*.'

The Judeo-Czech words in this 13th-century text are nearly identical to the forms we find in modern Czech: *veš* 'louse', *blechy* 'of a flea', and *bavlna* 'cotton'. Note that Judeo-Slavic is regularly referred to in this and other Hebrew texts as לשון כנען *leshon kena'an* 'the language of Canaan', and that Slavic-speaking territories were referred to by Jews as כנען *kena'an* 'Canaan'. This is not because of any supposed historical connection between the Slavs and the biblical Canaanites, but rather because Canaan was associated with slavery (cf. Genesis 9:25), and the ethnic term 'Slav' gave rise to the word 'slave' in Western Europe.

Though smaller than its Polish counterpart, the Czech Jewish community remained a prominent and well-established one throughout the medieval and early modern periods. The Jews of Prague experienced a golden age in the 16th century, producing a number of eminent scholars, the most famous of whom is Rabbi Judah Loew ben Bezalel (ca. 1525–1609), commonly referred to as the Maharal of Prague. The Maharal (the nickname is an acronym based on the initials of his title and name) was the author of various works of Jewish philosophy and mysticism, and he became a popular figure in Central and Eastern European Jewish folklore: according to legend, he was the creator of the Golem of Prague, a clay man animated by mystical means in order to protect the local Jews from antisemitic attacks. Like the Jews of Poland, the Jews of Prague typically spoke Yiddish rather than the local Slavic language, and they did not usually write Czech in the Hebrew alphabet, other than in the medieval commentaries mentioned earlier. However, there is at least one curious exception to this tendency. There are a small number of textiles (mainly Torah mantles) dating to the late 19th or early 20th centuries, which were woven for display in Czech synagogues and contain short donors' dedications in Czech written in Hebrew script. This unusual practice shows us that even though Czech, like Polish, was for much of history not in widespread use among Jews, it too has a place in the story of Jewish languages, not only in the medieval period, but also in modern times.

In addition to Polish, Czech, and Russian (see RUSSIAN), Jews have also spoken other Slavic languages, including Ukrainian, Bulgarian, Bosnian, and more. As with Polish and Czech, only very rarely do we find instances of these languages written down in Hebrew characters, as in, for example, a short Judeo-Bosnian poem found in a 19th-century manuscript from Sarajevo.

References and further study

Hill (2017) is a historical overview of Slavic-language sources written in Hebrew characters. Jewish coins with Hebrew-letter inscriptions are treated by Gumowski (1975), which includes many photographs. Goldberg (1985) is a critical edition of the royal privilege charters granted to Jews in Poland, and it includes the full text of the Judeo-Polish document discussed in this chapter. The Hasidic tale with the Polish sentence in Hebrew script can be found in Breitstein (1914). Polonsky (2009–12) is an extensive three-volume history of the Jews in Poland. The most comprehensive work on Judeo-Slavic glosses is that of Bláha et al. (2015), though it is written in Czech. It is from that work that the excerpts from *'Or Zarua'* were taken. Kybalová et al. (2003) includes discussion of Judeo-Czech inscriptions on textiles, with some images of examples from the Jewish Museum in Prague. Kulik (2014) is a discussion of early Judeo-Slavic. The Judeo-Bosnian poem was published in a Latin-letter transcription with a French translation by Šamić (1996).

32 Portuguese

There has been a Jewish community in the area of Portugal since at least as early as the 4th century CE. Jews there lived first under the rule of the Roman Empire and then, from the 5th century, under Germanic Christian rulers. The Muslim Arabs took over Iberia in the early 8th century, and remained in power until the 12th century; it is only after they were driven out of most of the modern territory of Portugal that we can begin to speak of a distinct Portuguese nation. Jews in medieval Portugal were active in the highest levels of power, as also in Christian and Muslim Spain. For example, the first king of Portugal, Alfonso I (ruled 1139–1185), had a Jewish treasurer, as did some later kings. In the 13th century, Portuguese Jews were given royal permission to manage their own legal and political affairs, and though their relative independence came at the price of heavy taxation, the community prospered under these semi-autonomous conditions. The independence of the Jewish community eventually provoked the anger of their Christian neighbours, and over the course of the 14th and 15th centuries, their situation gradually deteriorated.

We have a number of texts written in Portuguese in Hebrew characters from the 14th and 15th centuries, but almost nothing afterwards. This situation is comparable to the other Romance languages used by Jews (see CATALAN, FRENCH, ITALIAN, and PROVENÇAL), with the exception of Spanish, since there is an enormous literature in Judeo-Spanish (see LADINO) from after the Expulsion of 1492. The grammar and vocabulary of Judeo-Portuguese is essentially the same as that of other Portuguese texts from the same era; the only major distinguishing feature of Judeo-Portuguese is the use of the Hebrew script. In this regard, it is similar to Judeo-French and Judeo-Catalan, but very different from Ladino and most varieties of Judeo-Italian, which are uniquely Jewish languages in several ways.

There are only a small number of surviving Judeo-Portuguese texts, but they span a range of genres, and some of them are very long. The longest text, by far, is an extensive scientific treatise called או ליברו די מאג׳יקא *O livro de magika* 'The Book of Magic', which focuses heavily on astrology but also touches on geography, medicine, and other sciences; it contains over 800 pages and was probably written in the 14th or 15th century. Another one, או ליברו קונפרידו אינוש גויזוש דאש אישטרילאש *O livro kumprido enos guizos das estrelas* 'The Complete Book on the Decrees of the Stars', is an astrological text of almost 500 pages that can be dated to 1411; it is actually a translation of a Spanish translation (made by a Spanish Jew) of an Arabic treatise.

Other Judeo-Portuguese texts include a forty-page manual providing instruction in the preparation of coloured inks, dyes, and paints (called או ליברו די קומו שי פאזין אש קוריש *O livro de komo se fazen as kores* 'The Book of How Colours are Made'), which has been dated to sometime in the 15th century; two sets of instructions for the Passover *seder* appearing within Hebrew holiday prayer-books; and a few other smaller texts, including a treatise on ophthalmology that has been dated to 1300. Interestingly, most of the Judeo-Portuguese texts are scientific in nature, a testament to the fact that Spain and Portugal were great centres of scholarship in the medieval period, largely thanks to the scientific traditions brought by the Arabs.

The short treatise called *O livro de komo se fazen as kores* 'The Book of How Colours are Made' is actually quite interesting, because it describes in detail the labour-intensive processes required to make coloured inks and paints from scratch in the pre-modern era, using mercury, sulfur, flowers, eggs, sal ammoniac, and many other natural ingredients; even urine was used in the process of making certain colours! For example, to make a 'good green' (בואו וירדי *boo verde*) one must combine 'the juice of a blue-green lily' (סומו דו ליריאו אזול וירדי *sumo do lirio azul verde*) and 'alum water' (אגואה דאלונברי *agua d'alunbre*). Some of the methods for applying colour to paper are interesting. For example, when applying gold leaf to the page, the treatise instructs the reader as follows:

פואין או אורו אין סימא אי דיש אי ברוניאו מוי ביין קון דינטי די פורקו או די קאבאלו

puen o oro in sima e des e bruneo muy bien con dente de porko o de kavalo

'put the gold on it, and smooth very well with the tooth of a pig or horse'

In 1492, many Spanish Jews fled the Inquisition for Portugal, which had not yet adopted its neighbour's policy of expulsion. One of the most famous of the Spanish-Jewish refugees who fled to Portugal was the astronomer and mathematician Abraham Zacuto (1452–1515). Zacuto became the royal astronomer to King John II of Portugal (ruled 1481–1495), and Christopher Columbus relied heavily on Zacuto's astronomical tables when he sailed for the New World in 1492. (Incidentally, Columbus likely also had Jewish crewmembers on his journeys.)

In 1496, the Portuguese king, considering the negative economic ramifications of banishing the Jews from the country, decided against expulsion and instead adopted a policy of forced conversion to Christianity. Some Jews left the country at this point, while those who remained were forcibly baptized, even though many continued to practice Judaism secretly at home. In the mid-1500s, this situation was replaced by an official Inquisition policy, and many Jews fled to the newly Protestant cities of northern Europe, especially to Amsterdam, London, and Hamburg. These immigrant Portuguese-Jewish communities retained their Sephardic religious customs and, for many years, the Portuguese language. Between the 16th and the 19th centuries, Jews published many books in Portuguese, especially

A page from the Judeo-Portuguese treatise *O livro de komo se fazen as kores* 'The Book of How Colours are Made'. Lines 6–8 have the instruction that begins with פואין או אורו *puen o oro* 'take the gold'. Parma, Biblioteca Palatina, ms. Parm. 1959, fol. 14r.

in Amsterdam, but these all used the normal Portuguese alphabet rather than the Hebrew script. A notable exception was a small Hebrew–Judeo-Portuguese glossary called אור טוב *'Or Ṭov*, which was published in Amsterdam in 1675 and again in 1726.

Significantly, the Inquisition did not apply at first to Portuguese colonies abroad, so many Jews fled to these overseas destinations. In these colonies, the previous policy was still in effect, whereby the Jews were expected to live outwardly as Christians but were spared overt persecution; that is, Jews could still practice Judaism secretly, because they were not subject to close scrutiny. Some Jews went to Portugal's West African colonies, and even more went to Brazil. When the Inquisition did eventually come to the New World, persecution increased, and life became more difficult for the Jews. For this reason, the Jews living in Brazil welcomed the arrival of the Dutch and their attempts to conquer the colony from the Portuguese.

When the Dutch captured the Brazilian city of Recife in 1630, the Jews were able to begin practising Judaism openly. The Dutch established a colony called New Holland on the east coast of Brazil, and the Portuguese Jewish community that was already living there was joined by even more Jews coming from the Netherlands. When the Portuguese recaptured the colony in 1654, all the Jews had to leave. Most went to Amsterdam, but some went to New Amsterdam (later renamed New York) or elsewhere. Portuguese Jewish communities were also established in Philadelphia and Newport, Rhode Island, which is home to Touro Synagogue, the oldest synagogue in the United States. Other Portuguese Jews migrated to Dutch, French, and British colonies in the Caribbean, principally Curaçao (see PAPIAMENTU), but also others such as Suriname, Barbados, and Cayenne. These communities of Jewish refugees in the Americas preserved Portuguese for a time, but not in any distinctive variety—the Portuguese that they spoke and wrote was essentially the same as that used by Christians.

References and further study

Strolovitch (2017) is a survey of Judeo-Portuguese language and texts. Blondheim (1929) is an edition and English translation of *O livro de komo se fazen as kores* 'The Book of How Colours are Made'; the manuscript has been digitized and is available online (ms. 1959 of the Biblioteca Palatina in Parma). The two other major manuscripts, *O livro de magika* (Bodleian ms. Laud Or. 282) and *O livro kumprido enos guizos das estrelas* (Bodleian ms. Laud Or. 310) are also available to view online. Lichtenstein et al. (2007) is an overview of the history of the Jews of Portugal. See Arbell (2002) for a history of the Jewish settlements in the Caribbean. Mark and da Silva Horta (2011) is a comprehensive study of the Portuguese Jewish communities in West Africa.

33 Provençal

In the southern parts of France in the medieval period, the main language wasn't French, but rather a closely related language (with many local varieties) called Provençal. The southeastern part of France—the region known as Provence—was actually an independent territory for many centuries, and was not incorporated into the Kingdom of France until 1481. The earliest traces of the Provençal language come from around 1000 CE, and it is perhaps best known for its widespread use in the poems and songs of the medieval troubadours, lyric poets who flourished from the 12th to the 14th centuries. The troubadours, who either travelled from place to place performing at different courts or lived in one place under noble patronage, composed epic romances that gave Provençal a vibrant literary tradition. Their songs and poems typically focused on themes of love and chivalry. After the heyday of the troubadours had ended, the language continued to be used in writing for another couple of centuries.

By the 16th century, written Provençal had fallen out of use in favour of French, but varieties of the language have nevertheless continued to be spoken until the present day. Still, Provençal is today a highly endangered language, with only small numbers of speakers, mostly in their seventies or older. In modern times, the name Provençal, strictly speaking, refers only to the language variety spoken in the region of Provence itself. In other areas of southern France, the language is called Occitan, a term which is based on the fact that its historical word for 'yes' was *oc*, as opposed to the word *oui* (and its earlier form *oïl*), which is used in northern France.

There was a well-established Jewish community in Provence and the neighbouring areas during the medieval period, the origins of which may go back to at least the 1st century CE. The earliest concrete evidence of Jews living in Provence is from the town of Arles in the 5th century CE. The Jewish population of Provence was never that big to begin with, probably never reaching much more than 15,000. Towns in Provence with prominent Jewish communities included Marseilles, Arles, and Toulon. The chief occupation of the Jews in Provence was moneylending, but they also engaged in other types of work, such as medicine and agriculture, including the cultivation of vineyards. There was a major expulsion of the Jews from Provence at the turn of the 15th century, and they did not return until the 17th century.

Jews also lived in the nearby region of Comtat-Venaissin. This region was part of France until the late 13th century, when it became a Papal State, and it returned to French rule only in 1791, during the French Revolution. In contrast to Provence and other areas of France, the Jews of Comtat-Venaissin were never expelled en masse, though there were smaller-scale expulsions throughout the medieval and early modern periods. From the early 17th century onwards the Jews of Comtat-Venaissin were confined to the ghettos of four cities within the region: Avignon, Carpentras, Cavaillon, and L'Isle-sur-la-Sorgue. These cities, which came to be known by Jews as the 'four holy communities', served as places of refuge for Jews when they were expelled from Provence and the surrounding regions. However, the Jewish communities in these cities were always small, with populations generally numbering less than a thousand. The synagogues of these cities were closed during the French Revolution due to its anti-religious ideology.

The Jews of southern France spoke the Provençal language of their neighbours, and they occasionally wrote texts in that language using Hebrew letters. Only a handful of these texts have survived, including some liturgical poetry, two stories based on the Book of Esther, and some account books. By far the longest text that we have in Judeo-Provençal is a complete *siddur*, or prayer-book, which probably dates to the 15th century. This *siddur*, which is now housed at the University of Leeds (ms. Roth 32) and which covers over 200 pages of text, was made specifically as a gift for a young woman. We know this because on one of the first pages is a dedication written in large, gold letters that says אחותי היי לאלפי רבבות *ahoti hayi le-'alfe revavot* 'My sister, may you become thousands of myriads'. This blessing is based on the one given to Rebecca in the book of Genesis (24:60) when she leaves her family and sets off to meet her future husband Isaac. Still today it is used as a blessing of goodwill for new brides.

The fact that the *siddur* was intended for female use is no doubt the reason why it was written in Judeo-Provençal—that is, in the everyday spoken language. Jewish men were normally better educated in Hebrew than women were, and so a woman would have been more likely to need a translation of a Hebrew text. In fact, we know of other examples of non-Hebrew Jewish literature being written specifically for a female audience, such as the famous Yiddish-language epic *Bovo-bukh* (see YIDDISH, OLD AND EARLY MODERN).

The Judeo-Provençal *siddur* contains an especially remarkable feature that exists on account of the fact that it was intended to be used by a woman. In the section at the beginning of the *siddur* called ברכות השחר *birkhot ha-shahar* ('Blessings of the Dawn'), which consists of blessings traditionally recited by Jews at the beginning of each day, there is a list of sentences thanking God for everyday things that He has done, such as providing each individual with everything they need, giving strength to the tired, and healing the sick. In a traditional *siddur*, the following is one of the blessings included in this list:

ברוך אתה ה׳ אלהינו מלך העולם שלא עשני אשה

barukh 'atta YHWH *'elohenu melekh ha-'olam she-lo 'asani 'isha*

'Blessed are you the LORD our God, who has not made me a woman'

פֿיש אמי טוטץ בֿוש אופֿש בֿריֿנֿטו

שֿנֿט בֿמֿדיט נושטֿורי דֿייבֿ דֿלֿשֿנֿבֿלֿי לֿא

פֿייטֿנֿט פּֿשֿיש דֿאומֿי ' בֿמֿרֿינֿ טו שֿנֿט

בֿמֿריט נושטורי דֿייבֿ רֿיי דֿלֿשֿנֿבֿלֿי קֿי :

נון פֿיש מֿי שֿדֿווֿינֿטֿא ' בֿמֿרֿינֿ טו שֿנֿט

בֿמֿריט נושטורי דֿייבֿ רֿיי דֿלֿשֿנֿבֿלֿי קֿי

נון פֿיש מֿי גֿוֿיה בֿמֿרֿינֿ טו שֿנֿט בֿמֿריט

נושטורי דֿייבֿ רֿיי דֿלֿשֿנֿבֿלֿ קֿי פֿיש מֿי

פֿינֿה ' בֿמֿרֿינֿ טו שֿנֿט בֿמֿריט נושטורי

דֿייבֿ דֿיי דֿלֿשֿנֿבֿלֿי לֿו פֿֿרֿינֿט פּֿשֿר אדֿו

רֿגֿמֿינֿזֿנֿט דֿי מֿושֿטֿאֹולֿש אי בֿקֿוורֿינֿונֿט

דֿי מֿאֿשֿטֿופּֿירֿלֿאֿש אי דֿונֿא נֿזֿפֿאֿרֿט

אֿנֿטֿרֿי אי אֿנֿקֿלֿינֿא נֿזֿאֹורֿלֿנֿטֿאֹֿאֿט א

שֿוורֿיר אטֿו אי פֿאֿי אֿוֿידֿר מֿי אֿקֿבֿרֿא

דֿקֿומֿֿינֿזֿמֿטֿא אי נון פֿשֿש אֿוֿידֿר מֿי

A Judeo-Provençal *siddur* from the 15th century, written for a woman and including 'Blessed are you the LORD our God, who has made me a woman' (lines 7–9). Leeds, Brotherton Library, ms. Roth 32, fol. 4v. REPRODUCED WITH THE PERMISSION OF SPECIAL COLLECTIONS, LEEDS UNIVERSITY LIBRARY.

This blessing is obviously only appropriate for recitation by a male. Women have traditionally recited a variant blessing in its place:

ברוך אתה ה׳ אלהינו מלך העולם שעשני כרצונו

barukh ʾatta YHWH *ʾelohenu melekh ha-ʿolam she-ʿasani ki-rtsono*

'Blessed are you the LORD our God, who has made me according to his will'

In the Judeo-Provençal *siddur*, however, we find something almost totally unheard of in Jewish history. Instead of the standard female variant of the blessing, we find something much more positive:

בֶּנְדִּיג׳ טוּ שַנט בֶּנֶדִּיט נוֹשְטְרִי דְּייב רְיי דַּלשֶׁגְלִי קֵי פִּיש מִי פֶּינַה

bendich tu sant benezet nostre dieu rei dal segele que fis mi fenna

'Blessed are you the LORD our God, who has made me a woman'

Because of this explicitly pro-female blessing, we might consider this an early feminist *siddur*. Besides this *siddur*, we know of two Hebrew *siddurim* that contain the same positive female blessing, both of which were composed in Italy right around the time that our Judeo-Provençal *siddur* was composed. (One of these, from 1471, is now owned by the Jewish Theological Seminary in New York; the other, from 1480, is owned by the National Library of Israel.) Nowadays, it doesn't seem surprising to the modern reader that there should be a female equivalent of the male blessing, but in fact it wasn't until the 20th century that we find something approaching a true egalitarian liturgy within Judaism. This is a good example of how a text in a vernacular Jewish language can teach us about the diversity of pre-modern Jewish culture.

By the 20th century, the Jewish communities in southern France had dwindled to almost nothing, and those last remnants were all but wiped out in World War II. Still, in the 1970s there remained one last fluent speaker of the Jewish dialect of Provençal, Armand Lunel. The American linguist George Jochnowitz interviewed Lunel in 1968 and recorded some of the unique vocabulary and grammatical features of Lunel's speech. Lunel died in 1978, and his language largely died with him. However, even now, there are still some Jews in the South of France who remember and use certain Judeo-Provençal vocabulary and expressions (mostly of Hebrew origin) in their everyday speech.

References and further study

Some general works to do with the history of the Jews of the region are Lunel (2018), Shapiro (2007), and Szajkowski (2010). Two overviews of the Judeo-Provençal language are Strich with Jochnowitz (2017) and Jochnowitz (2018); for a short survey, see Guttel and Aslanov (2007). A description of Jochnowitz's encounter with the last speaker of Judeo-Provençal can be found in Jochnowitz

(1978). The first article to deal with the women's blessing in the Judeo-Provençal *siddur* is Jochnowitz (1981), although Jochnowitz was not aware of the existence of the two similar Hebrew *siddurim*. Those two are held by the Jewish Theological Seminary (ms. 8255) and the National Library of Israel (ms. Heb. 8°5492) and are digitally available online. The Judeo-Provençal *siddur* (ms. Roth 32) itself has yet to be published, but a digitized version of it can be found on the University of Leeds website:

https://explore.library.leeds.ac.uk/special-collections-explore/115456.

34 Russian

Beginning in the late medieval period, significant numbers of Jews migrated from Central to Eastern Europe (see also POLISH), and a considerable proportion ended up in czarist Russia. From the end of the 18th century until 1915, Jewish residence in the Russian Empire was generally restricted to the so-called Pale of Settlement, an area corresponding to present-day Belarus, Moldova, Lithuania, and parts of Ukraine, Latvia, Poland, and western Russia. Jews in the Pale of Settlement lived both in small towns (often called *shtetls*, a Yiddish word) and in larger cities. The Jews of the Pale made up more than 10% of the total population, and in certain areas they even constituted the majority. Cities with particularly large Jewish populations in the Pale included Warsaw, Odessa, Vilnius, Lodz, Kishinev, and Minsk.

By the end of the 19th century, there were almost five million Jews living in the Pale. Nearly all of them spoke Yiddish, and knowledge of Russian was still low. Still, there was a growing trend of Russification, which was brought on by several factors. First, over the course of the 19th century the czarist government established a network of Russian-language schools for the Jewish population. Jews had previously only studied in traditional Jewish religious schools, in which Yiddish was the medium of education. Second, there was a growing urbanization of the Jewish population, which led to greater contact with and use of Russian. Third, among the educated adherents of the Jewish Enlightenment movement, Yiddish came to be considered a substandard language, and they urged Jews to abandon it in favour of speaking Russian or German (see GERMAN and HEBREW, ENLIGHTENMENT). Finally, in the 1850s and 1860s, it became easier for Jews to live outside the Pale, and so the Jewish population of cities like Moscow and St. Petersburg began to increase. For those Jews outside the Pale, Russian became a symbol of upward mobility, and urban Jews who acquired an education and sought improved social status began to switch over to it. By 1926, the percentage of Yiddish native speakers had fallen sharply, to only around 70% in Russia, whereas in the mid-19th century it was nearly 100%.

This trend towards the abandonment of Yiddish in favour of Russian continued to gather momentum over the following decades, largely as a result of the oppressive actions of the new Soviet regime. The early Soviets had actually supported Yiddish as a minority language, but the government attitude changed radically in the 1930s, when Yiddish was forcibly suppressed. Soviet policies of resettlement, exile, and forced labour resulted in large numbers of Jews leaving the traditional Yiddish-speaking areas of Eastern Europe for far-flung regions of the USSR, such as Central Asia and Siberia, which further contributed to the shift from Yiddish to Russian. By the mid-20th century, the majority of Russian Jews were monolingual Russian speakers.

The Russian used by Jews in Russia is on the whole quite similar to that of non-Jewish speakers. However, there is an identifiable Jewish variety of Russian, which is a product of the Yiddish-speaking heritage. The Jewish Russian variety is sometimes called Odessa Russian; this is comparable to how Jewish English is often conflated with New York English in the minds of some Americans. Hallmarks of Jewish Russian include the use of Yiddish vocabulary, distinctive features of pronunciation and intonation, and the use of certain Yiddish word formations, such as the trivializing prefix *shm-*, as in магазин-шмагазин *magazin-shmagazin* 'store-shmore'.

In the 1960s, many Russian Jews applied for permission from the Soviet authorities to leave the country and immigrate to Israel, typically out of Zionist convictions, but also to escape difficult conditions and institutional antisemitism. Most of these Jews were refused exit visas and came to be known as refuseniks. The refuseniks were subjected to persecution and sometimes even imprisonment. In 1971, the emigration restrictions were relaxed somewhat, and around 160,000 Soviet Jews emigrated to Israel over the course of the 1970s and 1980s. With the collapse of the Soviet Union in the beginning of the 1990s, Jewish migration from Russia proceeded on a much larger scale. This huge influx of Russian-speaking Jews—eventually totalling more than 900,000 people—continued into the 2000s and has had a profound linguistic and cultural impact on Israel.

The circumstances of this most recent wave of Russian Jewish immigration are markedly different from those that came before it. Russian immigrants to the Land of Israel in the 19th and early 20th centuries came as adherents of a passionate Zionist idealism, as part of which they quickly shed their European identities and abandoned Russian in favour of Hebrew. The immigrants of the 1970s and 1980s also had strong Zionist ideals, and were generally unable to maintain close ties to Russia for political reasons. In contrast, the recent immigrants have considerable cultural and familial connections to Russia, which they have been able to sustain through visits and other forms of contact; moreover, the decision to relocate to Israel has less often been due to Zionist ideological beliefs, but rather has been largely driven by economic and other practical motivations. They also tend to have great pride in Russian language, literature, and culture, and often actively seek to preserve and cultivate their Russian-speaking heritage in Israel. For these reasons, and likely also because of the sheer size of their community, the new Israeli Russians have maintained the Russian language to a much larger extent than has been the case with earlier immigrants to Israel (whether from Russia or elsewhere).

Today, following more than twenty years of this large-scale immigration, Israel has one of the biggest Russian-speaking populations outside of the former Soviet Union. Roughly 15% of the population of Israel, over a million people, speak Russian. It is the country's third most widely used language, after Hebrew and Arabic.

The vast majority of these Russian speakers came only in the 1990s, and their presence has significantly changed the linguistic landscape of Israel. While the Russian-Israeli immigrants have by and large learned Hebrew, and their children generally speak Hebrew natively, Russian is still widely used in the community. Russians in Israel have access to Israeli Russian television, radio, newspapers, music, and other forms of media. This Russian-language media is quite visible in public spaces in Israel; for example, Russian radio can be heard on city buses, and many TV Hebrew programmes broadcast on Israeli channels are subtitled in Russian as a matter of course. There are even Russian-Israeli Internet celebrities. Many government services are available in Russian, and some politicians even campaign in Russian—sometimes almost exclusively so. All this has also served to strengthen the preservation of Russian in Israel, and consequently, there are large numbers of second- and even third-generation Russian Israelis who are bilingual in Russian and Hebrew. An example of the prevalence of Russian language and culture in Israel is the fact that many Israelis have taken to referring to the secular New Year festivities of December 31/January 1 as נובי גוד *novi god*, from the Russian Новый Год *novy god* (literally 'New Year'), which is celebrated by many Israelis, despite the fact that it is not a Jewish holiday.

The pervasiveness of Russian has sometimes provoked a reaction from other Israelis, some of whom resent the fact that the Russian community has not completely acculturated according to the traditional Zionist ideal. Russian remains very much a community language in Israel: despite its large number of speakers, its widespread public visibility, and the fact that it is offered as an optional language of study in many Israeli high schools, it is relatively rare for Israelis not from Russian backgrounds to study or speak the language. There is also no bilingual provision for Russian speakers in mainstream Israeli primary and secondary schools, so Russian-speaking parents who want their children to be instructed in the language generally have to send them to Russian after-school programmes.

Since the 1990s, a rich Russian-language cultural scene has emerged in Israel, including literature, theatre, and music. Israeli novelists of Russian background have created a new type of Israeli literature in the Russian language, often reflecting the experience of Russian Jews in Israel. This literature has even gained acclaim in Russian-speaking communities worldwide. There is a bilingual Russian–Hebrew theatre company based in Tel Aviv, called *Gesher* 'Bridge', which stages productions of dramatic works by classic European and Russian playwrights such as Shakespeare and Chekhov, as well as classic works of early 20th-century Jewish theatre and original plays composed in Israel and elsewhere. Russian-Israeli musicians compose and perform songs in Russian. One well-known musical group is Gevolt, a heavy metal band that was founded in 2001 by a group of Russian Jews who had come to Israel as teenagers in the 1990s, and who sing in both Russian and Yiddish.

The Russian spoken in Israel has, not surprisingly, developed some unique characteristics as a result of its ongoing intensive contact with Hebrew. For example, Israeli Russian has adopted a considerable number of Hebrew nouns denoting concepts relating to Israeli life (e.g., мазган *mazgan* 'air conditioning', from

Hebrew מזגן *mazgan*; and тахана *takhana* 'bus stop, bus station', from Hebrew תחנה *takhana*). As you can see, these Hebrew loanwords are written in the Russian alphabet. They have also been incorporated into the grammatical structure of Russian; that is, they appear with Russian case and plural endings. Israeli Russian has also created new verbs based on Hebrew nouns, such as метапельить *metapel'it'* 'to work as a caregiver', from the Hebrew noun מטפלת *meṭapelet* '(female) caregiver', and хаморить *xamorit'* 'to work like a donkey', from the Hebrew noun חמור *ḥamor* 'donkey'.

The late 20th- and early 21st-century trajectory of Russian in Israel is remarkable. Russian has gone from a language spoken by a Diaspora Jewish community to an extremely visible and prominent component of Israeli public life and has, despite lack of official status or much state support, become the country's third major language alongside Hebrew and Arabic. In addition, since becoming established in Israel, it has begun to develop into a distinctly Israeli type of Russian; a similar trajectory has also been observed in the case of Israeli Amharic (see AMHARIC).

References and further study

Gitelman (2001) is a history of the Jews of Russia and the Soviet Union in the 20th century. See Verschik (2017, 2018) for overviews of the distinctive features of Jewish Russian (as used in Russia). Yelenevskaya (2015) is a sociolinguistic study of Russian in contemporary Israel. Perelmutter (2018) is a detailed survey of the history and linguistic features of Israeli Russian. Mendelson-Maoz (2015) has a chapter on Russian-Israeli literature, and includes a discussion of the *Gesher* theatre.

35 Tajik (Bukhari)

Bukhara, a populous city in Central Asia along the so-called Silk Road, has been a prominent centre of Persian language and culture for over a thousand years, at times rivalling great Islamic centres of learning like Baghdad. From the 1500s until 1920, Bukhara was the capital of an independent state called the Emirate of Bukhara. During most of this period (until 1868), the Bukharan rulers also controlled the ancient Silk Road city of Samarkand, another important centre of learning. The term 'Bukharan Jews' refers to Jews from Bukhara itself, as well as Jews from Samarkand and smaller towns within the former Emirate of Bukhara. There were also communities of Bukharan Jews in Central Asia outside the traditional boundaries of the Emirate, most notably in the Silk Road city of Tashkent. Bukharan Jews often had to live in their own quarters of town (ghettos) and wear badges or other identifying items of clothing, but nevertheless were able to prosper.

The Bukharan Jews traditionally spoke a variety of Persian called Bukhari or Judeo-Tajik. Judeo-Tajik is very similar to the language of the Bukharan Muslim majority, which is just called Tajik. Many Bukharan Jews also spoke Uzbek, the local Turkic language, in addition to Tajik (see Turkish). Like most Jewish communities, Bukharan Jews wrote their Persian dialect in the Hebrew script and used Hebrew vocabulary to denote Jewish religious and cultural concepts, but besides this, there were apparently no marked differences between the Jewish and Muslim varieties of Tajik. Tajik in general, however, has some grammatical differences from other types of Persian, and also contains a significant amount of vocabulary deriving from Turkic languages. It is difficult to say exactly when Judeo-Tajik became a language distinct from Judeo-Persian, and scholars debate this point. Some works of Judeo-Persian poetry were produced by the Bukharan Jewish community in the 16th–18th centuries, and though some local dialectal features can be identified, these are best considered part of the greater world of Judeo-Persian (see Persian) rather than as representative of a separate Judeo-Tajik language. In the 19th century, we begin to see works that look more distinctive from Judeo-Persian, and in the 20th century, political policies helped further distinguish Tajik from Persian, and hence also Judeo-Tajik from Judeo-Persian.

The Bukharan Jewish community probably dates back well over a thousand years. One tradition, coming from the community itself, identifies the first Jewish settlers of Bukhara as members of the lost Ten Tribes who were exiled by the

Assyrians in the 8th century BCE (see also Tᴀᴛ). According to that Bukharan Jewish tradition, the biblical place name Khabor, which is mentioned in 2 Kings 17:6 as one of the places where the king of Assyria exiled the Ten Tribes of Israel, is to be identified with Bukhara, since the names share the same consonants (though in a different order).

The 12th-century Jewish traveller Benjamin of Tudela, who visited Central Asia only about fifty years before Genghis Khan's Mongol hordes ravaged the area, mentions meeting Jews who claimed to be descended from the lost Ten Tribes. He does not specifically mention Bukhara in his book of travels, but he does refer to Samarkand, which he says had over 50,000 Jewish inhabitants, including some who he describes as wealthy and learned. Even if the figure of 50,000 is a vast exaggeration, as is likely the case, it nevertheless shows us that the Samarkand Jewish community was a large and established one by the 12th century. Bukhara became an important Jewish centre later, in the 16th century. By the 1830s, Bukhara was reported to have a Jewish population of approximately 10,000, many of whom made their living as dyers and silk merchants. According to visitors' reports, many Jews could be recognized by their hands, which were perpetually stained blue from dye.

In the 1860s, Tashkent and Samarkand were annexed by the Russian Empire, and although Bukhara itself remained the capital of a nominally independent state, it grew heavily reliant on Russia as well. After the arrival of the Russians, the Jews gained increased freedom to trade with the Russian Empire, and their range of occupations increased. Bukharan Jewish merchants expanded their businesses, and until the end of the 19th century, they reportedly held a near monopoly on the cloth-dyeing and cotton trades in the area. Also in this period, many Bukharan Jews moved out of Bukhara into neighbouring areas that were completely under Russian control, because life there was easier and freer for them. In this way, the Jewish population of Bukhara decreased, while that of Samarkand and Tashkent grew. The Jews who remained in Bukhara suffered increasing discrimination and hardship. However, on the whole they were economically successful.

Around the turn of the 20th century, there were roughly 20,000 Jews in the whole region of Bukhara, with around 4000–5000 residing in the city of Bukhara itself. The Bukharan Jewish community was quite international and well travelled. When the British Jewish scholar Elkan Adler visited Bukhara in 1897, he reported that among the Jews he met were individuals who had visited places as diverse as Jerusalem, China, India, Moscow, Paris, and London. This was in large part due to the fact that many of the Bukharan Jews were merchants.

Already in the 1860s, Bukharan Jews began to immigrate to Jerusalem, which was then part of the Ottoman Empire, and in 1893, a Bukharan settlement was founded there. It is a testament to the prosperity of the Bukharan Jews that within five years of its establishment, the community grew to an impressive 179 houses, two synagogues, and two schools. This Jerusalem community became an intellectual centre for the Bukharan Jews back home in Central Asia as well.

With the end of the 19th century came the beginnings of publication in Judeo-Tajik. The first printed book in Judeo-Tajik was a translation of the biblical book of Psalms, published in Vienna in 1883. There were around a hundred books published in Judeo-Tajik, all using the Hebrew alphabet, and most of these were produced by the nascent community in Jerusalem. Many of the books were translations of traditional religious texts. We also find translations of 19th-century Hebrew fiction from Eastern Europe, like Abraham Mapu's popular novel אהבת ציון *'ahavat tsiyyon* 'The Love of Zion' (see HEBREW, ENLIGHTENMENT), and translations of other famous non-Jewish works, like Shakespeare's *Comedy of Errors*. In the same period (1910), the first Judeo-Tajik newspaper was established in Central Asia, though this lasted only until the outbreak of World War I.

After 1900, the Jews in Central Asia began to suffer increased hostility from the local Muslim population, and life grew more difficult for them. In the early 1920s, what was once the Emirate of Bukhara became part of the Soviet Union. Most of it was incorporated into the new Soviet Republic of Uzbekistan, while the eastern portion became part of the new Soviet Republic of Tajikistan. In 1924, the Soviet authorities officially changed the name of the Persian dialect of these regions to Tajik, and the distinctive dialectal features of Tajik were emphasized, so as to maximize the distinction between Persian and this new Tajik language. They did this to obscure the cultural and historical connections between the Soviet territories and Persia (modern Iran). The Jewish dialect—that is, Judeo-Tajik, or Bukhari—was essentially the same as the Tajik language spoken by Muslims, but because it was written in the Hebrew script, it was recognized as a separate language by the Soviet government. Already in 1923, Judeo-Tajik had become the official language of instruction in a newly established network of Jewish schools.

Soviet rule brought educational reforms to the Bukharan Jews, and Judeo-Tajik literary production increased. Bukharan Jews living in the Uzbekistani cities of Samarkand, Bukhara, and the capital Tashkent published a number of new Judeo-Tajik newspapers, using the traditional Hebrew script, with the first of these appearing in 1925. The image shows the front page of one of these newspapers, *Rushnai* (meaning 'Light'), which was published in Samarkand in the 1920s. The 1920s also saw the publications of dozens of books in Judeo-Tajik, as well as the establishment of amateur theatre groups.

Around 1928–1929, Soviet policy shifted, and the Central Asian populations, including the Tajik-speaking Jews, were forced to adopt the Latin alphabet. (See TAT for discussion of a similar issue in Azerbaijan and Dagestan.) So Judeo-Tajik lost its most distinctive feature, namely the use of the Hebrew alphabet, though the Latin alphabet used for Judeo-Tajik included two additional letters (ḥ and ə) to denote the sounds that were found only in words of Hebrew origin, namely those written in Hebrew with the letters ח *ḥ* and ע '. (Other additional letters to the Latin alphabet, like ɋ and z, were used also in standard Tajik at that time.) Jews continued to write in Tajik, including some important literary works of fiction, but their language was essentially that of Muslim Tajik speakers, except for the use of occasional words derived from Hebrew. In the early 1930s a literary journal in Judeo-Tajik was established, as was a professional theatre in Samarkand (in 1932) and a publishing house in Tashkent, which issued propaganda works, textbooks, and original literary creations. The main literary genre was theatrical drama

The front page of the Judeo-Tajik newspaper *Rushnai* ('Light'), 5 July 1926.

intended for performance. Many of these were translations from original Uzbek plays; curiously, one of the major themes of these plays was the issue of women's rights, especially with regard to polygamy, an issue which was relevant to Uzbek Muslim life, but not to Bukharan Jewish life. Other themes were those that were typical of Jewish writing in the early Communist era throughout the Soviet Union, including Jewish agricultural settlement of the land and the role of the Jews in the Russian Revolution of 1917.

By the late 1930s, the policies of the Stalinist regime had become much less enlightened, to the detriment of Judeo-Tajik. The government no longer recognized Judeo-Tajik as a distinct language, and all Tajik writing was mandated to be done in the Cyrillic (Russian) alphabet. That is to say, Tajik and Judeo-Tajik were no longer distinguished in written form, and so Judeo-Tajik effectively died out in its homeland. Beginning in 1938, there was a wave of imprisonments and deportations of Bukharan Jewish writers, newspapers and publishing houses were shut down, theatrical activities stopped, and the Judeo-Tajik schools were closed. In this period the spoken language also saw a severe decline, with many Jews shifting to Russian. Jews continued to make important contributions to Tajik literature, though there was no longer anything distinctive about their language as compared to non-Jewish writers. By 1940, Judeo-Tajik literary activity ceased completely, and there have been no further publications in the language in the former Soviet Union until the present day.

For most of the 20th century, Bukhara retained a strong Jewish presence, but with the collapse of the Soviet Union in 1990, the majority of Bukharan Jews emigrated from their homeland, with most of them settling in Israel or the US. While there are still as many as 200,000 Bukharan Jews worldwide, most of them are in Israel (around 100,000) and the United States (around 50,000). Fewer than 10,000 Bukharan Jews remain in Central Asia. As a result of the rapid shift to Russian that began around 1940, coupled with the subsequent large-scale emigration that separated Bukharan Jews from their linguistic homeland, the Judeo-Tajik language has become severely endangered.

References and further study

Borjian (2017) provides an overview of Judeo-Tajik language and literature. Rzehak (2008) provides some additional details regarding political language policy and other linguistic matters. See Zand (2007) for a survey of the Bukharan Jewish community in general and Zand (1991) and Loy (2015) for more in-depth surveys of their literature and culture. See Burton (1994–96) for an overview of Bukharan Jewish history.

36 Tat (Juhuri)

Judeo-Tat is a language variety traditionally spoken by the Jews of Azerbaijan and Dagestan, the so-called Mountain Jews. Native speakers, of which there are at least several thousand remaining, call the language Juhuri (with stress on the last syllable), a term that actually just means 'Jewish' in that language. (This can be compared to how the word Yiddish means 'Jewish' in the Yiddish language.) They also often refer to their language as Gorsky, which is a Russian term that literally means 'Mountain (language)'. Judeo-Tat belongs to the Iranian language family; it is related to both Persian and Tajik (see PERSIAN and TAJIK), though speakers of Judeo-Tat are generally able to understand those languages only imperfectly and with difficulty. Judeo-Tat is also distinguished from the language called Tat or Tati, which is spoken by about 30,000 Muslims in the same region, though Judeo-Tat and Tat have a high degree of similarity. There are four distinct dialects of Judeo-Tat, based on geography, but the differences between them are quite few.

The Mountain Jews have a very long history of settlement in Azerbaijan and Dagestan. They have probably been living there since at least the time of the Sasanian Empire (226–651 CE), or perhaps even earlier. In fact, according to some local Jewish traditions, they settled in the region already in the biblical period, as early as the 8th century BCE, when the northern Ten Tribes were exiled from the Kingdom of Israel by the invading Assyrians. Azerbaijan and Dagestan were under the Persian sphere of influence until the 19th century, when those regions were annexed by the Russian Empire. At that time, the population of Mountain Jews was probably in excess of 200,000.

European Jews became aware of the existence of the Mountain Jews in the 17th century via fragmentary reports, and by the mid-18th century there were more frequent articles in Russian periodicals about these Jews, who were by that time already living under Russian rule. There was also some contact between Mountain and European Jews. For example, some Mountain Jews travelled to Lithuania in the 19th century in order to study in the famous Ashkenazi Talmudic academies there, and the first books in Judeo-Tat were published in Vilnius, Lithuania, which was a centre of Hebrew and Yiddish literary activity.

In the late 19th century, the Mountain Jews became increasingly urbanized, and by the early 20th century more than half of them were already living in cities, such as Baku and Quba in Azerbaijan and Makhachkala and Derbent in Dagestan. In

Derbent, they made up a quarter of the city's population. There were also small communities of Mountain Jews living in Jerusalem from the 19th century onwards, and there was a significant wave of immigration to Israel in the 1970s. Emigration increased greatly in the 1990s, after the fall of the Soviet Union, when the majority of Mountain Jews moved away from their homeland, settling mostly in Israel and the United States, as well as elsewhere in the West.

Judeo-Tat has a rich oral tradition of folktales, poems, and proverbs, no doubt with a long history. However, the earliest known written texts—all using the Hebrew alphabet—date to only the early 1800s. Moreover, until the 20th century the language was used only to write everyday documents such as letters and business records, rather than anything we can call literature. Only in the early 20th century did Judeo-Tat develop a more established written literary tradition. The first book published in Judeo-Tat was a translation of a Russian-language nonfiction book on Zionism, which appeared in 1908 under the title of *Metleb Siyüniho* 'The Goal of the Zionists'. The following year saw the publication of a Hebrew prayer-book with a Judeo-Tat translation. (The translator of both of these books, Asaf Pinhasov, was executed by the Soviets a decade later.) The first Judeo-Tat newspaper, though short-lived, was established in 1915 in Baku.

In the early Soviet period (the 1920s and early 1930s), there was a policy of active state support for regional languages, and Judeo-Tat benefited from this. As a result of this linguistic policy, we see the appearance of the first textbook for Judeo-Tat in the 1920s, and the language began to be taught in schools. In 1938, Judeo-Tat became one of the ten official languages of Dagestan.

In the 1920s, amateur and professional Judeo-Tat theatre troupes were established, performing various genres of plays, including dramas and musicals. Some of the plays addressed topical issues affecting the Judeo-Tat-speaking Jews; for example, a play called *Du Biror* 'Two Brothers', which appeared around 1930, is a story of the clash between the traditional Mountain Jewish lifestyle and the new Soviet one. Some of the Judeo-Tat theatres remained active until the end of the Soviet period.

The 1930s also saw the emergence of original prose and poetry written in Judeo-Tat. Between the 1950s and 1980s, there continued to be a small but steady stream of publications in Judeo-Tat, including novels, short stories, and poetry, and limited publication of Judeo-Tat newspapers. The literary works often provide a window into Mountain Jewish life both before and after the Communist Revolution. Currently the main centre of Judeo-Tat publication is in Israel, but even there, numbers of writers are very small.

As mentioned previously, from its beginnings and continuing into the early Soviet period, Judeo-Tat writing was done using the Hebrew alphabet. In 1929, the Hebrew alphabet was officially replaced by the Latin alphabet for all publishing. One Judeo-Tat newspaper, founded in Dagestan in 1928, was published at first in Hebrew, but gradually switched over to the Latin alphabet starting in 1930. In fact, the newspaper itself was used to help introduce the new Latin writing system and to introduce readers to new Judeo-Tat words. Beginning in 1938, the Latin alphabet was in turn replaced by the Cyrillic alphabet that was used for Russian.

Both the Latin and Cyrillic scripts were modified so that they could represent all the sounds of Judeo-Tat. There were actually two different variants of the Cyrillic script used to write Judeo-Tat, one used in Azerbaijan and one used in Dagestan.

To see the striking differences between the various scripts that have been used for Judeo-Tat over the past hundred years, compare the following Judeo-Tat sentence, taken from the introduction to the 1909 prayer-book mentioned earlier (p. viii), presented in four different alphabets: 1. Hebrew; 2. Latin; 3. Dagestani Cyrillic; 4. Azerbaijani Cyrillic. (The original publication has only the Hebrew script.)

1. ג׳והורון דרבּנד ניסא וַרסירא אמבּרא גָף הָי אָן ג׳והורון גורזנא רָא גורזנא אן דרבּנדא דרבּנד
    אן קובּה רא קובּה אָנו הָיגֵרא.

2. *Çuhurun Dərbənd nisə vərəsirə ambərə gofhoj ən çuhurun Guroznərə, Guroznə—ən Dərbəndə, Dərbənd—ən Cٳubərə, Cٳubə—ən uhojgərə.*

3. *Жугьурун Дербенд нисе вересире амбаре гофгьой эн жугьурун Гурознере, Гурозне—эн Дербенде, Дербенд—эн Гъубере, Гъубе—эн угьойгере.*

4. *Чуһурун Дәрбәнд нисә вәрәсирә амбарә гофһоj эн чуһурун Курознәрә, Курознә—эн Дәрбәндә, Дәрбәнд—эн Губәрә, Губә—эн уһоjкәрә.*

'Jews of Derbent do not understand many words of the Jews of Grozny, Grozny—of Derbent, Derbent—of Quba, Quba—of others'

There is today no official standard writing system for Judeo-Tat; it is most commonly written in a form of the Cyrillic alphabet (either the Azerbaijani or Dagestani variety), but occasionally some publications appear in the Latin alphabet.

Judeo-Tat has a number of distinctive features besides its historical use of the Hebrew alphabet. It has large numbers of words borrowed from neighbouring Turkic languages, as well as vocabulary of Hebrew and Aramaic origin. We expect that words for Jewish religious practices should come from Hebrew and Aramaic, and this is often the case. Interestingly, however, some words connected with common Jewish religious practices come from Arabic or Persian rather than Hebrew, for example, *heloli* 'kosher', which derives from Arabic حلال *ḥalāl* 'permissible'; *ḥerimi* 'non-kosher', from Arabic حرم *ḥaram* 'forbidden'; and *nimaz* 'synagogue', from Persian نماز *namāz* 'prayer'. Some of the Judeo-Tat names for Jewish holidays differ from those commonly found in other Jewish languages. For example, Passover is called *nisonu*, which comes from the name of the Hebrew month of *Nisan*, during which Passover is observed. Hebrew words were also used by the Mountain Jews when they did not want to be understood by their non-Jewish neighbours, as happened also in other Jewish communities (see PERSIAN). There are also some grammatical differences between Judeo-Tat and the neighbouring Muslim Tat dialects; for example, Muslim Tat expresses the present tense of verbs by means of a prefix *ba-*, which is absent in Judeo-Tat.

The Mountain Jews have traditionally been multilingual, in a region which is highly linguistically and ethnically diverse. In Azerbaijan, Judeo-Tat speakers normally also know Azeri (a Turkic language), while further north in Dagestan

שחרית

וּלְיִרְאָה וּלְאַהֲבָה אֶת שְׁמֶךָ: בָּרוּךְ אַתָּה יְהֹוָה
הַבּוֹחֵר בְּעַמּוֹ יִשְׂרָאֵל בְּאַהֲבָה:

שְׁמַע יִשְׂרָאֵל יְיָ אֱלֹהֵינוּ יְיָ אֶחָד:

בלחש בָּרוּךְ שֵׁם כְּבוֹד מַלְכוּתוֹ לְעוֹלָם וָעֶד:

וְאָהַבְתָּ אֵת יְיָ אֱלֹהֶיךָ בְּכָל לְבָבְךָ וּבְכָל נַפְשְׁךָ וּבְכָל
מְאֹדֶךָ: וְהָיוּ הַדְּבָרִים הָאֵלֶּה אֲשֶׁר אָנֹכִי מְצַוְּךָ
הַיּוֹם עַל לְבָבֶךָ: וְשִׁנַּנְתָּם לְבָנֶיךָ וְדִבַּרְתָּ בָּם בְּשִׁבְתְּךָ בְּבֵיתֶךָ
וּבְלֶכְתְּךָ בַדֶּרֶךְ וּבְשָׁכְבְּךָ וּבְקוּמֶךָ: וּקְשַׁרְתָּם לְאוֹת עַל יָדֶךָ
וְהָיוּ לְטֹטָפֹת בֵּין עֵינֶיךָ: וּכְתַבְתָּם עַל מְזֻזוֹת בֵּיתֶךָ וּבִשְׁעָרֶיךָ:
וְהָיָה אִם שָׁמֹעַ תִּשְׁמְעוּ אֶל מִצְוֹתַי אֲשֶׁר אָנֹכִי מְצַוֶּה אֶתְכֶם
הַיּוֹם לְאַהֲבָה אֶת יְיָ אֱלֹהֵיכֶם וּלְעָבְדוֹ בְּכָל לְבַבְכֶם

תורא, ארי תרסירא ארי דוסד־דשדא נום־תורא: ברוכאי תו
ה' ביכדנָר קַיִיף יו ישראל רא אא דוסדי רבז:
(שמע) . שינב ישראל ה' כודימו ה' יאפ־יני:
(ברוך) . ברוכאי נום חורמת פדרג'הי יו אה עולם המישא:
(ואהבת) . וַא דוסד־דָר ה' כודָי תורא אה המאי דול
תורבָז, אה המאי ג'ון תורבז, אה המאי מָל תורבז: וַא בְּשות
נו אי נֶף הא, מה פָרמו דרנום אתו אימודוז אַחַרי דול־תו:
כו אישורה ארי כוד־הָאי־תו, וא גו אישורה אה נושדא־כי
תו אה כונאי־תו, אה רַפדכי־תו אה רַח, אה כיסירא־כָי תו אה
אה בכושדא־כי תו: וַא בְּסָד אישורה ארי נושונא אסרי דָס־
תו, וַא בְּשות־גֶנו ארי פושני בָגֶד אה עֶרלוקי ג'ום הָאי־תו:
וַא נובוס־אישורה אַסרי יָן דָר־הָאי כונאי תו וַא דרבזא
הָאי תו:
(והיה) . וַא מיבו אַנֵר שינירֶן שַׁנירית־נָא אה מצוה־האי
מא מה פָרמו דרנום אישמורה אימורֶז ארי דוסד־דשדא ה'

— 83 —

A page from the Hebrew–Judeo-Tat prayer-book published by Asaf Pinhasov (Vilnius, 1909).

they have also usually had knowledge of other Turkic languages and/or Caucasian languages such as Chechen. Russian became an increasingly dominant language beginning in the 19th century, when Azerbaijan and Dagestan became part of the Russian Empire. From the 1920s onwards, more and more Mountain Jews began to learn Russian, with the result that Russian influence on Judeo-Tat became much heavier. In the 1940s, Judeo-Tat instruction in schools was replaced by Russian, and subsequently the use of Judeo-Tat began to decline both in speech and writing. By the 1950s most Mountain Jews were typically fluent in Russian, and Judeo-Tat often became a second language for them. The post-Soviet emigration of Jews from the Caucasus, combined with the lack of Judeo-Tat education in schools, only weakened the language's status further.

The number of Mountain Jews worldwide is probably well over 100,000, and they remain proud of their traditional culture. In the United States, the community is centred in Brooklyn, New York, where they have their own synagogue (Ohr HaMizrach) and website (Gorsky Jews). Mountain Jews also live all over Israel, and they have at least one dedicated synagogue in Israel in Tirat Carmel, in the vicinity of Haifa. In most Mountain Jewish communities, however, the Judeo-Tat language is no longer being passed down to the younger generations, and like many other Jewish language varieties, it is now considered to be endangered. The number of remaining speakers is uncertain, but there are probably no more than 20,000, with some estimates placing the figure as low as 3000. One exception to the decline in speaker numbers is a small, exclusively Jewish town near Quba in Azerbaijan called Qırmızı Qəsəbə ('Red Town'), where Judeo-Tat is still being learned by children in the 21st century. Interestingly, Qırmızı Qəsəbə is perhaps the only all-Jewish town outside of Israel or the United States.

References and further study

Shalem (2018) is an overview of Judeo-Tat; our sample text in four different scripts comes from his chapter. Borjian (2017) contains a discussion of the language as well, and Authier (2012) is a descriptive grammar. Mikdash-Shamailov (2002) is a general book-length work on the history and culture of the Mountain Jews. For a shorter survey of Mountain Jewish culture with an emphasis on Judeo-Tat literature, see Zand (1991). See also Zand (1985, 1986) for more detailed surveys of Judeo-Tat literature and drama.

37 Turkish (and Uzbek)

In the 19th century, the Turkish Ottoman Empire encompassed not only the present-day country of Turkey but also modern Israel, Lebanon, Syria, and Iraq, and much of North Africa, Arabia, and the Balkans. The Ottoman Empire ruled over Jews from a variety of backgrounds, who spoke a number of different languages. The majority of Jews within the Ottoman Empire were members of Sephardic communities, descendants of Jews expelled from Spain and Portugal, whose primary language was Ladino (see LADINO), or members of Arabic-speaking communities (see ARABIC, MODERN). Very few Jews in the Ottoman Empire would have spoken Turkish as their first (or second) language, though some in Turkish-speaking areas surely learned it to a degree, in order to communicate with their neighbours.

A very few texts in Turkish in Hebrew characters are known from the 16th to 19th centuries, but these seem to be isolated examples, and not part of any larger literary trend. The earliest, and longest, is a 16th-century transcription of an Ottoman Turkish history called تواريخ آل عثمان *tevarih-i al-i osman* ('A History of the People of Osman'). Much shorter, but perhaps more interesting, is a Judeo-Turkish text on the plague from the 17th or 18th century. Bound together with this is a Greek (Christian) text, in the margins of which is a Hebrew–Judeo-Turkish glossary, with words in no apparent order. From the way that it is written, it seems to be a random list rather than a glossary intended for distribution. In another manuscript, from the 18th or 19th century, we find a *piyyuṭ* (liturgical poem) of just a few dozen lines, alternating between Hebrew and Judeo-Turkish. An even shorter poem, from the early 19th century, mixes Hebrew and Judeo-Turkish within the same line. Of these texts, only the *Tevarih-i Al-i Osman* has ever been published.

Another interesting text is a short Judeo-Arabic–Judeo-Turkish glossary from the 16th century, which was found in the Cairo Genizah (see ARABIC, MEDIEVAL). This text begins with the Judeo-Arabic heading נתעלם כלם אתורכי *naṭa'allam kilām at-turkī* 'let's learn Turkish!' and is followed by a list, in two columns, of about four dozen words in both Judeo-Arabic (no doubt the native language of the writer) and Judeo-Turkish. We know that the writer was a merchant, because there is an accounting list in the same manuscript in the same handwriting. The merchant obviously felt that it was useful to know some basic Turkish words for his business dealings; this is reminiscent of a Judeo-Persian–Judeo-Malay glossary from India, discussed in another chapter (see MALAY). As with any language learner, the writer made a number of errors. For example, he wrote *karbus* קרבוס for Turkish *karpuz* 'watermelon'. The following are some sample words from the glossary:

Judeo-Arabic	*fars* פרס	*mawya* מוויה	*'ummi* אומי	*fawq* פוק	*yabki* יבכי
Judeo-Turkish	*at* את	*su* סו	*anne* אנה	*yukarı* יוקרי	*ağlar* אגלר
English	'horse'	'water'	'mother'	'up'	'he weeps'

In 1839, a series of reforms were introduced by the Ottoman government, largely as a reaction to growing national movements within the Empire. The government sought to promote a unified Ottoman nationalist movement, in part by granting equal rights to non-Muslim communities. Further reforms pertaining to religious equality were instituted in 1856. As a consequence of these reforms, Jews had greater opportunities for employment in the Ottoman government, although they were still held back by the fact that so few of them were literate in Turkish. When the famous British Jewish philanthropist Moses Montefiore visited Istanbul in 1840, he encouraged the chief rabbi there to make Turkish a compulsory subject in Jewish schools, but he seems to have had little immediate success with that idea.

One of the means used to encourage Jews to learn Turkish, and thereby to better integrate into Ottoman society, was the printing of newspapers in Judeo-Turkish— that is, in Turkish printed in Hebrew characters. During the Ottoman period, when Turkish was written in a version of the Arabic alphabet, the written language was rather difficult to learn. This was in part because the Arabic alphabet was unsatisfactory for writing Turkish, and in part because the written language was quite different from the spoken language, especially because the former made heavy use of Persian and Arabic loanwords. By publishing Turkish in Hebrew characters, Jewish readers could be introduced to a simpler version of the language, closer to the spoken variety. The publisher of these Judeo-Turkish newspapers, Moses Fresco, wrote explicitly that his aim was 'to familiarize the community I belong to, as far as possible, with the official language of the eternal state we belong to'. Three such newspapers are known, though each was published only for a short time. *Şarkiye* ('The East') appeared in 1864, *Zaman* ('The Time') in 1872, and *Üstad* ('The Master') from 1889 to 1891. The last of these was actually a bilingual periodical, with some articles in Judeo-Turkish and others in Ladino.

By the turn of the 20th century, the great majority of Ottoman Jews still spoke Ladino as their first language. The new Jewish schools that opened in the last decades of the 19th century, operated by the Paris-based Alliance Israélite Universelle, provided some teaching of Turkish, but French was the primary medium of instruction. And of course Hebrew was used for all religious purposes. So even as knowledge of Turkish improved, it was still often the fourth language studied.

The Ottoman Empire was badly defeated in World War I, and the sultan was deposed in 1922. The new Republic of Turkey was established in 1923, guided by principles of nationalism and secularism. The new leader, Mustafa Kemal Atatürk, instituted a policy of Turkification, which included heavy pressure from the government for all its citizens to learn Turkish. Turkish became the language

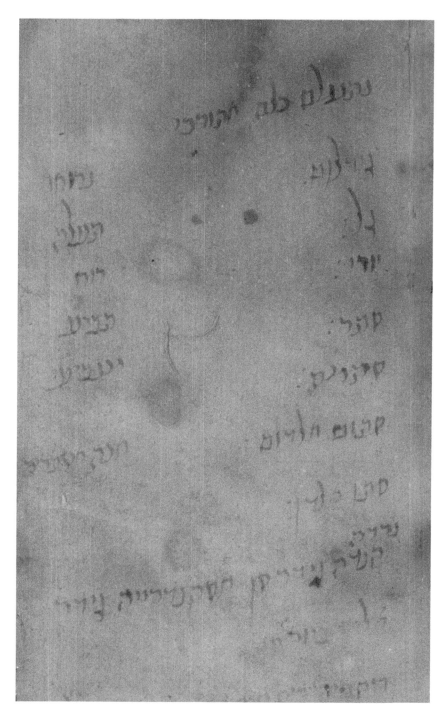

The first page of a Judeo-Arabic–Judeo-Turkish glossary from the 16th century, with the heading נתעלם כלם אתורכי *nataʿallam kilām at-turkī* 'let's learn Turkish!'. Cambridge University Library, T-S Ar. 30.295, fol. 4v. COURTESY OF THE SYNDICS OF CAMBRIDGE UNIVERSITY LIBRARY.

קיקרי   חתקט

לווורה און

כייק (מידיקא

חאב'אדיס מאחאלייה

(נוב'ידאדיס לוקאליס)

קוילא טא

קף יהרדהן ג

"לאמחסי אינ

חאלרם כיר י

נייכי כוונדהן

שאק חוודוודי

דה (קאואל)

עיין אולווכדיב

כ'ינאיהטוימיז עוסמאנלי באנקאסי מוודירי
איקיהן סהלהניקה טאעיין אולונמיש אולדהן
מוסיוו "דאיינכטוז" ניוומוט קאפלאמאלי אי
קיי סופ'רא טאקוימי אידרא (רינאלאר) איט
מישלהר כ'ה חוווהרלהריכדה :

עוסמאנלי באנקאסינין איומיר שועכההסי
(סוקסירסאל) מהאהמיורלהרי טאראפ'יכדאן
מוודירלהרי "נילוס דאיינכטוז" יאדינייאר
(סוב'ינור) דיר , איומיר 1 קיימהנין אהב'
כ'הל (ריסימבכרי) 1889 עוכאהרהסי יאוילמיש
דיר .

כיר מוורה

קיהסין ניוווני

רהנג "כהרלהרי

להרי דכר קיכ

ניכדהן ניהב"כ

כיר ג"וק יאה

לא אילקאמד

קצא סהקיי

מאגניסאדהן סומא יה יחצילמאקה"ם אולדהן
דיומיד יולינין אקקהיסאהרס קאדאר אולדהן קיס
מי (פ'ארטי) מווקיהטמהאל סוורכטאדה כיטמיש
אולמאבלה ניהג"הן פ'אואר אירטיסי ניוווני רהס
מי"קאווסאדי (איניגורדהר) אינ'רא אולווגמיש
דיר .

A Judeo-Turkish article from the bilingual (Judeo-Turkish and Ladino) newspaper אוסטאד *Ustad*, from 22 January 1890. Notice the unusual position of final *kaph* (ך) in lines 3 and 4 of the article.

of education in Jewish schools, and the Jewish community quickly became linguistically and culturally Turkish. The 20,000 or so Jews in Turkey today speak and write Turkish just as their neighbours do.

So the Judeo-Turkish texts of the 19th century, the newspapers aimed at furthering the knowledge of Turkish among the Jews, can be seen as a sort of experiment, or as a step along the path to the Turkification of the Jewish communities of Turkey. For scholars of Jewish languages, the texts are quite noteworthy for the peculiar adaptation of the Hebrew alphabet that they used. For example, Judeo-Turkish texts use the Hebrew letter ה (the consonant *h* in Hebrew) to represent the vowel *e*, while to represent the consonant *h*, they use ך, which in Hebrew is used only to represent the sound *kh* at the end of a word. Since the letter ך in Hebrew is never used at the beginning or in the middle of a word, its use in Judeo-Turkish is kind of like seeing an English capital letter in the middle of a word. For example, in one newspaper we find the Judeo-Turkish phrase דהר ג״יאהארשאנבא *her chaharshanba* 'every Wednesday', corresponding to modern Turkish *her çarşamba*.

The Uzbek language, a member of the Turkic language family and therefore a relative of Turkish, also has a Jewish connection. Bukharan Jews living in Bukhara, Samarkand, Tashkent, and other towns in the modern country of Uzbekistan primarily spoke Judeo-Tajik (see Tajik), but many of the men also spoke Uzbek, which was (and remains) a widely used language in those towns. Around 1900, a well-known Bukharan rabbi in Jerusalem named Shim'on Ḥakham made a Judeo-Tajik translation of a late 18th-century Hebrew work titled תוכן עלילות *Tokhen ʿAlilot*, which is about the biblical Joseph and his brothers. In one passage, the story explains how Joseph's ten older brothers all were able to speak Aramaic, since they had been born in the city of Haran (in Aram), while Joseph's younger brother, Benjamin, did not, since he was born in Canaan (Israel). Therefore, after the older brothers sell Joseph into slavery and want to discuss what they have done, they use Aramaic to keep from being understood by Benjamin. In Shim'on Ḥakham's Judeo-Tajik version of the story, he translates the Aramaic into Judeo-Uzbek—that is, Uzbek in Hebrew script—for a total of about eleven lines of text. One line reads תָא קַגִ'ין גֵּה גֵ'יה פִּיכִּיר אֵיתִיב אוֹזִי בִּיז נִי קִילְגַּן יַמָאן אִישִׁי בִּיז דַן *ta qachangacha fikir etip özibizni qilgan yaman ishibizdan* 'How long shall we not admit our evil deed and be ashamed of it?' Shim'on adds a parenthetical explanation that the use of Uzbek for translation is very appropriate in this case, because Bukharan men, who knew Uzbek from their business dealings in the countryside, sometimes used the language when they wanted to keep their conversations from being understood by their wives and children.

References and further study

Very little has been written about Judeo-Turkish. Mignon (2017) is the only overview of the material. The manuscript with the Judeo-Turkish historical text, published by Marazzi (1980), is held by the Bodleian Library in Oxford (ms. Heb. e 63, folios 106r–121v). The glossary and the text on the plague are in a manuscript owned by the British Library (ms. Add. 15455, folios 1v–8v), as is the longer

Hebrew–Judeo-Turkish poem (Or. 12352, folios 7r–7v). The shorter poem is found in a manuscript in the Jewish Theological Seminary (ms. 1420, fol. 20a). The glossary from the Genizah is held the Cambridge University Library (T-S Ar. 30.295, fols. 4r–5r) and was published by Arad (2017). All of these manuscripts, with the exception of the one at Oxford, are currently available online. Copies of some of the Judeo-Turkish newspapers can be found in the National Library of Israel. The Judeo-Uzbek passage of Shimʻon Ḥakham is included in the introduction of Paper (1986).

38   Urdu (and Marathi)

Apart from the Cochin Jews (see MALAYALAM), there were two other major Jewish communities in India, called the Baghdadis and the Bene Israel (literally 'children of Israel'). These two Jewish groups have very different histories from that of the Cochin Jews and indeed from each other. They did not settle in India at the same time, and they have traditionally spoken different languages.

There is no scholarly consensus as to when the Bene Israel community arrived in India. Documentary evidence goes back only to the 17th century, though the community is likely well over a thousand years old. The tradition of the Bene Israel themselves is that their ancestors ended up in India when they were shipwrecked off the coast near Mumbai (formerly called Bombay), though dates for this supposed shipwreck range from the 8th century BCE to the 6th century CE. The Bene Israel have traditionally lived mostly in rural villages in western India, in the Maharashtra region. They have always been the largest of the three Indian Jewish communities; in the 1830s the Bene Israel population consisted of around 8000 people, and by the 1940s it had increased to almost 25,000. The majority of the Bene Israel have since immigrated to Israel or elsewhere, and probably only a few thousand remain in India, mostly now in urban locations. The Bene Israel community in Israel numbers in the tens of thousands, though, as with most other immigrant groups, they have become well integrated and assimilated into Israeli society.

The Bene Israel traditionally spoke Marathi, a member of the Indo-Aryan language family and a close relative of Hindi, with which it shares an alphabet called Devanagari. It is the primary language of the Maharashtra region (and its capital Mumbai), and, with over eighty million native speakers, is one of the most widely spoken languages in India. By the 19th century (and likely much earlier), knowledge of Hebrew in the Bene Israel community was extremely limited, and many of the customs of Rabbinic Judaism had been lost. In 1832, a Christian missionary named John Wilson published a Hebrew grammar in Marathi, intended specifically for the education of the Bene Israel, and this greatly helped spread familiarity with Hebrew. Missionaries also made Marathi translations of the Bible accessible to the Bene Israel. Around the same time, teachers from the Cochin Jewish community came to live and work among the Bene Israel, introducing them to traditional Jewish liturgy and customs.

The combined work of the Christian missionaries and Cochin Jews led to something of a renaissance of the Bene Israel community. From the mid-19th to the mid-20th century, dozens of Hebrew religious books were published—including prayer-books, Passover Haggadot, and other religious texts—often with Marathi translations, though in each case the Marathi was printed in the native Devanagari script. Moreover, there is no evidence that the Marathi used by Jews was any different from that of their non-Jewish neighbours. In one Haggadah, from 1911, even the Hebrew text was printed in the Devanagari script, which means that at least some Jews felt more comfortable with that script than with the Hebrew alphabet. There is also a manuscript prayer-book from the early 20th century in which we find a small amount of Judeo-Marathi (that is, Marathi written in Hebrew script). The prayer-book is in Hebrew, but some of the prayer headings and instructions are in Marathi, sometimes written in Devanagari script and sometimes written in Hebrew script.

While most Bene Israel traditionally spoke Marathi, those in other areas speak or have spoken Konkani (a close relative of Marathi) or Gujarati, which is the primary language of the Gujarat region (the northwestern neighbour of the Maharashtra region). The Gujarati capital of Ahmedabad once had upwards of 2000 Jews, mainly Bene Israel, though today the community numbers only about 100–200 people. One fascinating linguistic artefact from the Gujarati Jewish community comes in the form of a handwritten notepad from around the turn of the 20th century. The notepad belonged to a Persian-speaking Jewish clothing merchant and mostly contains words and phrases in Judeo-Persian and Judeo-Malay (see MALAY), and even one page with Gujarati script. On another page, which lists the address of a shop in Ahmedabad (using English letters), we find the words אסתירי *istiri* 'iron' and טופי *ṭopi* 'hat', which are the perhaps the only words ever written in Judeo-Gujarati.

In the 18th and 19th centuries, Middle Eastern Jews (chiefly from Baghdad in Iraq and Aleppo in Syria) settled both in Mumbai and in the northeastern city of Kolkata (formerly called Calcutta), where they founded thriving communities. These Indian Jews are called the Baghdadis, after the Iraqi city from which many of them came. The Baghdadi Jews traditionally spoke Judeo-Arabic (see ARABIC, MODERN), and in the 19th and early 20th centuries a number of Judeo-Arabic books and periodicals were printed in India. Some Baghdadi Jews also adopted Urdu, at least as a second (or third or fourth) language, in many cases probably for business purposes, since it is one of the most widely used languages in India. In its spoken form, Urdu is essentially the same language as Hindi, but Urdu is more closely associated with Muslim speakers and is written in the Arabic script, whereas Hindi is more closely associated with Hinduism and is written in the native Devanagari script. Moreover, texts in Urdu tend to use more words borrowed from Arabic, while those in Hindi tend to use more words borrowed from Sanskrit, which is the language of Hindu sacred texts. With its Arabic script and numerous Arabic loanwords, Urdu would have evoked some sense of familiarity among Baghdadi Jews.

There are at least four existing texts in Judeo-Urdu—that is, in the Urdu language written in Hebrew script—all apparently from the late 19th century. These

हग्गादा शेल पेसाह.

इगदाल एलोहीम हाय वेइशत्तब्बाह निमसा
वेएन एथ एल मेसीऊथो एहाद बेएन याहीद केइ
हूदो नेअलाम वेगाम एन सोफ लेआहादूथो एन
लो देमूथ हग्गूफ वेएनो गूफ लो नाआरोख एलाव
केदूशाथो कादमोन लेखोल दाबार आशेर निबरा
रीशोन वेएन रेशीथ लेरेशीथो हिन्नो. आदोन
ओलाम लेखोल नोसार योरे गेदुलाथो उमालखूथो
शेफा नेबूआथो नेथानो एल आनशें सेगुलाथो
वेथिफआरतो लो काम बेइसराएल केमोशे ओद
नाबी उमब्बीत एथ तेमूनाथो तोराथ एमेथ
नाथान लेअम्मो एल आल याद नेबीओ नेएमान
बेथो लो याहालीफ हाएल वेलो यामीर दाथो
लेआलामीम लेजूलाथो सोफे वेयादआ सेथारेनू
मब्बीत लेसोफ दाबार बेकादमूथो गोमेल लेईश
हासीद केमिफआलो नोथेन लेराशा रा केरीशाआथो
इशलाह लेकेस यामीन मेशीहेनू लिफदोथ महक्के केस
येगूआथो मेथीम येहय्ये एल बेरोथ हासदो बारूख
आद आद शेम तेहिल्लाथो एले शेलोश एसरे
लेइक्करीम तोराथ मोशे नेएमान उमीसिबाथो.

A Hebrew Haggadah in Devanagari (Marathi) script, printed in Bombay (1911), p. 5. The header reads हग्गादा शेल पेसाह *haggada shel pesah* (= Hebrew הגדה של פסח *haggada shel pesaḥ* 'Passover Haggadah'), and is followed by the words इगदाल एलोहीम हाय *igdal elohim hay* (= Hebrew יגדל אלוהים חי *yigdal 'elohim ḥay* 'may the living God be exalted'), the beginning of a well-known prayer.

A page from a manuscript of the 19th-century play *Indar Sabhā* in Judeo-Urdu. British Library, ms. Or. 13287, fol. 25r. © The British Library Board.

are an Urdu play (اِندر سبها *Indar Sabhā*) transcribed into Hebrew script, known both from a manuscript version and from a lithograph version; another Urdu play (لیلی مجنو *Laila Majnu*) transcribed into Hebrew script, which was actually published (Bombay, 1888); a short Hebrew–Judeo-Urdu glossary containing about a thousand entries; and a sort-of phrasebook, preserved only in fragmentary form. There is also a Hebrew *siddur* (prayer-book) from 1837 that has some instructions written in Judeo-Urdu. Occasional words in Judeo-Urdu may also be found in a few other Hebrew manuscripts from India. Although the glossary is linguistically the most interesting, the fragmentary phrasebook has some rather curious entries. For example, we find in it phrases like סַמְבּוּסַךּ גַּרֶם הֵי *sambūsak garam he* 'the samosa is hot' and אַגַּר הַם גֻ֗וֹת בּוֹלֵיגָ֗א *agar ham jʰūṭ bole-gā* 'if I tell a lie'.

References and further study

Slapak (2003) is a nice overview of the different Jewish communities in India, with many photographs. Roland (1998) is a more in-depth study. Musleah (1975) and Manasseh (2013) focus on the Baghdadi community, while Isenberg (1988) focuses on the Bene Israel. Rubin (2016) is a study of the Hebrew–Judeo-Urdu glossary, including photographs of the entire manuscript; it also has some discussion of the other Judeo-Urdu texts. The example of Judeo-Gujarati appears on fol. 39v (and again on fol. 44v) of the aforementioned notepad, which is held in the British Library (ms. Or. 13914); it is available to view online. The prayer-book with Judeo-Marathi, formerly part of the Valmadonna collection, is now in the National Library of Israel (ms. Heb. 8°9191) and is also available to view online.

39 Yiddish, Old and Early Modern

When people think of Jewish languages, Yiddish is probably—other than Hebrew—the first one that comes to mind. In North America, the UK, Australia, South Africa, and many other places, it has traditionally been the language of most Jewish immigrants. It is also the Jewish language—again, other than Hebrew—with the most highly developed literary tradition. Before World War II, some 75%–80% of Jews worldwide spoke Yiddish, and so for a long time it could reasonably be described as the world's most important Jewish language. Over the course of the last 75 years, there has been a marked decline in the number of Yiddish speakers, yet it remains the language of more than half a million Jews around the world (see YIDDISH, MODERN STANDARD and YIDDISH, MODERN HASIDIC).

The exact origins of Yiddish are not totally understood, but we know that when Jews began to move into Germanic-speaking areas of Central Europe, by around 1000 CE, they adopted the local Germanic dialects. The first written traces of a language that might be an early form of Yiddish appear in the commentaries of Rashi, the famous Jewish scholar who lived in France from 1040 to 1105 CE. Rashi wrote his commentaries on the Bible and the Talmud in Hebrew, but sometimes provided short translations or definitions in another language in order to clarify difficult Hebrew terms that his readers might not have understood. In most cases the other language was Judeo-French (Old French in Hebrew characters; see FRENCH), but occasionally Rashi would instead use a Germanic word, also written in Hebrew characters. For example, when trying to explain the meaning of the Hebrew word פרגוד *pargod* 'breeches' in the Babylonian Talmud (Shab. 120a), Rashi used the term קני הוזן *kni hozn* 'knee-trousers', which is related to the modern Yiddish words קני 'knee' and הויזן *hoyzn* 'trousers'. Rashi himself spoke French, but had studied in the German-speaking towns of Mainz and Worms, and he must have anticipated that his commentaries would be read by Jews from those communities as well.

The earliest complete sentence in Yiddish is found inside a Hebrew *maḥzor*, or holiday prayer-book, which was written in 1272, most likely in the German city of Würzburg or Nürnberg. The prayer-book is known as the Worms Maḥzor because it was used for hundreds of years in the synagogue in the city of Worms. The Yiddish sentence is actually written inside the letters of a very large Hebrew word. The Hebrew word begins a prayer (for dew!), and the Yiddish sentence inside it has nothing to do with the prayer. Rather, the Yiddish is a message to the readers, wishing them a good day:

גוֹט טַק אִים בְּטַגָא שֶׁ וַיר דִּיש מַחֲזוֹר אִין בֵּית הַכְּנֶסֶת טְרַגָא

gut tak im betage se vayr dis makhazor in bes hakneses trage

'May a good day shine for the one who carries this *maḥzor* to the synagogue'

Beginning in the 1300s, we begin to see the emergence of a real Yiddish literature, and by the 15th century, Yiddish grammar and vocabulary begin to look increasingly distinct from the German dialects of the Jews' Christian neighbours. Of course, because Yiddish was from its very beginnings written in Hebrew letters, it always looked different from German in written form.

Until around the year 1600, scholars usually refer to the language as Old Yiddish. Old Yiddish literature is very diverse, including fables, poetry, Bible translations and commentaries, adaptations of European epic romances, and even scientific and medical writings. There were also non-literary texts, like letters and other types of everyday writing.

The most prominent author of the Old Yiddish period is known in Yiddish as Elye Bokher, in Hebrew as Eliyahu ha-Levi, and in English usually as Elijah Levita. Elye was born in the German city of Neustadt in 1469, but spent much of his life in Italy, where he died, in Venice, in 1549. (Incidentally, there were Yiddish-speaking communities in Venice and some other Italian cities, which provided refuge for Jews fleeing persecution in Germany. On the influence of Yiddish on Judeo-Italian, see ITALIAN.) Elye was a Hebrew and Aramaic grammarian, who taught Hebrew to a number of prominent Christians in Italy and who worked for many years in the publishing business in both Italy and Germany. Most of his scholarly works were written in Hebrew, but he also composed some works in Yiddish intended for a popular audience. His most famous work is the epic בבא דאנטונה *bovo d'antona* ('Bovo of Antona'), more commonly known as בבא־בוך *bovo-bukh* ('Bovo-book'), which is regarded as the greatest masterpiece of early Yiddish literature.

Bovo-bukh, written in 1507 in northern Italy, is a story is about a young man born into nobility who becomes a lowly stable boy, falls in love with a princess, and by virtue of his bravery and chivalrous deeds wins the hand of the girl and is restored back to his proper station in life. The story includes romance, intrigue, battles, and everything else one would expect to find in a medieval epic tale. *Bovo-bukh* is actually an adaptation of the Italian epic romance *Bovo d'Antona*, which itself was based on the Anglo-Norman epic *Bevis of Hampton*. Elye's version follows the general plotline of the Italian epic, but with many changes to the details. Some of these changes were clearly done in order to make the story more relatable to a Jewish readership. The many Christian references in the Italian version are excised or turned into a Jewish equivalent. For example, the children of Bovo and his wife are baptized in the Italian tale, but circumcized in Elye's version.

Elye himself made it clear that he intended the work for a female audience. This is probably why he chose to write it in Yiddish rather than Hebrew, since at that time women were not as well educated in Hebrew as men. Elye's intentions can be seen in the following extract from the introduction to the epic (note also the rhyming lines):

ikh elye levi der shrayber	איך אליה לוי דער שרייבר
diner aler frumen vayber	דינר אלר ורומן וייבר
mit ern un mit tsukhtn	מיט אירן אוני מיט צוכטן
un ikh los mikh alzo bedukhtn	אוני איך לוש מיך אלזו בידוכטן
un shtet oykh vol tsu glaben	אוני שטיט אויך וואל צו גלבן
das mir etlekhe froyen far ubl haben	דש מיר איטלכֿי ורויאן בור אובל הבן
varum ikh nit oykh fur zey druk	וארום איך ניט אויך בֿור זיא דרוק
mayner taytsh bukher ayn shtuk	מיינר טייטש בוכֿר אײן שטוק
das zey zikh mogn dinen dermayen	דש זיא זיך מוגן דינן דר מייאן
un shaboses un yamim toyvim dinen layen	אוני שבתות אוני ימים טובים דינן לייאן

'I, Elijah Levita the writer, servant of all pious women with honour and courtesy, feel distressed that I have offended some women because I have not also printed one of my Yiddish books for them so that they can take delight in them, and read them on the Sabbath and festivals.'

Some of the most interesting texts from the Old Yiddish period come from private letters. While these may not be classified as true literature, they are still a great source on the use of the Yiddish language, and they offer a fascinating window into the everyday lives of medieval Yiddish speakers. When the Cairo Genizah, a treasure trove of hundreds of thousands of old Jewish documents that had been preserved in a synagogue there, was discovered in the late 19th century (see ARABIC, MEDIEVAL), researchers were amazed to find a handful of texts in Yiddish, including letters. The presence of Yiddish texts attests to the fact that there were Yiddish speakers living in the Middle East at least as early as the 16th century. There is a set of correspondence in Yiddish between a woman named Rachel, who was living in Jerusalem, and her son Moshe, who was living in Cairo. The letters, written in the 1560s, include such timeless motherly gems as the following:

מיין ליבר זון יצ׳ו מיר איז זֵיר בנג דז איך בעו׳ אזו לנג קיין בריב בֿון דיר ניט האב גיהט

mayn liber zun y[ishmerehu] ts[uro] v[ihayyehu] mir iz zer bang das ikh be'avo[noyseyne] azo lang keyn briv fun dir nit hab gehat

'My dear son—may God protect him and keep him alive—I am very upset that I (for my sins) have not received a letter from you in such a long time'

Continuing in the same manner, she also says:

מיין זון הקב״ה זול דיר עז מוחל זיין דז דו מיך האשט אזו מצער גיוועזן

mayn zun hak[odesh] b[orekh] h[u] zol dir es moykhl zayn das du mikh hast azo metsaer gevezn

'My son, may the LORD, blessed be He, forgive you for causing me misery'

But despite her being hurt at her son's negligence in writing, she still expresses her love for him with lines like this one:

איך ביט אימדר דען רופא נאמן דו זאלשט קיין קרנקייט האבן איך זאל בור דיר ליידן

ikh bet imder den royfe neyman du zolst keyn krankayt haben ikh zol fur dir layden

'I always ask of the Faithful Healer [God] for you not to have any illness; I should suffer instead of you'

She also gives her son advice and guidance on various practical and ethical issues:

איך ביט דיך זיר גי דו מינשט דז דו קנשט אין דען באך ניט באדן זא קן עז דיר ניט שאדן

ikh bet dikh zeyr gey du minst das du kenst in den bakh nit boden zo ken es dir nit shoden

'I beg of you, go as little as possible to bathe in the river, so it won't do you any harm'

ווען דו עפז גוטז טושט זייא דיך ניט מתפאר שנ' הצנֵיע לכת עם אלהיך

ven du epes guts tust zay dikh nit mispaer shen[eʾemar] hatsneaʿ lekhet ʾim ʾelohekha

'When you do something good, don't boast, as it is written [in the Bible, Micah 6:8]: walk humbly with your God'

Not only do these letters prove that medieval Yiddish-speaking mothers worried about their sons just as much as mothers do today, but they also show us that Yiddish writing could be found in unexpected places, such as in medieval Egypt. These letters are also special because they were written by a woman, at a time when most writing was done by men. In fact, there was another, even more substantial and important Yiddish text written by a woman about a century and a half later.

The work is a volume of memoirs composed by a woman called Glikl of Hameln. Glikl, who lived from 1645 to 1719, was a well-to-do German Jewish widow and businesswoman, who chronicled her life and that of her family, as well as detailing events affecting the German Jewish community of her time. Glikl's memoirs give us a valuable insight into the everyday family life of Jews in Central Europe in the 17th and 18th centuries, and her work is full of fascinating details about the trials and tribulations experienced by her family. For example, she tells a story about how, when a plague struck, her wealthy grandparents suddenly became destitute and had their lives turned upside down. She describes these events, beginning before the arrival of the plague, saying that her grandfather had the following:

גנצי קיסטין פול גילדני קעטין ושארי תכשיטות אונ' גנצי גרוישי בייטלין מיט מרגליות
דאז אין דער זעלבי צייט אויף מאה פרסאות זוא קיין עושר גיוועזין וועלכיש אביר בעו"ה

ניט לנג גיווערהרט. איזט ב״מ דבר אויף גיקומין איזט מיין גרויש פאטיר אונ׳ עטליכי קינדר
גישטארבין. מיין גרויש מויטר זעליג האט נאך איבעריג גיהאלטין ב׳ ליידיגי בנות איזט מיט
אינין בעירום ובחוסר כל ארויז גאנגין אונ׳ מיר פאר צילט ווי זיא זיך נעביך מוזין גיניטן.
[. . .] אלזו האט זיך מיין ליבי גרויש מוטיר מיט אירי ביידי יתומי׳ גרוש צרות גניט און
ממש פון איין הויז צום אנדרן מוזין קריכין עד כי יעבור הזעם. דאך דער דבר האט זיך לקצת
אויף גיהערט האט זיא איר בית ווידר וואלין ביוואונין אונ׳ לאזין אויז וועטרין איר זאכין
אביר דאר האט זיא ווינ19ק גיפונדין.

*gantse kistn ful gildene keten veshayre takhshites un gantse groyse bay-
tlen mit margolyes doz in der zelbe tsayt oyf meye parses zo keyn oysher
gevezen velkhes ober be'avo[noyseyne] ha[rabim] nit lang gevert. izt b[ar]
m[inen] deyver oyz gekumen izt mayn groys foter un etlekhe kinder gesh-
torben. mayn groys muter zelig hot nokh iberig gehalten 2 leydige bones izt
mit inen be'eyrem uvekhoyser kol aroyz gangen un mir far tselt vi zi zikh
nebekh muzin genitn. . . . alzo hot zikh mayn libe groys muter mit ire beyde
yesoymi[m] gros tsores genit un mamesh fun eyn hoyz tsum andern muzen
krikhen ad ki ya'avor haza'am. dokh der deyver hot liktsas oyf gehert hot
zi ir bays volen vider bevonen un lozen oyz vetren ir zakhen ober dor hot
zi venik gefunden.*

'Whole boxes full of golden chains and other kinds of jewels, and whole
big bags of pearls; at that time there was no such wealth for a hundred
miles. Unfortunately, however, it didn't last long. A plague—God help
us—came, and my grandfather and several children died. My late grandmother was left behind with two unmarried daughters. She left with them,
taking absolutely nothing, and she used to tell me what she had to endure,
poor thing. . . . So my beloved grandmother and both her orphan daughters endured great sorrows and had to make their way from one house to
another until the turmoil passed. After the plague had died down somewhat,
she wanted to go back to live in her house and air out her things, but she
found very little there.'

Glikl goes on to relate how her grandmother got back onto her feet after the total
loss of the family fortune. This is just one of many times in Glikl's story that death
and hardship forced her or a member of her family to rebuild their lives. Her story
is truly amazing to read.

No discussion of early Yiddish literature would be complete without mention of the *Tsenerene* (צאינה וראינה). The *Tsenerene*, written sometime at the
end of the 16th century, is a loose translation of parts of the Bible (the Torah,
Haftarot, and the Five Scrolls), interspersed with expansions of the biblical
stories based on later Jewish legends. For example, in the beginning of the
biblical Book of Esther, we learn that King Ahasuerus of Persia ruled over
127 provinces. The *Tsenerene* adds that the reason Ahasuerus merited this
distinction was because he married Esther, a descendant of the biblical matri-
arch Sarah, who lived to be 127 years old. This interpretation is similar to an
explanation found in early medieval Aramaic Targumim to the Book of Esther,

The earliest dated Yiddish text (1272), which appears in the Worms Maḥzor. National Library of Israel, ms. 4°781, fol. 54r. The Yiddish text is written in red ink inside the large letters. COURTESY OF THE NATIONAL LIBRARY OF ISRAEL.

A 16th-century Yiddish letter found in the Cairo Genizah. Line 5 contains the complaint that begins מיין ליבר זון *mayn liber zun* 'my dear son'. Cambridge University Library, T-S Misc 36.L.1, fol. 1v. COURTESY OF THE SYNDICS OF CAMBRIDGE UNIVERSITY LIBRARY.

which are many centuries older than the *Tsenerene*. (See ARAMAIC, ANCIENT AND MEDIEVAL for a discussion of the Targumim.) Another noteworthy addition to the biblical narrative that we find in the *Tsenerene* story of Esther comes in a description of King Ahasuerus' military exploits, where it says that he was משוגע *meshuge* ('crazy').

The *Tsenerene* was composed for readers who did not know enough Hebrew to understand the Torah portions in the original. It was intended to be used by both men and women, and that was indeed the case, but because women were usually less educated in Hebrew than men, it came to be commonly known as the 'Women's Bible'. The *Tsenerene* became one of the most well-known and beloved Eastern European Jewish literary works, and was perhaps the most popular and widely read Yiddish book of all time, even into the 20th century.

Yiddish literature from its beginnings until the 18th century had its stronghold in Western and Central Europe, especially in the German-speaking territories. Beginning in the 17th century, as Jewish communities in Eastern Europe grew quite large, the centre of the Yiddish-speaking world shifted eastward. Yiddish more or less died out in Western and Central Europe in the 18th century, as the status of Jews in those regions rose and they became more acculturated to the local non-Jewish environment. As part of this process, they abandoned Yiddish in favour of non-Jewish languages like German and Dutch. In Eastern Europe, where Jews remained more segregated, Yiddish continued to flourish and evolve (see YIDDISH, MODERN STANDARD).

References and further study

Baumgarten (2005) is an introduction to Old Yiddish literature. Frakes (2004) is a comprehensive selection of Old Yiddish texts with nice introductions to each extract but no English translations. It includes a discussion of and further details on the Worms Maḥzor. The Worms Maḥzor is located in the National Library of Israel (ms. 4°781) and can be viewed online; the Yiddish sentence appears on fol. 54r. Frakes (2014) consists of English translations of major Old Yiddish epics, including *Bovo-bukh*. Frakes (2017) is a textbook of Old Literary Yiddish. The most comprehensive edition of *Bovo-bukh* is Rosenzweig (2016). The most complete edition of the Yiddish letters from the Cairo Genizah are in Turniansky (1984). No complete English translations have ever been published. All the letters are now in the collections of the Cambridge University Library, except for one, which is in the National Library of Israel. See Turniansky (2019) for a comprehensively annotated English translation of Glikl's memoirs. Elbaum and Turniansky (2010) provide an overview of the content and publication history of the *Tsenerene*.

40 Yiddish, Modern Standard

As mentioned in the previous chapter, Yiddish was a thriving language used by the Jews in Central and Eastern Europe from the medieval period onwards, with a flourishing written tradition. However, in the middle of the 19th century, Yiddish emerged as a modern literary language on a completely different scale. This revolutionary development was actually an unexpected, and indeed quite accidental, by-product of the rise of Hebrew as a literary language during the Haskalah (Jewish Enlightenment) of the late 18th and 19th centuries (see HEBREW, ENLIGHTENMENT). Around this time, the Yiddish spoken in Western Europe largely died out and was replaced by the state languages of those regions (mostly German, Dutch, and to a lesser extent French). By contrast, the Yiddish spoken in Eastern Europe had millions of speakers and a growing population. Jewish writers who wanted to create a modern literary language for Jews began writing prolifically in Hebrew, but to their frustration soon realized that their readership was not as large as they had hoped. This was because most Eastern European Jews had only partial knowledge of Hebrew, as opposed to Yiddish, which nearly all of them spoke. As a result, around the middle of the 19th century, some of these Hebrew writers turned to Yiddish, practically against their will, and began to compose novels and short stories in the language which they almost unanimously deemed as inferior to Hebrew. Moreover, they thought Yiddish to be generally unsuitable as a literary vehicle, regarding it as simply a corrupt and debased form of German, and something less than a real language. Almost overnight, these writers who felt that they had toiled in vain for a relatively small Hebrew readership became bestselling authors, gaining widespread fame and recognition among the Yiddish-speaking population of Eastern Europe.

Thus, modern Yiddish literature was born. In this formative period, Yiddish acquired its own trio of "classic" writers, the first of whom was Mendele Moykher Sforim, the pen-name of Sholem Jacob Abramovitch (1836–1917). Affectionately called the grandfather of Yiddish literature (as well as the grandfather of Hebrew literature, for his Hebrew compositions!), Mendele wrote about the Jewish experience in Eastern Europe through the persona of an itinerant book peddler (מוכר ספרים *moykher sforim* means 'book peddler' in Yiddish), describing life in the *shtetl*, the kind of small town where many Eastern

European Jews lived throughout the 19th and early 20th centuries. The other two members of this classic trio of Yiddish writers were Sholem Aleykhem (1859–1916)—another pen-name, this one meaning 'hello!' in Yiddish—and Y. L. Peretz (1852–1915), both of whom composed novels, short stories, and poetry on a wide variety of topics. Sholem Aleykhem is particularly famous for his humorous stories of Tevye the Milkman, a pious Jew with a penchant for quoting (and misquoting) the Hebrew Bible, Mishnah, and Talmud. The stories about Tevye are based around him and his family, including his seven daughters, many of whom come home with a match viewed as unsuitable by their father (including a Communist and a non-Jew). Tevye's stories were made famous in English and many other languages in the form of the musical *Fiddler on the Roof*. Over the following decades, in addition to these and numerous other writers of original Yiddish literature, many classics of world literature were translated into Yiddish, including works by authors as diverse as Aeschylus, Miguel de Cervantes, Victor Hugo, Henry Wadsworth Longfellow, Leo Tolstoy, and Arthur Conan Doyle.

During the two decades between the end of World War I and the outbreak of World War II, besides a great flurry of literary activity, there was also a booming Yiddish press. Numerous dailies and weeklies were published from across the political spectrum, not only in Eastern Europe but also in North America, Argentina, Mexico, England, and elsewhere. (Palestine was an exception, since Yiddish there was viewed as a threat to Modern Hebrew and actively suppressed.) Yiddish musical theatre became hugely popular in Yiddish-speaking communities worldwide, and this eventually sowed the seeds for a very successful Yiddish film industry, based mainly in Poland and the United States, with its heyday in the 1930s. The most popular film of this period was ייִדל מיטן פֿידל *yidl mitn fidl* 'Yiddle with His Fiddle' (Poland, 1936), a romantic musical comedy that tells the story of a girl who disguises herself as a boy and wanders the Polish countryside making her living as an itinerant musician. The Yiddish film industry, like many other aspects of Yiddish language, literature, and culture in Eastern Europe, was cut tragically short by the Holocaust.

The Yiddish spoken in Eastern Europe traditionally had three main dialects: one centred in the territory corresponding to present-day Lithuania, Latvia, and Belarus, another centred in the areas corresponding to present-day Poland and Hungary, and a third centred in the areas corresponding to present-day Ukraine and Romania. The differences between these dialects pertain mostly to pronunciation, particularly of the vowels. For example, the sound *oy* does not exist in Lithuanian Yiddish, so the word וווינען 'to live', which is pronounced as *voynen* by Yiddish speakers from Poland, Hungary, Ukraine, and Romania, is pronounced as *veynen* by Lithuanian speakers, making it a homophone of the verb וויינען *veynen* 'to cry'. This means that in Lithuanian Yiddish, the question וווּ וווינסטו *vu veynstu* 'where do you live' sounds identical to וווּ וויינסטו *vu veynstu* 'where do you cry?' As a result, Lithuanian Yiddish speakers developed the idiomatic question וווּ לאַכסטו *vu lakhstu*, which literally means 'where do you laugh?', to ask where someone lives.

The following chart illustrates some of the most common differences in the pronunciation of vowels between the main dialects of Eastern European Yiddish (as well as Standard Yiddish, a literary variety that will be discussed a bit later):

Lithuanian	Polish	Ukrainian	Standard	English
זון *zun*	זון *zin*	זון *zin*	זון *zun*	'son'
קויפֿן *keyfn*	קויפֿן *koyfn*	קויפֿן *koyfn*	קויפֿן *koyfn*	'to buy'
זאָגן *zogn*	זאָגן *zugn*	זאָגן *zugn*	זאָגן *zogn*	'to say'
זיין *zayn*	זיין *zaan*	זיין *zan*	זיין *zayn*	'to be'
שיין *sheyn*	שיין *shayn*	שיין *sheyn*	שיין *sheyn*	'beautiful'

In some regional varieties of Yiddish there are also different pronunciations of consonants. Perhaps the most striking of these was a variety of Yiddish, once found in a small area located within what is now Lithuania, which completely lacked the sound *sh*; speakers instead substituted the sound *s*. Because of this, that variety is known as *sabesdiker losn* 'Sabbath language', which would be pronounced as *shabesdiker loshn* (שבתדיקער לשון) in other varieties of Yiddish.

There are also some grammatical differences between the traditional Eastern European dialects of Yiddish. For example, Polish and Ukrainian Yiddish, as well as Standard Yiddish, have a system of three noun genders (masculine, feminine, and neuter) for nouns (just as certain other European languages such as German and Russian do). Each gender is marked by a different form of the definite article (the word for 'the'): masculine nouns take the form דער *der*, whereas feminine nouns take די *di*, and neuter nouns take דאָס *dos*. By contrast, Lithuanian Yiddish has only two noun genders, masculine and feminine (like Spanish or French); it does not have a neuter gender at all. Thus, nouns that are neuter in other varieties of Yiddish are either masculine or feminine in Lithuanian Yiddish. For example, the phrase 'the house' is דאָס הויז *dos hoyz* in Polish and Ukrainian Yiddish, but די הויז *di heyz* in Lithuanian Yiddish.

In the 1920s and 1930s, the traditional Eastern European dialects of Yiddish were augmented by the introduction of Standard Yiddish, which became a quasi-official variety of the language. Standard Yiddish was developed by the YIVO Institute, an organization founded in 1925 by the prominent Yiddish linguist Max Weinreich (1894–1969) and several likeminded colleagues. YIVO, originally headquartered in Vilnius, Lithuania, was designed to serve as a scholarly centre for research on Yiddish, and one of its early aims was the establishment of a standard form of the language—something that had never existed. The work of YIVO led to the creation of a standardized spelling system for Yiddish, as well as a pronunciation system based largely around the Lithuanian dialect but with some elements of Polish and Ukrainian Yiddish (e.g., the sound *oy*), and a grammatical system based largely on

Polish and Ukrainian Yiddish. During World War II, YIVO's headquarters moved to New York, where it remains to this day. The YIVO spelling system has become the standard all around the Yiddish-speaking world, outside of ultra-Orthodox circles (see YIDDISH, MODERN HASIDIC), and Standard Yiddish is almost always the type taught in Yiddish classes at universities and summer schools.

People often think of Yiddish as being very close to German, or even a dialect of German. While it is true that Yiddish and German are closely related (see YIDDISH, OLD AND EARLY MODERN), there are many differences between the two languages in both pronunciation and grammar (in addition to the fact that Yiddish is written in the Hebrew alphabet). One grammatical difference between Yiddish and German is their different ways of forming the past tense. Standard German has two past tenses, a simple past and a perfect. The simple past is etymologically related to the English simple past tense and is formed by means of vowel changes or suffixes; for example, the simple past of the German verb *schreiben* 'to write' is *schrieb* 'wrote' (with a vowel change), and the past tense of the German verb *lieben* 'to love' is *liebte* 'loved' (with a suffix comparable to the English *-ed*). The German perfect tense is formed by means of a helping verb (*haben* 'to have' or *sein* 'to be') and functions similarly to the English present perfect—for example, *ich habe geschrieben* 'I have written'. By contrast, Yiddish has only one past tense, formed by means of a helping verb, and this serves as the equivalent of both German past tenses. So in Yiddish, איך האָב געשריבן *ikh hob geshribn* means both 'I wrote' and 'I have written'.

Yiddish also differs from German in its word order. While German is infamous for putting the verb at the end of complex clauses, Yiddish behaves more like English. For example, compare the following two sentences, both meaning 'I wrote the letter while I waited for the train with my friend yesterday':

German

> *Ich schrieb den Brief, während ich mit meinem Freund auf den Zug <u>wartete</u>*
> (literally 'I wrote the letter while I with my friend for the train <u>waited</u>')

Yiddish

> איך האָב געשריבן דעם בריוו בשעת איך האָב געוואָרט אויף דער באַן מיט מײַן חבֿר
> *ikh hob geshribn dem briv beshas ikh <u>hob gevart</u> oyf der ban mit mayn khaver*
> (literally 'I wrote the letter while I <u>waited</u> for the train with my friend')

In addition to differences in pronunciation, grammar, and vocabulary between the two sentences, we see that the verb 'waited' appears in the middle of the Yiddish sentence (as in English) but at the very end of the sentence in German.

Sometimes Yiddish and German differ in their vocabulary. Around 70%–85% of Yiddish vocabulary is Germanic and often very similar to German—and indeed English; compare, for example, Yiddish האַנט *hant* vs. German *Hand* 'hand', Yiddish פֿינגער *finger* vs. German *Finger* 'finger', Yiddish פֿיש *fish* vs. German *Fisch* 'fish', and Yiddish זינגען *zingen* vs. German *singen* 'to sing'. However, Yiddish has many "false friends" with German, meaning that a Yiddish word sounds like an etymologically related German word but has a different meaning. For example, the Yiddish verb שמעקן *shmekn* means 'to smell', while the similar-sounding German verb *schmecken* means 'to taste'. The Yiddish word יאָרצײַט *yortsayt* (literally 'year-time') denotes the anniversary of a death, while the German equivalent *Jahreszeit* means 'season'. The Yiddish phrase שוואַרץ-יאָר *shvarts yor*, which literally means 'black year', is used to mean 'devil', whereas the German equivalent *schwarze Jahr* has only the literal meaning 'black year'.

Around 12%–20% of Yiddish vocabulary derives from Hebrew and Aramaic. This includes a lot of basic vocabulary, such as משפחה *mishpokhe* 'family', דירה *dire* 'apartment, flat', לבֿנה *levone* 'moon', and חיה *khaye* 'animal'. The Hebrew/Aramaic component of Yiddish is not restricted to nouns, but rather also includes many commonly used verbs (e.g., חתמענען *khasmenen* 'to sign' and גנבֿענען *ganvenen* 'to steal'), as well as adverbs, conjunctions, and other particles (e.g., כּמעט *kimat* 'almost', אפֿשר *efsher* 'maybe', and בשעת *beshas* 'while'). And of course, most Yiddish words referring to Jewish religious culture derive from Hebrew and Aramaic—for example, תּפֿילה *tfile* 'prayer', סידור *sider* 'prayer-book', יום טובֿ *yontef* 'Jewish festival'.

Eastern European Yiddish has a rich stock of Slavic vocabulary (around 3%–10%), mostly from Polish and Ukrainian, acquired during the many centuries of Yiddish life surrounded by speakers of these languages. (Note that Western Yiddish, which was spoken in Germany, the Netherlands, and Switzerland, never acquired this Slavic component.) Again, the Slavic vocabulary in Yiddish permeates all aspects of the language, including nouns (e.g., קאַפּעליוש *kapelyush* 'hat', פּושקע *pushke* 'tin can', and פּלימעניק *plimenik* 'nephew') adjectives (e.g., נודנע *nudne* 'boring', זשעדנע *zhedne* 'greedy', and טשיקאַווע *tshikave* 'funny'), verbs (e.g., האָרעווען *horeven* 'to work hard', בלאָנדזשען *blondzhen* 'to be lost', and קאָרמענען *kormenen* 'to feed'), adverbs (e.g., פּאַמעלעך *pamelekh* 'slowly'), and conjunctions and other particles (e.g., כאָטש *khotsh* 'although' and נו *nu* 'well? come on!'). All of this means that intelligibility between Yiddish and German can be quite a challenge, because most Yiddish sentences are likely to have some non-Germanic words, some grammatical features that differ from standard German, and perhaps some Germanic words with meanings not found in German.

The Holocaust dealt a catastrophic blow to Yiddish language and culture, as the majority of the six million Jews killed were Yiddish speakers. This irreparable loss, combined with widespread assimilation and abandonment of Yiddish by those Jews who emigrated from Eastern Europe before or after the War, Stalinist oppression of Yiddish in the Soviet Union, and opposition to the language in favour of Modern Hebrew in Palestine (and later Israel), led to a precipitous drop in the number of Yiddish speakers by the mid-20th century. A Yiddish-speaking population estimated at 11 million before World War II has been reduced to perhaps less than a million today. Despite this severe decline, Yiddish continues to play an important role in contemporary Jewish society. First, it remains the primary language of hundreds of thousands of Hasidic Jews worldwide (see YIDDISH, MODERN HASIDIC).

אַן ענציקלאָפּעדיע פֿון סתם מענטשן

שוין אויף ייִדיש אויך

שלום בערגער (ניו-יאָרק)
ספּעציעל פֿאַר „פֿאָרווערטס"

דורך דער געשיכטע פֿרווּט יעדער פֿאָלק, וואָס פֿאַרמאָגט אַ ליטעראַטור, אַריַבערגעמען אין איין בוך, אָדער ביכער, דאָס גאַנצע וויסן. די געשיכטע פֿון וויסן איז אויך די געשיכטע פֿון קאַטעגאָריזירן וואָס מע ווייסט.

לויט די כּללים פֿון 21סטן יאָרהונדערט, דאַרפֿן זיך באַטייליקן אין אַן ענציקלאָפּעדיע אַקאַדעמיקערס פֿון אַ צאָל פֿאַרשיידענע פֿעלדער. געוויינטלעך, באַשליסן די רעדאַק־ טאָרן פֿון די ענציקלאָפּעדיעס, וועי עס וועט אַנטריַבען אַ געוויסן אַרטיקל – און יענער באַשלוס קען זיַן אַ ביז גאָר גורלדיקער פֿאַרן פֿאַרשטאַנד פֿון די קומעדיקע דורות, וואָס פֿאַרשטייען דעם דאָזיקן לימוד דורך יענעמס ברילן. וועי געדענקט ניט, וועי די השערה, וואָס מע האָט זיך אַרומגעטראָגן דערמיט זינט די שול־יאַרן, איז אין אַ רגע חרוב געוואָרן דורך פֿאַקטן, וואָס זיַנען פֿריִער ניט פֿאַרגעשטעלט געוואָרן?

צווישן די אויסגאַבעס, וואָס האָבן זיך שטאַרק געביטן אין דער אינטערנעט־תקופֿה, געפֿינט זיך אויך די ענציקלאָפּעדיע. בשעת די אַלגעמיינע ענציקלאָפּעדיע ווערט אַגערענעצט צו אַ געוויסער אַקאַדעמישער עליטע, האָבן די דאָזיקע אויפֿגעקומענע „פּראָיעקטן פֿון אפֿענעם מקור" אויפֿן אינטערנעט פֿאַרבעטן מחברים אָנטייל צו נעמען אין פֿאַרזאַמלען און פֿאַרשרייבן.

ביז סוף 90ער האָבן עקזיסטירט אַ צאָל אַזוינע פּראָיעקטן, אַ טייל ווי בנוגע צו מער טראַדיציאָנעלע עקספּערטן־ענציקלאָפּעדיעס. זינט 2001 האָט אָבער די אויבערהאַנט די גרויסע אינטערנעץ־ענציקלאָפּעדיע, מיטן נאָ־ מען „וויקיפּעדיע", אַ צונויפֿהעפֿט פֿון האַ־ וויַיש וואָרט „וויקי" (גיך) און „[ענציקלאָ־ פּ]עדיע". אַזוי ווערט באַצייכנט אַ וועבזיַטל, וואָס יעדער לייענער באַיִנער מעג עס רעדאַקטירן.

די דאָזיקע אָריגינעלע (ענגליש־שפּראַכיקע) וויקיפּעדיע נעמט שוין אַריַן מער ווי אַ מיליאָן

אינטערנעץ־ענציקלאָפּעדיע,

אויסמעקן גרויסע טיילן טעקסט, וואָס יענער האָט איבער זיַ לאַנג געהאָרעוועט. ווי אַזוי פֿונקציאָנירט דאָס אויף אַן אמת?

פֿון איין זיַט, קען מען זאָגן, אַז דער דעמאָקראַטישער צוגאַנג צוגעזאַמט פֿון דעם דאָזיקן פּראָיעקט, איז ניט קיין אילוזיע. יעדער (צווישן געוויסע גרענעצן) מעג צושריַבען זיַנע פֿאַר ווערטעס. פֿון דעסט וועגן איז וויקיפּעדיע נאָך אַלץ, מער וויניקער, אַ פֿאַרלאָזלעכער מקור פֿון פּשוטע פֿאַקטן. בײַ טייל איינעס איז די קוואַליטעט פּונקט אַזוי גוט, ווי בײַ מער טראַדיציאָנעלע ענציקלאָפּעדיעס.

צוריקגערעדט, קענען פֿאַלשע ידיעות דערפֿירן צו ניט־פֿאַרוויסגעזעענע רעזולטאַטן. נאָך מער קאָנקרעט: טייל היסטאָרישע (אָדער סתם „פּאָפּ"־קולטורעלע) פֿיגורן, וואָס זיַנען נאָך צווישן די לעבעדיקע, האָט מען געפֿונדן אַראָפּרעסן און מוציא־שם־רע זיַן אויף די שפֿאַלטן פֿון וויקיפּעדיע. ווער שמועסט נאָך וועגן די אַלע קאָנטראָווערסיעלע טעמעס, וואָס ציִען צו טשודאַקעס פֿון אַלע סאָרטן?

פֿאַר אָן אַ שיעור אינטערעסאַנטע איַנגעשאַפֿטן וואָס מע קען אַרומרעדן. לאָמיר אָבער דאָ זיך אָפּשטעלן אויפֿן הויפּט־פּרינציפּ פֿון דער וויקיפּעדיע – דאָס, וואָס יעדער מעג זיַן אַ שריַבער אָדער אַ רעדאַקטאָר. יעדער מעג אַנפֿילן אַ בלויז צווישן די טעמעס, צונויפֿגיסן צוויי אַרטיקלען אין איינעם, אָדער אַפֿילו

A recent article about Wikipedia in Yiddish, from Forverts, *an American Yiddish newspaper.*

In addition, since the 1970s, there has been a growing interest in Yiddish outside of Hasidic circles, with Yiddish university courses, evening classes, and intensive summer schools springing up in various locations around the world. Some graduates of these courses and summer schools have gone on to become fluent in Yiddish and even speak the language to their children, so that for the first time there is a very small new generation of native speakers of Standard Yiddish (which was previously just a written language used alongside the traditional spoken Yiddish dialects of Eastern Europe).

21st-century Yiddish has kept up with the developments of society, and speakers have coined new words for modern concepts and inventions. Today, one meets words such as בליצפּאָסט *blitspost* 'email', צעלקע *tselke* 'mobile phone, cell phone', מיקראָכוואַלניק *mikrokhvalnik* 'microwave', איבערניץ *ibernits* 'recycling', and the recently coined term הערקלערן *herklern* 'to mansplain', which is based on the word דערקלערן *derklern* 'to explain' combined with the word הער *her* 'gentleman, mister'. A fun new Yiddish word is שטרודל *shtrudl*, which is used (as it is also in Modern Hebrew) to refer to the symbol @ that appears in email addresses, because the shape of the symbol looks like a slice of strudel pastry.

There is also a significant online Yiddish presence, including פֿאָרווערטס *Forverts*, a New York-based Yiddish newspaper (published in print form from 1897 to 2019) and an associated YouTube channel that produces Yiddish-language programmes on cooking, travel, and more. וויבערטײטש *Vaybertaytsh* is a Yiddish-language feminist podcast, and the popular language-learning app Duolingo has a Yiddish programme in development. There are even two heavy metal bands, the Sweden-based Dibbukim and the Israel-based Gevolt, that sing traditional Yiddish folk and theatre songs in a metal style!

References and further study

Weinreich (2007a, 2007b), D. Katz (2011), and Kahn (2017c) provide overviews of Yiddish language and literature. D. Katz (1987) and N. Jacobs (2005) are reference grammars of Yiddish. Lansky (2004) offers a very accessible popular account of Yiddish studies in the 20th century. Howe, Wisse, and Shmeruk (1987) is a bilingual anthology of Yiddish poetry. Greenbaum (2010) contains a discussion of the Yiddish press, Steinlauf (2010) is an overview of Yiddish theatre, and Hoberman (2010) is a history of the Yiddish film industry.

41 Yiddish, Modern Hasidic

Many people today think of Yiddish as a dying language, spoken only by Ashkenazi Jews who were born before World War II. It is widely believed that the language was not really passed on to younger generations and that in the 21st century it is spoken only by very elderly people. In fact, while this is generally true outside of the ultra-Orthodox (also known as Haredi) Jewish world, within ultra-Orthodox society Yiddish is actually alive and well, with more than half a million fluent speakers worldwide, including many young adults and children.

Most ultra-Orthodox Yiddish speakers belong to one of the various Hasidic groups that have flourished since the emergence of that Jewish spiritual movement in late 18th-century Ukraine (see HUNGARIAN). Over the course of the 19th and early 20th centuries, these groups spread throughout much of Jewish Eastern Europe, acquiring large numbers of followers, most of whom were Yiddish speaking. Hasidic dynasties were established in various locations in Poland, Hungary, Romania, Ukraine, and elsewhere in Eastern Europe. The dynasties were led by a *rebbe*, a charismatic spiritual leader whose followers would come to his court to listen to his wisdom and seek his advice. The dynasties were typically named for the places in which they were based, such as Belz (a town in present-day Ukraine), Satmar (now Satu Mare, Romania), and Ger (now Góra Kalwaria, Poland).

The Holocaust had a cataclysmic effect on the Hasidic world, with entire communities destroyed and others severely damaged. After the Holocaust, many surviving *rebbes* and the remnants of their followers managed to rebuild their lost communities outside of their traditional Eastern European homelands. Many Hasidic groups settled in Israel (particularly in Jerusalem and Bnei Brak, near Tel Aviv), while other large centres emerged in North America (particularly New York and Montreal), in the United Kingdom (London and Manchester), and in Belgium (Antwerp). In contrast to the non-Hasidic immigrant Jewish communities that abandoned Yiddish in favour of Modern Hebrew, English, and other languages, these newly established Hasidic communities generally continued speaking Yiddish. They were also joined by new members, including some who were Yiddish-speaking themselves and others who learned Yiddish in order to integrate into Hasidic society. Thus, while in the non-Hasidic Jewish world, Yiddish underwent a process of severe decline in the 1950s, 1960s, and 1970s, Yiddish continued to thrive and grow in Hasidic communities.

In the 21st century, Yiddish remains the first language of many Hasidic communities around the world. Not only is it the language of thousands of homes, but it is also the language of instruction in many Hasidic schools and yeshivas. Hasidic Yiddish has, in fact, become the most widely spoken type of Yiddish today. Because the Yiddish spoken by Hasidic Jews has evolved largely in isolation from so-called "secular" Yiddish over the past 80 years, and because it has no connection to the standard, academic variety of Yiddish that emerged in the 1920s and 1930s (see YIDDISH, MODERN STANDARD), it has developed some fascinating features that distinguish it from other varieties of the language.

One striking example of the linguistic development of Hasidic Yiddish is the complete loss of grammatical gender. Most prewar dialects of Yiddish, including the standard literary variety (see YIDDISH, MODERN STANDARD), resembled German and several other European languages such as Latin, Greek, and Russian, in that they had a system of grammatical gender for nouns, with three different categories called 'masculine', 'feminine', and 'neuter'. (Readers may be more familiar with Romance languages such as Spanish and French, which have only two grammatical genders—for example, Spanish *el camino* 'the road', a masculine word, vs. *la casa* 'the house', a feminine word.) The exception was Lithuanian Yiddish, which distinguished only two grammatical genders: masculine and feminine. This system of three grammatical genders—or two in Lithuania—was true of the prewar Yiddish used by both Hasidic and non-Hasidic speakers. One consequence of having these different genders was that the form of the definite article (i.e., the word for 'the') varied depending on whether the noun in question was masculine, feminine, or neuter. If a noun was preceded by an adjective, that would get a different ending too, depending on the gender of the noun. For example, the Yiddish word מאַן *man* 'man' is masculine, so the Yiddish phrase 'the good man' would be דער גוטער מאַן *der guter man*, whereas 'the good woman' would be די גוטע פֿרוי *di gute froy*, and 'the good book' (a neuter noun) would be דאָס גוטע בוך *dos gute bukh*. Gender distinction survives in the standard variety of Yiddish (see YIDDISH, MODERN STANDARD), as well as in the speech of some non-Hasidic ultra-Orthodox Jews and that of the relatively small number of remaining speakers of the traditional Eastern European Yiddish dialects outside of the ultra-Orthodox world.

Contemporary Hasidic Yiddish differs dramatically from this historical and standardized model because it has completely lost grammatical gender. In this sense, it is like English, in which there is only one form of the word for 'the'. Instead of the three forms דער *der*, די *di*, and דאָס *dos*, Hasidic Yiddish has developed a new, invariable definite article, דע *de*, which is used with all nouns regardless of their gender in earlier forms of the language. Moreover, adjectives appearing before a noun all end in ע- *-e*, rather than changing their shape depending on the gender of the noun. So, for example, in contemporary spoken Hasidic Yiddish one hears דע גוטע מאַן *de gute man* 'the good man', דע גוטע פֿרוי *de gute froy* 'the good woman', and דע גוטע בוך *de gute bukh* 'the good book', with גוטע דע *de gute* in each case. Because Hasidic Yiddish, like other forms of the language, has a long written tradition, speakers often still employ the older forms of the definite article, דער *der*, די *di*, and דאָס *dos* in writing, rather than using the new form דע *de*; however, they generally use the older forms indiscriminately (and, from the point of view of previous generations of Yiddish speakers, incorrectly!), because they no longer know the historical gender associated with each noun.

Throughout the history of Yiddish, speakers have borrowed words from surrounding languages. This is why Yiddish has a significant number of loanwords from Slavic languages such as Polish and Ukrainian (see YIDDISH, MODERN STANDARD). Today, many speakers of Hasidic Yiddish are bilingual in the majority language of the country in which they live, usually English or Modern Hebrew, and Hasidic Yiddish has borrowed a lot of vocabulary from these dominant languages. Perhaps surprisingly, Hasidic Yiddish has borrowed many more foreign words than the Yiddish used by non-Hasidic speakers. For example, while in prewar and modern Standard Yiddish, the word for 'window' is פֿענצטער *fentster*, many Hasidic Yiddish speakers in the United States instead say ווינדע *vinde*, from English 'window'. Likewise, while the verb 'to walk' in prewar and modern Standard Yiddish is גיין *geyn*, Hasidic Yiddish speakers may say וואקען *voken*, from English 'walk'.

Over the past eighty years, differences have also crept into the meanings of Yiddish words as used by Hasidic speakers as compared to their meanings in the Yiddish used outside of the Haredi (ultra-Orthodox) world. For example, the word for 'thank you' in Standard Yiddish is אַ דאַנק *a dank* (a Germanic word etymologically related to the English word 'thank'); by contrast, Hasidic speakers usually say שכויח *shkoyekh* (a word derived from a Hebrew phrase meaning 'well done').

Yiddish is highly visible in the major Hasidic centres around the world. For example, one can see Yiddish signs and advertisements on buildings, and there are shops selling Yiddish books, newspapers, and games. There are also Hasidic libraries, where it is possible to read or borrow Yiddish books. As noted earlier, Yiddish is frequently the language of instruction in Hasidic schools, with many of the textbooks written in Yiddish. Yiddish is also used in many Hasidic workplaces as the main language of conversation, and Yiddish signs are visible on Jewish shops and notice boards. In Brooklyn, which has a particularly large Hasidic population, it is even possible to buy subway tickets from vending machines using Yiddish! There are also some towns in upstate New York, such as Kiryas Joel and Monsey, that are populated mostly by Yiddish-speaking Hasidic Jews, and in these towns, officially produced Yiddish signs for public services such as buses are a common feature of the landscape. There are also rest stops off the highway in upstate New York with signs in Yiddish.

There is a thriving Yiddish publishing industry within the Hasidic community. There are Hasidic newspapers and magazines from New York, London, and Israel that are written either entirely or partly in Yiddish, and a wide variety of Yiddish books are produced for children and adults. Books for younger children include illustrated tales of the lives of famous *rebbes* and episodes from Jewish history, as well as educational books teaching young readers how to conduct themselves ethically and put Jewish laws into practice in their everyday lives. For older children and adults, there are also novels of all kinds; one popular youth series, called 21 אונטער 1 דאך *21 unter eyn dakh* '21 under One Roof', relates the everyday adventures of a Yiddish-speaking Haredi family with twenty-one children living in Israel. In

The front cover of the second volume of the Yiddish children's book series אונטער 21
דאך 1 *21 unter 1 dakh* '21 Under 1 Roof', published in 2018.

one of the books, the family travels to London for a wedding and has all kinds of exciting encounters, such as a meeting with the Queen at Buckingham Palace. Other types of books include nonfiction works on Jewish history, the teachings of Hasidic *rebbes*, ethical writings, commentaries on classic Jewish texts, and discussions of Jewish law. There are even books unconnected to Judaism, ranging from cookbooks to manuals of handwriting analysis. Particularly widespread is popular fiction aimed at female readers. Such books are usually set in contemporary times, and the plots deal with intrigue, espionage, crime, and other dramatic topics, but they are populated by Haredi characters and contain ethical messages approved by rabbinical authorities. The great popularity of these novels—which are widely sold in Haredi bookshops in Israel, New York, London, and Antwerp and are commonly available in libraries serving a Haredi clientele—highlights the vibrancy of Yiddish as a literary language in the contemporary Hasidic world. This large body of modern Hasidic Yiddish writing has very different literary norms from those of non-Hasidic Yiddish, not only in grammar and vocabulary (as described earlier), but even sometimes in basic spelling.

While Hasidic communities typically avoid radio and television, there have been a few films made with Hasidic Yiddish-speaking actors. One such film, produced in the United States in 2005, is called געשעפט א *a gesheft* 'A Deal', which contains dialogue entirely in Yiddish. The film tells the story of a childhood rivalry between two Hasidic boys, which develops into a decades-long feud featuring dramatic scheming, tragic consequences, and ultimately a happy ending. In 2017, another film entirely in Yiddish and featuring Hasidic actors was produced in the United States. The film, called מנשה *menashe* 'Menashe', was shot in Brooklyn and is loosely based on a true story of a Hasidic man who fought for the right to raise his son alone after the death of his wife.

In sum, Hasidic Yiddish is a thriving modern language, used by many hundreds of thousands of speakers worldwide, and with its own media and literature. While Standard Yiddish remains the subject of courses and textbooks in universities and summer schools, Hasidic Yiddish is the variety that is the most widely spoken and that is the most likely to survive into the future.

References and further study

Biale et al. (2018) is a comprehensive survey of Hasidic history and culture, and Wodziński (2018) is a historical atlas of Hasidism. See Belk, Kahn, and Szendrői (2020) for a detailed discussion of the absence of grammatical gender in contemporary London Hasidic Yiddish. Assouline (2017) is a sociolinguistic study of Yiddish as used by ultra-Orthodox speakers in Israel. Sadock and Masor (2018) is an overview of the Yiddish of the Bobov Hasidic community in New York, and Krogh (2018) discusses various aspects of the language of the Satmar Hasidic community in New York.

42 Zulu (Fanagalo)

The Bantu language family contains about 500 distinct languages (perhaps more, depending on how one distinguishes dialects from languages), which are spread out across the entire southern half of the African continent. In total there are probably more than 300 million Africans—about 25% of the total African population—who speak one or more Bantu languages. The most widely known and widely used Bantu language is Swahili, which is spoken as a first or second language by around ninety million people in East Africa, mainly in Tanzania, Kenya, and Uganda.

The second most widely spoken Bantu language is Zulu. Though just one of eleven official languages in South Africa, Zulu is actually the language most widely spoken in South African homes, with roughly twelve to thirteen million speakers, or around 22% of the population. It is used as a second language by another fifteen million or so people, which means that is it spoken and understood by about 50% of all South Africans. Zulu has a very unusual system of sounds, in that it makes use of three "click" consonants. Clicks are extremely rare among the languages of the world, and in fact are found almost exclusively among the languages of southern Africa. The clicks, along with a rather complex grammatical system, can make Zulu quite challenging to learn for outsiders.

Zulu also serves as the base for a pidgin language called Fanagalo. A pidgin is a language that develops from extended contact between two or more groups of people that do not share a common language. By definition, a pidgin is no one's native language (unlike a creole; see PAPIAMENTU), and it is typically used only in limited environments, like at work or when two parties meet to conduct some sort of business; in fact, most scholars believe that the term *pidgin* comes from the pronunciation of the word *business* in Chinese Pidgin English (a pidgin used from the 17th to 19th centuries between English and local Chinese traders in China). Pidgins are normally based on a single language—either the language of the local majority or the language of a colonial or trading power—combined with elements from the other native languages of those who use the pidgin. Pidgins are by nature simplified languages, with vastly reduced grammatical structures and a limited lexicon as compared with the source language.

Fanagalo developed in the 19th century, when large numbers of British and Afrikaner (Boer) settlers—including Jews—migrated to the region that became the British Colony of Natal (founded in 1843) and today comprises the South African province of KwaZulu-Natal (established in 1994). Beginning in 1860, the British imported large numbers of indentured labourers from India to Natal to work on plantations, and many of these Indians eventually became landowners and merchants themselves. Zulu was the language of the majority of the black population, but it is just one of many languages in the region. Fanagalo—a pidginized version of Zulu, with some lexical elements taken from English, Afrikaans, and other sources—developed as a means of communication between black labourers and their white or Indian employers, on farms, in the home, and in other work environments. When the South African mining industry (especially diamond and gold mining) exploded in the late 19th century, Fanagalo became the common language of the mine workers, who came from a variety of linguistic backgrounds. The language even spread to mines outside of South Africa, in countries like Zambia and Zimbabwe. At one point there were millions of people who made use of Fanagalo at work—especially in the mining industry—and today the number of speakers is probably still at least 200,000. Fanagalo has always remained a pidgin, meaning that it has never developed into a language with native speakers; those who use it in the present day still do so only in certain restricted circumstances, particularly in the mining industry.

In the 20th century, a number of textbooks and phrasebooks of Fanagalo were published in South Africa. Some were intended specifically for use by those employed by mining companies, while others were aimed at employers of domestic servants. In these various books and in other early publications, Fanagalo is also sometimes called Fanakalo, Basic Bantu, or Kitchen Kaffir. In the 19th century and into the first few decades of the 20th century, the term *kaffir* was used in a way comparable to how English *negro* was used in that same era, and it did not necessarily have a derogatory sense. However, since the adoption of Apartheid in 1948, the term has had a clear pejorative sense, and it was long used as a racial slur in South Africa. Now it is legally considered hate speech to direct the word *kaffir* at someone; in 2016, a white South African woman was actually jailed for using the word against several black police officers. It is so offensive today that one often hears it referred to in South Africa as "the K-word", just as in other English-speaking countries people prefer to say "the N-word" rather than utter the offensive slur that it refers to.

One Fanagalo dictionary from 1947 (mistitled *Conversational Zulu for the Home*) contains only about 1500 words, but includes the word 'Jew'. A textbook from about the same period (called *Basic Bantu*) includes 'Jew' (but not 'Christian' or 'Muslim') in a rather short list of geographic and ethnic adjectives that is clearly limited to words one might need in South Africa. These books attest to the fact that there was a sizeable Jewish population in the region at the time. In fact, a Jewish presence in South Africa goes back to the beginning of the 19th century, though the overall Jewish population remained very small until the 1880s, when Eastern European Jews began to immigrate in significant numbers. By the turn of the 20th century, the total number of Jews in South Africa was about 38,000. The number peaked at about 118,000 in the 1970s and 1980s, but by the year 2001, it had decreased to about 70,000, some 48,000 of whom lived in Johannesburg. The great majority of Jews settled in Johannesburg and Cape Town—the two largest South African cities, both far from the Natal region—but a significant number settled in Durban, the third largest city in South Africa, and the largest city of today's KwaZulu-Natal province. The Jewish population of Durban was around 1250 by 1905, and 6050 in 1969, but down to only 2750 in 2004.

In fact, there has been an influential Jewish presence in Durban almost since its founding in 1824. The British Jew Nathaniel Isaacs (1808–1872) was one of the first European settlers in the city, arriving in 1825, though he lived only six years or so in Natal before returning to England. Isaacs even spent some time among the Zulus in the 1820s, during which he associated with the famous Zulu king Shaka, and he subsequently published a very valuable account of his travels (1836). (In one passage, he tells how he prescribed the making of chicken soup for a sick Zulu man; the patient later died.) Another British Jew, Daniel De Pass (1839–1921), was one of the pioneers of the sugar industry in Natal, and sugar remains the major industry of the modern province of KwaZulu-Natal. Jonas Bergtheil (1819–1902), a Bavarian-born Jew, was a member of the first legislative assembly of Natal, at a time when Jews were not yet allowed to serve in Parliament in England. Matthew Nathan (1862–1939), a member of a prominent British Jewish family, was governor of the Natal Colony from 1907 to 1909. When he was appointed governor of the Gold Coast (present-day Ghana) in 1900, he became the first Jewish governor of a British colony.

Some Jews living in Natal did learn Zulu, but many more learned the much simpler Fanagalo, in order to communicate with their black employees, whether they be domestic servants or industrial labourers. It was precisely with this need in mind that an anonymous author published a short Yiddish–Fanagalo dictionary, printed in London around 1904, under the title די קאפֿירישע שפּראכע פֿון די שווֹארצע מענשען אין אפֿריקא *di kafirshe shprakhe fun di shvartse mentshen in afrike* 'The *Kaffir* Language of the Black People in Africa'. (At the time, the term *kaffir* would not have been considered offensive.) It contains a little more than 200 Yiddish words, each with a Fanagalo translation written in both Hebrew letters and English letters. A short introduction in Yiddish by the author explains that the dictionary is intended to be used by Jewish employers with their black employees. After this, but before the alphabetical dictionary, the author instructs the reader as follows (in Yiddish):

ווען דער קאָפֿיר וועט וועלין קויפֿען, וועט ער פֿרעגען: באַס, אַס, פֿינאַ, טענגאַ. (מיין הער, איך ברויך קויפֿען)

פֿרעגט איהם דער וויסער: אוטענגאַני? (וואָס ווילסטו קויפֿען?)

וועט אייך דער שוואָרצער ענטפֿערען: אומפּאַשלאַ (סחורה), אָדער ער וועט אָן רופֿען דיא סחורה, וועלכע ער ברויכט.

ven der kafir vet veln koyfn, vet er fregn: bas, as, fina, tenga (mayn her, ikh broykh koyfn)

fregt im der vayser: utengani? (vos vilstu koyfn?)

vet aykh der shvartser entfern: umpashla (skhoyre), oder er vet on rufn di skhoyre velkhe er broykht.

'When the *kaffir* wants to buy something, he will ask: *bas, as, fina, tenga* (sir, I need to buy)

The white person asks him: *utengani*? (What do you want to buy?)

The black person will answer you: *umpashla* (goods), or he will name the goods that he needs.'

In general, the author's knowledge of Fanagalo seems to be rather poor, or at least his attempts at transcription are not very good. For example, the numbers one through five are given in the dictionary as מינגע (*minne*), מאבילע (*mabile*), מאטאטי

אײנצינע ווערטער.

א.

קאפיר׳ש.	קאפיר׳ש	אידיש
Kaeena	קאעענא	איהרע
Ingubn	איננובו	א דעקע
Maduku	מאדוקו	א טיכעל
Mgodla	מגאדלא	א זאק .
Minuaj	מינואי	א שוועסטער
Induna	אינדונא	א קאפיטאן
Coss	קאסס.	א קייזער
Madala	מאדאלא	אלטע
Kopela	קאפעלא	אליין, זעלבסט
Maphana	מאפאנא	איננעל
Massawensa	מאסאוועננא	ארבייטען
Sawensa	סאוועננא	ארבייט
Makanda	מאקאנרא	אייער
Imbisa	אימביזא	א מאס
Sislalu	וישלאלו	א שמול
Taphula	טאפולא	א טיש
Mlungu	מלונגו	א וויסער מענש
Inkomu	אינקאמו	אקס
Mahatschie	מאהאטששי	א פערד
Umphula	אומפולא	א טינד
Imphu	אימפו	א שעפס

A page from the Yiddish–Fanagalo glossary, with the Fanagalo in both Hebrew and English characters (London, ca. 1904).

(*matati*), מאַני (*mani*), and זאָסלאַני (*zaslani*). In fact, the correct Fanagalo forms are *munye*, *mabile* (or *mabili*), *matatu*, *mane*, and *hlanu* (or *mahlanu*). And the phrase *as fina tenga* 'I need to buy' seems to be a bit garbled. The intended form was probably *sifuna tenga*, which actually means 'we need to buy'. ('I need to buy' is either *ngifuna tenga* or *mina funa tenga*.)

One of the more interesting aspects of the Yiddish–Fanagalo dictionary is how the author transcribed the more unusual sounds of Zulu and Fanagalo. One such sound is written in both Zulu and Fanagalo as *hl*. This sound is called a voiceless lateral fricative, and is pronounced like an *l*, but without any vibration of the vocal cords. The sound exists in many languages, including Welsh (spelled *ll*), and actually, it was the way that the Hebrew letter שׂ *sin* was pronounced in early biblical times. (By the end of the first millennium BCE, Hebrew שׂ *sin* was pronounced the same as Hebrew ס *samekh*; we know this because contemporary writers sometimes confused the two in spelling.) In the Yiddish–Fanagalo dictionary, the author transcribed this sound either with סל *sl* (as in זאָסלאַני *zaslani* 'five', for Fanagalo *hlanu*) or with של *shl* (as in the word אומפאַאַשלאַ *umpashla* 'goods', for Fanagalo *mpahla*). And, of course, there are the famous click sounds, although these are relatively rare in Fanagalo. One Fanagalo word with a click is *mncane* 'young'. The letter *c* in Zulu and Fanagalo orthography represents a dental click, a sound that in English we use as an indication of disapproval (written *tsk! tsk!* or *tut-tut!*). In our dictionary, the word for 'young' is given as מוטשאַנאַ *mutshana*, with the click sound represented by the Hebrew/Yiddish letters טש *t* + *sh*.

This dictionary is probably the only example of Fanagalo or any other Bantu language written in Hebrew script. It is thus a unique volume, even if the text itself is largely uninteresting. It is also a rather unpleasant reminder of the status of the black population of South Africa for much of modern history. On the other hand, it is yet another reminder of how Jews used the alphabet with which they were most familiar in order to write down the local language, no matter how far removed from Hebrew.

References and further study

Saron and Hotz (1955) and Mendelsohn and Shain (2008) are general histories of South African Jewry. Isaacs (1836) is Nathaniel Isaacs' account of his time among the Zulus. An accessible overview of Fanagalo is Mesthrie and Surek-Clark (2013); information on other pidgins can be found in that same volume and the other volumes in the series.

Bibliography

Abegg, Martin Jr., Peter Flint, and Eugene Ulrich. 1999. *The Dead Sea Scrolls Bible: The Oldest Known Bible Translated for the First Time into English*. San Francisco: Harper Collins.

Aḥituv, Shmuel. 2008. *Echoes from the Past: Hebrew and Cognate Inscriptions from the Biblical Period*. Jerusalem: Carta.

Aitken, James K., and James Carleton Paget, eds. 2014. *The Jewish-Greek Tradition in Antiquity and the Byzantine Empire*. Cambridge: Cambridge University Press.

Althaus, Hans-Peter. 2014. *Zocker, Zoff & Zores: Jiddische Wörter im Deutschen*, 4th edn. Munich: C.H. Beck.

———. 2015. *Chuzpe, Schmus & Tacheles: Jiddische Wortgeschichten*, 3rd edn. Munich: C.H. Beck.

———. 2019. *Kleines Lexikon deutscher Wörter jiddischer Herkunft*, 4th edn. Munich: C.H. Beck.

Anbessa Teferra. 2017. Jewish Amharic. In *Handbook of Jewish Languages*, revised and updated edn., ed. Lily Kahn and Aaron D. Rubin, pp. 8–21. Leiden: Brill.

———. 2018. Hebraized Amharic in Israel. In *Languages in Jewish Communities, Past and Present*, ed. Sarah Bunin Benor and Benjamin Hary, pp. 489–519. Berlin: De Gruyter Mouton.

Aprile, Marcello. 2012. *Grammatica storica delle parlate giudeo-italiane*. Galatina, Italy: Congedo.

Arad, Dotan. 2017. "Let's Learn Turkish": A Turkish-Arabic Glossary from the Cairo Genizah. *Turcica* 48:451–73.

Arbell, Mordechai. 2002. *The Jewish Nation of the Caribbean: The Spanish-Portuguese Jewish Settlements in the Caribbean and the Guianas*. Jerusalem and New York: Gefen.

Assouline, Dalit. 2017. *Contact and Ideology in a Multilingual Community: Yiddish and Hebrew Among the Ultra-Orthodox*. Berlin: Mouton De Gruyter.

Authier, Gilles. 2012. *Grammaire juhuri, ou judéo-tat, langue iranienne des Juifs du Caucase de l'est*. Wiesbaden: Ludwig Reichert.

Banitt, Menahem, ed. 1972. *Le Glossaire de Bâle*, 2 vols. Jerusalem: Israel Academy of Sciences and Humanities.

———. 1995–2005. *Le Glossaire de Leipzig*. Jerusalem: Israel Academy of Sciences and Humanities.

Bar-Moshe, Assaf. 2019. *The Arabic Dialect of the Jews of Baghdad: Phonology, Morphology, and Texts*. Wiesbaden: Harrassowitz.

Baum, Ilil. 2016. Hebrew-Catalan Medieval Wedding Songs: Satirical Function of the Hebrew Component and Other Linguistic Aspects. *Journal of Jewish Languages* 166–202.

———. 2019. Jofre (Jaufre): The Circulation of Arthurian Romances among Late Medieval Catalan Jews. *Journal of Medieval Iberian Studies* 11:222–49.

Baumgarten, Jean. 2005. *Introduction to Old Yiddish Literature*. Ed. and trans. Jerold C. Frakes. Oxford: Oxford University Press.

Beit-Arié, Malachi. 1985. *The Only Dated Medieval Manuscript Written in England (1189 CE)*. London: Valmadonna Trust Library. Partially reprinted in Malachi Beit-Arié, *The Makings of the Medieval Hebrew Book*, pp. 129–41. Jerusalem: Magnes, 1993.

Belk, Zoë, Lily Kahn, and Kriszta Eszter Szendrői. 2020. Complete Loss of Case and Gender within Two Generations: Evidence from Stamford Hill Hasidic Yiddish. *Journal of Comparative Germanic Linguistics* 23.

Benbassa, Esther. 1999. *The Jews of France: A History from Antiquity to the Present*. Trans. M.B. DeBevoise. Princeton: Princeton University Press.

Benor, Sarah Bunin. 2018. Jewish English in the United States. In *Languages in Jewish Communities, Past and Present*, ed. Sarah Bunin Benor and Benjamin Hary, pp. 414–30. Berlin: De Gruyter Mouton.

Benor, Sarah Bunin, and Benjamin Hary. 2018. *Languages in Jewish Communities, Past and Present*. Berlin: De Gruyter Mouton.

Ben-Rafael, Miriam, and Eliezer Ben-Rafael. 2018. Jewish French in Israel. In *Languages in Jewish Communities, Past and Present*, ed. Sarah Bunin Benor and Benjamin Hary, pp. 544–68. Berlin: De Gruyter Mouton.

Berger, David. 1979. *The Jewish-Christian Debate in the High Middle Ages: A Critical Edition of the Niẓẓaḥon Vetus with an Introduction, Translation, and Commentary*. Philadelphia: Jewish Publication Society.

Bhayro, Siam. 2017. Judeo-Syriac. In *Handbook of Jewish Languages*, revised and updated edn., ed. Lily Kahn and Aaron D. Rubin, pp. 631–34. Leiden: Brill.

Biale, David, et al. 2018. *Hasidism: A New History*. Princeton: Princeton University Press.

Bieder, Joan. 2007. *The Jews of Singapore*. Singapore: Suntree Media.

Bláha, Ondřej, et al., eds. 2015. *Kenaanské glosy ve středověkých hebrejských rukopisech s vazbou na české země* [Knaanic Glosses in Hebrew Manuscripts with Links to Czech Territory]. Prague: Academia.

Blanc, Haim. 1964. *Communal Dialects in Baghdad*. Cambridge, MA: Harvard University Press.

Blondheim, David S. 1929. An Old Portuguese Work on Manuscript Illumination. *Jewish Quarterly Review* 19:97–135.

Boulton, Marjorie. 1960. *Zamenhof: Creator of Esperanto*. London: Routledge and Kegan Paul.

Bons, Eberhard, and Jan Joosten, eds. 2016. *Die Sprache der Septuaginta/The Language of the Septuagint*. Gütersloh: Gütersloher.

Borjian, Habib. 2017. Judeo-Iranian Languages. In *Handbook of Jewish Languages*, revised and updated edn., ed. Lily Kahn and Aaron D. Rubin, pp. 234–97. Leiden: Brill.

Borovaya, Olga. 2012. *Modern Ladino Culture: Press, Belles Lettres, and Theatre in the Late Ottoman Empire*. Bloomington: Indiana University Press.

Bos, Gerrit, and Guido Mensching. 2005. The Literature of Hebrew Medical Synonyms: Romance and Latin Terms and Their Identification. *Aleph* 5:169–211.

Breitstein, Solomon Zalman. 1914. שיחות חיים [Talks of Life]. Piotrkow.

Breuer, Edward, trans. 2018. *Moses Mendelssohn's Hebrew Writings*. New Haven: Yale University Press.

Bunis, David M. 2017. Judezmo (Ladino). In *Handbook of Jewish Languages*, revised and updated edn., ed. Lily Kahn and Aaron D. Rubin, pp. 366–451. Leiden: Brill.

————. 2018. Judezmo (Ladino/Judeo-Spanish): A Historical and Sociolinguistic Portrait. In *Languages in Jewish Communities, Past and Present*, ed. Sarah Bunin Benor and Benjamin Hary, pp. 185–238. Berlin: De Gruyter Mouton.

Burton, Audrey. 1994–96. Bukharan Jews, Ancient and Modern. *Jewish Historical Studies* 34:43–68.

Carmi, T. 2006. *The Penguin Book of Hebrew Verse*. London: Penguin.

Cassuto, Umberto. 1929. Un'antichissima Elegia in Dialetto Giudeo-Italiano. *Archivio Glottologico Italiano* 22–23:349–403.

Centassi, René, and Henri Masson. 2001. *L'homme qui a défié Babel*. Paris: L'Harmattan.

Chazan, Robert. 1973. *Medieval Jewry in Northern France: A Political and Social History*. Baltimore: The Johns Hopkins University Press.

Chetrit, Joseph. 2017. Jewish Berber. In *Handbook of Jewish Languages*, revised and updated edn., ed. Lily Kahn and Aaron D. Rubin, pp. 118–29. Leiden: Brill.

————. 2018. Judeo-Berber in Morocco. In *Languages in Jewish Communities, Past and Present*, ed. Benjamin Hary and Sarah Bunin Benor, pp. 70–93. Berlin: De Gruyter Mouton.

Clackson, James. 2008. An Armenian/Judaeo-Arabic Word-List in Cambridge. In *Between Paris and Fresno: Armenian Studies in Honor of Dickran Kouymijian*, ed. Barlow Der Mugrdechian, pp. 241–46. Costa Mesa, CA: Mazda.

Cohen, David. 1964–75. *Le parler arabe des juifs de Tunis*, 2 vols. The Hague: Mouton.

Cohen, Marcel. 1912. *Le parler arabe des Juifs d'Alger*. Paris: H. Champion.

Cole, Peter. 2007. *The Dream of the Poem: Hebrew Poetry from Muslim and Christian Spain 950–1492*. Princeton: Princeton University Press.

Dalven, Rachel. 1990. *The Jews of Ioannina*. Philadelphia: Cadmus.

Daniels, Peter T. 2018. Uses of Hebrew Script in Jewish Language Varieties. In *Languages in Jewish Communities, Past and Present*, ed. Benjamin Hary and Sarah Bunin Benor, pp. 602–26. Berlin: De Gruyter Mouton.

Darmesteter, Arsène. 1909. *Les gloses françaises de Raschi dans la Bible. Accompagnées de notes par Louis Brandin, et précédées d'une introduction par Julien Weill*. Paris: Durlacher.

Dean-Olmsted, Evelyn, and Susana Skura. 2017. Jewish Latin American Spanish. In *Handbook of Jewish Languages*, revised and updated edn., ed. Lily Kahn and Aaron D. Rubin, pp. 490–503. Leiden: Brill.

Debenedetti Stow, Sandra. 1980. Due poesie bilingui inedite contro le donne di Šemu'èl da Castiglione (1553). *Italia* 2:7–64.

————. 1983. Ḥarara, pizza nel XIV secolo. *Archivio glottologico italiano* 68:80–81.

Díaz Mas, Paloma. 1992. *Sephardim: The Jews from Spain*. Trans. George K. Zucker. Chicago: University of Chicago Press.

Diner, Hasia R. 2004. *The Jews of the United States: 1654 to 2000*. Berkeley: University of California Press.

Elbaum, Jacob, and Chava Turniansky. 2010. *Tsene-rene. YIVO Encyclopedia of Jews in Eastern Europe*, online edn., ed. Jeffrey P. Edelstein et al. www.yivoencyclopedia.org.

Emmanuel, Isaac S., and Susan A. Emmanuel. 1970. *History of the Jews of the Netherlands Antilles*, 2 vols. Cincinnati: American Jewish Archives.

Endelmann, Todd M. 2002. *The Jews of Britain: 1656 to 2000*. Berkeley: University of California Press.

Enoch, Reuven. 2008. בראשית :א .לתורה גרוזיה יהודי של המסורתי התרגום :תבסילי] *Tavsili*: The Traditional Oral Translation of the Bible in Judeo-Georgian: A Critical Edition of Genesis]. Jerusalem: Magnes.

―――. 2009. עיונים בתבסילי לספר בראשית [The Study of *Tavsili* According to the Book of Genesis]. Jerusalem: Magnes.

―――. 2014. התרגום המסורתי של יהודי גרוזיה להגדה של פסח [The Passover Haggadah in Jewish Georgian: A Critical Edition]. Jerusalem: Magnes.

―――. 2017. Jewish Georgian. In *Handbook of Jewish Languages*, revised and updated edn., ed. Lily Kahn and Aaron D. Rubin, pp. 178–93. Leiden: Brill.

Fassberg, Steven E. 2017. Judeo-Aramaic. In *Handbook of Jewish Languages*, revised and updated edn., ed. Lily Kahn and Aaron D. Rubin, pp. 64–117. Leiden: Brill.

Feliu, Eduard. 2006–07. Les traduccions hebrees del *Regiment de Sanitat* d'Arnau de Vilanova. *Tamid* [Societat Catalana d'Estudis Hebraics] 6:45–141.

Feliu, Francesc, and Joan Ferrer. 2011. Judaeo-Catalan: In Search of a Mediaeval Dialect That Never Was. Trans. John Francis Elwolde. *Journal of Medieval Iberian Studies* 3:41–60.

Firkavičiūtė, Karina, and Halina Kobeckaitė, trans. 2018. *Kiči Bijčiek* [The Little Prince], by Antoine de Saint-Exupéry. Neckarsteinach, Germany: Tintenfaß.

Flesher, Paul V.M., and Bruce Chilton. 2011. *The Targums: A Critical Introduction*. Waco: Baylor University Press.

Fontaine, Resianne, and Gad Freudenthal. 2013. *Latin-into-Hebrew: Texts and Studies*, 2 vols. Leiden: Brill.

Fortis, Umberto. 2006. *La parlata degli ebrei di Venezia e le parlate giudeo-italiane*. Florence: Giuntina.

Fox, Margalit. 2007. *Talking Hands: What Sign Language Reveals about the Mind*. New York: Simon and Schuster.

Frakes, Jerold C. 2004. *Early Yiddish Texts 1100–1750*. Oxford: Oxford University Press.

―――, ed. and trans. 2014. *Early Yiddish Epic*. Syracuse: Syracuse University Press.

―――. 2017. *A Guide to Old Literary Yiddish*. Oxford: Oxford University Press.

Friedlaender, Israel. 1908. Ein Autograph des Maimonides. *Monatschrift für Geschichte und Wissenschaft des Judentums* 52:621–25.

Fudeman, Kirsten A. 2006. The Old French Glosses in Joseph Kara's Isaiah Commentary. *Revue des études juives* 165:147–77.

―――. 2008. Restoring a Vernacular Jewish Voice: The Old French Elegy of Troyes. *Jewish Studies Quarterly* 15:190–221.

―――. 2010. *Vernacular Voices: Language and Identity in Medieval Northern France*. Philadelphia: University of Pennsylvania Press.

Gamliel, Ophira. 2009. *Jewish Malayalam Women's Songs*. Unpublished Ph.D. dissertation, The Hebrew University of Jerusalem.

―――. 2013. Voices Yet to Be Heard: On Listening to the Last Speakers of Jewish Malayalam. *Journal of Jewish Languages* 1:135–67.

―――. 2017. Jewish Malayalam. In *Handbook of Jewish Languages*, revised and updated edn., ed. Lily Kahn and Aaron D. Rubin, pp. 504–17. Leiden: Brill.

Garr, W. Randall, and Steven E. Fassberg. 2016. *A Handbook of Biblical Hebrew*, 2 vols. Winona Lake, IN: Eisenbrauns.

Gitelman, Zvi. 2001. *A Century of Ambivalence: The Jews of Russia and the Soviet Union, 1881 to the Present*, 2nd edn. Bloomington: Indiana University Press.

Glickman, Mark. 2011. *Sacred Treasure—The Cairo Genizah: The Amazing Discoveries of Forgotten Jewish History in an Egyptian Synagogue Attic*. Woodstock, VT: Jewish Lights.

Golb, Norman. 1998. *The Jews in Medieval Normandy: A Social and Intellectual History*. Cambridge: Cambridge University Press.

Goldberg, Jacob. 1985. *Jewish Privileges in the Polish Commonwealth: Charters of Rights Granted to Jewish Communities in Poland-Lithuania in the Sixteenth to Eighteenth Centuries—Critical Edition of Original Latin and Polish Documents with English Introductions and Notes*. Jerusalem: Israel Academy of Sciences and Humanities.

Goldstein, Jonathan, ed. 1999. *The Jews of China*, 2 vols. Armonk, NY: M.E. Sharpe.

———. 2015. *Jewish Identities in East and Southeast Asia*. Berlin: De Gruyter.

Greenbaum, Avraham. 2010. Newspapers and Periodicals. In *YIVO Encyclopedia of the Jews in Eastern Europe*, online edn., ed. Jeffrey P. Edelstein et al. www.yivoencyclopedia.org.

Grelot, Pierre. 1992. *What Are the Targums: Selected Texts*. Trans. Salvator Attanasio. Collegeville, MN: The Liturgical Press.

Gruber, Mayer, ed. 2004. *Rashi's Commentary on Psalms*. Leiden: Brill.

Gumowski, Marian. 1975. *Hebräische Münzen im mittelalterlichen Polen*. Graz: Akademische Druck- u. Verlagsanstalt.

Guttel, Henri, and Cyril Aslanov. 2007. Judeo-Provençal. In *Encyclopaedia Judaica*, 2nd edn., ed. Michael Berenbaum and Fred Skolnik, vol. 11, pp. 559–60. Detroit: Macmillan Reference USA.

Ha-Elion, Moshe, and Avner Perez, trans. 2011–14. *Shay Le-Navon: La Odisea trezladada en ladino i ebreo del grego antiguo*, 2 vols. Ma'aleh Adumim: Yeriot.

Halper, B. 1921. *Post-Biblical Hebrew Literature: An Anthology*, 2 vols. Philadelphia: The Jewish Publication Society of America.

Harris, Tracy K. 1994. *Death of a Language*. Newark: University of Delaware Press.

Haverkamp, Alfred. 2018. Germany. In *The Cambridge History of Judaism. Volume VI: The Middle Ages: The Christian World*, ed. Robert Chazan, pp. 239–81. Cambridge: Cambridge University Press.

Heath, Jeffrey. 2002. *Jewish and Muslim Dialects of Moroccan Arabic*. London: Curzon.

Henriquez, May. 1988. *Ta asina o ta asana? Abla, uzu i kustember sefardí*. Curaçao: May Henriquez.

Hertz, Deborah. 2018. Judaism in Germany (1650–1815). In *The Cambridge History of Judaism. Volume VII: The Early Modern World, 1500–1815*, ed. Jonathan Karp and Adam Sutcliffe, pp. 737–62. Cambridge: Cambridge University Press.

Hill, Brad Sabin. 2017. Judeo-Slavic. In *Handbook of Jewish Languages*, revised and updated edn., ed. Lily Kahn and Aaron D. Rubin, pp. 600–18. Leiden: Brill.

Hoberman, J. 2010. *Bridge of Light: Yiddish Film between Two Worlds*, 2nd edn. Hanover, NH: Dartmouth College Press.

Hoestermann, Cordelia. 2013. German Influence on Hebrew. In *Encyclopedia of Hebrew Language and Linguistics*, ed. Geoffrey Khan et al., vol. 2, pp. 53–57. Leiden: Brill.

Hoffman, Adina, and Peter Cole. 2011. *Sacred Trash: The Lost and Found World of the Cairo Geniza*. New York: Schocken.

Howe, Irving, Ruth R. Wisse, and Khone Shmeruk. 1987. *The Penguin Book of Modern Yiddish Verse*. New York: Penguin.

Isaacs, Nathaniel. 1836. *Travels and Adventures in Eastern Africa*, 2 vols. London: Edward Churton.

Isenberg, Shirley Berry. 1988. *India's Bene Israel: A Comprehensive Inquiry and Sourcebook*. Berkeley: Judah L. Magnes Museum.

Jacobs, Bart. 2012. *Origins of a Creole: The History of Papiamentu and Its African Ties*. Berlin: De Gruyter Mouton.

Jacobs, Neil G. 2005. *Yiddish: A Linguistic Introduction*. Cambridge: Cambridge University Press.

Jankowski, Henryk. 2014. Two Karaim Religious Poems by Isaac ben Abraham Troki. *Karaite Archives* 2:35–57.

———. 2017. Karaim and Krymchak. In *Handbook of Jewish Languages*, revised and updated edn., ed. Lily Kahn and Aaron D. Rubin, pp. 452–89. Leiden: Brill.

Jobes, Karen H., and Moisés Silva. 2000. *Invitation to the Septuagint*. Grand Rapids, MI: Baker Academic.

Jochnowitz, George. 1978. Shuadit: La langue juive de Provence. *Archives juives* 14:63–67.

———. 1981. . . .Who Made Me a Woman. *Commentary* 71:63–64.

———. 2018. Judeo-Provençal in Southern France. In *Languages in Jewish Communities, Past and Present*, ed. Benjamin Hary and Sarah Bunin Benor, pp. 129–44. Berlin: De Gruyter Mouton.

Kahn, Lily. 2013. Maskilic Hebrew. In *The Encyclopedia of Hebrew Language and Linguistics*, ed. Geoffrey Khan et al., vol. 2, pp. 581–85. Boston: Brill.

———. 2017a. The Book of Ruth and Song of Songs in the First Hebrew Translation of *The Taming of the Shrew*. *Multicultural Shakespeare* 16:13–28.

———. 2017b. *The First Hebrew Shakespeare Translations: Isaac Edward Salkinson's Ithiel the Cushite of Venice and Ram and Jael, A Bilingual Edition and Commentary*. London: UCL Press.

———. 2017c. Yiddish. In *Handbook of Jewish Languages*, revised and updated edn., ed. Lily Kahn and Aaron D. Rubin, pp. 642–748. Leiden: Brill.

Kahn, Lily, and Aaron D. Rubin, eds. 2017. *Handbook of Jewish Languages*, revised and updated edn. Leiden: Brill.

Kahn, Lily, and Sonya Yampolskaya. Forthcoming. *A Reference Grammar of Enlightenment Hebrew*. Leiden: Brill.

Kaplan, Steven. 1992. *The Beta Israel (Falasha) in Ethiopia: From Earliest Times to the Twentieth Century*. New York: New York University Press.

Katz, Dovid. 1987. *Grammar of the Yiddish Language*. London: Duckworth.

———. 2011. Language: Yiddish. In *YIVO Encyclopedia of Jews in Eastern Europe*, online edn., ed. Jeffrey P. Edelstein et al. www.yivoencyclopedia.org.

Katz, Nathan. 2000. *Who Are the Jews of India?* Berkeley: University of California Press.

Khan, Geoffrey. 1990. *Karaite Bible Manuscripts from the Cairo Genizah*. Cambridge: Cambridge University Press.

———. 1999. *A Grammar of Neo-Aramaic: The Dialect of the Jews of Arbel*. Leiden: Brill.

———. 2004. *The Jewish Neo-Aramaic Dialect of Sulemaniyya and Ḥalabja*. Leiden: Brill.

———. 2008. *The Jewish Neo-Aramaic Dialect of Urmi*. Piscataway, NJ: Gorgias.

———. 2009. *The Jewish Neo-Aramaic Dialect of Sanandaj*. Piscataway, NJ: Gorgias.

———. 2011. North-Eastern Neo-Aramaic. In *The Semitic Languages: An International Handbook*, ed. Stefan Weninger et al., pp. 708–24. Berlin: De Gruyter Mouton.

———. 2017. Judeo-Arabic. In *Handbook of Jewish Languages*, revised and updated edn., ed. Lily Kahn and Aaron D. Rubin, pp. 22–63. Leiden: Brill.

———. 2018. Jewish Neo-Aramaic in Kurdistan and Iran. In *Languages in Jewish Communities, Past and Present*, ed. Sarah Bunin Benor and Benjamin Hary, pp. 9–34. Berlin: De Gruyter Mouton.

———. 2019a. The Neo-Aramaic Dialects of Eastern Anatolia and Northwestern Iran. In *The Languages and Linguistics of Western Asia: An Areal Perspective*, ed. Geoffrey Haig and Geoffrey Khan, pp. 190–236. Berlin: De Gruyter Mouton.

———. 2019b. The Neo-Aramaic Dialects of Northern Iraq. In *The Languages and Linguistics of Western Asia: An Areal Perspective*, ed. Geoffrey Haig and Geoffrey Khan, pp. 305–53. Berlin: De Gruyter Mouton.

———. 2019c. The Neo-Aramaic Dialects of Western Iran. In *The Languages and Linguistics of Western Asia: An Areal Perspective*, ed. Geoffrey Haig and Geoffrey Khan, pp. 481–532. Berlin: De Gruyter Mouton.

Khan, Geoffrey et al., eds. 2013 *Encyclopedia of Hebrew Language and Linguistics*, 3 vols. Leiden: Brill.

Kiwitt, Marc, ed. 2013. *Les gloses françaises du glossaire biblique B.N. hébr. 301. Édition critique partielle et étude linguistique*. Heidelberg: Winter.

Kiwitt, Marc, and Stephen Dörr. 2017. Judeo-French. In *Handbook of Jewish Languages*, revised and updated edn., ed. Lily Kahn and Aaron D. Rubin, pp. 138–77. Leiden: Brill.

Kizilov, Mikhail. 2007. Two *Piyyutim* and a Rhetorical Essay in the (Northern) Troki Dialect of the Karaim Language by Isaac ben Abraham of Troki. *Judaica: Beiträge zum Verstehen des Judentums* 63:64–75.

———. 2015. *The Sons of Scripture: The Karaites in Poland and Lithuania in the Twentieth Century*. Berlin: De Gruyter.

Klagsbrun Lebenswerd, Joshua Patrick. 2017. Jewish Swedish. In *Handbook of Jewish Languages*, revised and updated edn., ed. Lily Kahn and Aaron D. Rubin, pp. 619–30. Leiden: Brill.

———. 2018. Jewish Swedish in Sweden. In *Languages in Jewish Communities, Past and Present*, ed. Sarah Bunin Benor and Benjamin Hary, pp. 431–52. Berlin: De Gruyter Mouton.

Komoróczy, Szonja Ráhel. 2018. Yiddish in the Hungarian Setting. In *Jewish Languages in Historical Perspective*, ed. Lily Kahn, pp. 92–107. Leiden: Brill.

Korzhenkov, Aleksander. 2010. *The Life of Zamenhof*. Trans. Ian M. Richmond. Ed. Humphrey Tonkin. New York: Mondial.

Krivoruchko, Julia. 2017. Judeo-Greek. In *Handbook of Jewish Languages*, revised and updated edn., ed. Lily Kahn and Aaron D. Rubin, pp. 194–225. Leiden: Brill.

Krogh, Steffen. 2018. How Yiddish Is Haredi Satmar Yiddish? *Journal of Jewish Languages* 6:5–42.

Kulik, Alexander. 2014. Jews and the Language of Eastern Slavs. *Jewish Quarterly Review* 104:105–43.

Kutscher, E.Y. 1982. *A History of the Hebrew Language*. Ed. Raphael Kutscher. Jerusalem: Magnes.

Kybalová, Ludmila, et al. 2003. *Textiles from Bohemian and Moravian Synagogues: From the Collections of the Jewish Museum in Prague*. Prague: The Jewish Museum.

Lansky, Aaron. 2004. *Outwitting History: How a Young Man Rescued a Million Books and Saved a Vanishing Civilization*. Chapel Hill, NC: Algonquin Books.

Lazar, Moshe, ed. 1999. *Sefarad in My Heart: A Ladino Reader*. Lancaster, CA: Labyrinthos.

Lehmann, Matthias B. 2018. Linguistic Transformations: Ladino (Judeo-Spanish). In *The Cambridge History of Judaism. Volume VII: The Early Modern World, 1500–1815*, ed. Jonathan Karp and Adam Sutcliffe, pp. 257–73. Cambridge: Cambridge University Press.

Leslau, Wolf. 1963. *Falasha Anthology*. New Haven, CT: Yale University Press.

Leslie, Donald. 1963–66. The Chinese-Hebrew Memorial Book of the Jewish Community of K'aifeng. *Abr-Nahrain* 4(1963–64):19–49; 5(1964–65):1–28; 6(1965–66):1–52.

————. 1972. *The Survival of the Chinese Jews: The Jewish Community of Kaifeng*. Leiden: E. J. Brill.

Leviant, Curt, ed. and trans. 2003. *King Artus: A Hebrew Arthurian Romance of 1279*. Syracuse: Syracuse University Press.

Lévy, Isaac Jack. 1989. *And the World Stood Silent: The Sephardic Poetry of the Holocaust*. Urbana: University of Illinois Press.

Lichtenstein, Aaron, et al. 2007. Portugal. In *Encyclopaedia Judaica*, 2nd edn., ed. Michael Berenbaum and Fred Skolnik, vol. 16, pp. 14–409. Detroit: Macmillan Reference USA.

Loy, Thomas. 2015. Rise and Fall: Bukharan Jewish Literature of the 1920s and 1930s. In *Iranian Languages and Literatures of Central Asia: From the Eighteenth Century to the Present*, ed. Matteo De Chiara and Evelin Grassi, pp. 307–36. Paris: Association pour l'avancement des études iraniennes.

Lunel, Armand. 2018. The Jews of the South of France. Trans. Samuel N. Rosenberg. *Hebrew Union College Annual* 89:1–157.

Mainz, Ernest. 1949. Quelques poésies judéo-arabes du manuscrit 411 de la Bibliothèque du Vatican. *Journal Asiatique* 237:51–83.

Manasseh, Rachel. 2013. *Baghdadian Jews of Bombay: Their Life & Achievements*. Great Neck, NY: Midrash Ben Ish Hai.

Marazzi, Ugo. 1980. *Tevārīḥ-i Āl-i Osmān: Cronaca anonima ottomana in trascrizione ebraica*. Naples: Istituto Universitario Orientale.

Mark, Peter, and José da Silva Horta. 2011. *The Forgotten Diaspora: Jewish Communities in West Africa and the Making of the Atlantic World*. Cambridge: Cambridge University Press.

Matsa, Joseph. 1971–81. השירה היהודית ביוונית [Jewish Poetry in Greek]. *Sefunot* 15:235–365.

Maurer, Philippe. 1998. El Papiamentu de Curazao. In *America Negra: panoramica actual de los estudios linguisticos sobre variedades hispanas, portuguesas y criollas*, ed. Matthias Perl and Armin Schwegler, pp. 139–217. Frankfurt am Main: Vervuert.

————. 2013. Papiamentu. In *The Survey of Pidgin and Creole Languages*, ed. Susanne Maria Michaelis et al., vol. 2, pp. 163–81. Oxford: Oxford University Press.

May, Harry S. 1971. *The Vale of Tears (Emek Habacha)*. The Hague: Martinus Nijhoff.

Meir, Irit. 2013. Sign Language in Hebrew. In *Encyclopedia of Hebrew Language and Linguistics*, ed. Geoffrey Khan et al., vol. 3, pp. 561–68. Leiden: Brill.

Meir, Irit, and Wendy Sandler. 2008. *A Language in Space: The Story of Israeli Sign Language*. New York: Lawrence Erlbaum.

Mendelsohn, Richard, and Milton Shain. 2008. *The Jews in South Africa: An Illustrated History*. Johannesburg: Jonathan Ball.

Mendelson-Maoz, Adia. 2015. *Multiculturalism in Israel: Literary Perspectives*. West Lafayette, IN: Purdue University Press.

Mesthrie, Rajend, and Clarissa Surek-Clark. 2013. Fanakalo. In *The Survey of Pidgin and Creole Languages*, ed. Susanne Maria Michaelis et al., vol. 3, pp. 34–41. Oxford: Oxford University Press.

Mignon, Laurent. 2017. Judeo-Turkish. In *Handbook of Jewish Languages*, revised and updated edn., ed. Lily Kahn and Aaron D. Rubin, pp. 635–41. Leiden: Brill.

Mikdash-Shamailov, Liya, ed. 2002. *Mountain Jews: Customs and Daily Life in the Caucasus*. Jerusalem: Israel Museum.

Mlotek, Chana. 2010. Folk Songs. In *YIVO Encyclopedia of Jews in Eastern Europe*, online edn., ed. Jeffrey P. Edelstein et al. www.yivoencyclopedia.org.

Moreen, Vera Basch. 1995. A Supplementary List of Judaeo-Persian Manuscripts. *British Library Journal* 21:71–80.

————. 2000. *In Queen Esther's Garden: An Anthology of Judeo-Persian Literature*. New Haven: Yale University Press.

Musleah, Ezekiel N. 1975. *On the Banks of the Ganga: The Sojourn of the Jews in Calcutta*. North Quincy, MA: The Christopher Publishing House.

Myhill, John. 2004. *Language in Jewish Society: Towards a New Understanding*. Clevedon: Multilingual Matters.

Natale, Sara. 2017. *L'elegia giudeo-italiana: Edizione critica e commentate*. Pisa: Pacini.

Nathan, Eze. 1986. *History of the Jews in Singapore, 1830–1945*. Singapore: Herbilu.

Neusner, Jacob. 1994. *Introduction to Rabbinic Literature*. New York: Doubleday.

Noy, David. 1993. *Jewish Inscriptions of Western Europe. Volume 1: Italy (excluding the City of Rome), Spain and Gaul*. Cambridge: Cambridge University Press.

———. 1995. *Jewish Inscriptions of Western Europe. Volume 2: The City of Rome*. Cambridge: Cambridge University Press.

Olszowy-Schlanger, Judith. 2015. *Hebrew and Hebrew-Latin Documents from Medieval England: A Diplomatic and Palaeographical Study*, 2 vols. Turnhout, Belgium: Brepols.

Paper, Herbert H. 1986. *The Musā-nāma of R. Shim'on Ḥakham*. Cincinnati: Hebrew Union College Press.

Patterson, David. 1964. *Abraham Mapu: The Creator of the Modern Hebrew Novel*. London: East and West Library.

———. 1988. *A Phoenix in Fetters: Studies in Nineteenth and Early Twentieth Century Hebrew Fiction*. Savage, MD: Rowman and Littlefield.

Perelmutter, Renee. 2018. Israeli Russian in Israel. In *Languages in Jewish Communities, Past and Present*, ed. Sarah Bunin Benor and Benjamin Hary, pp. 520–43. Berlin: De Gruyter Mouton.

Polliack, Meira, ed. 2003. *Karaite Judaism: A Guide to Its History and Literary Sources*. Leiden: Brill.

Polonsky, Antony. 2009–12. *The Jews in Poland and Russia*, 3 vols. Oxford: Littman Library of Jewish Civilization.

Quirin, James. 1992. *The Evolution of the Ethiopian Jews: A History of the Beta Israel (Falasha) to 1920*. Philadelphia: University of Pennsylvania Press.

Rendsburg, Gary A. 2003. A Comprehensive Guide to Israelian Hebrew: Grammar and Lexicon. *Orient* 38:5–35.

Roland, Joan G. 1998. *Jewish Communities of India: Identity in a Colonial Era*, 2nd edn. New York: Routledge.

Rosenhouse, Judith. 2017. Jewish Hungarian. In *Handbook of Jewish Languages*, revised and updated edn., ed. Lily Kahn and Aaron D. Rubin, pp. 226–33. Leiden: Brill.

Rosenzweig, Claudia. 2016. *Bovo d'Antona by Elye Bokher. A Yiddish Romance*. Leiden: Brill.

———. 2020. 'To a King, to a Pig', A Yiddish Poem on the Ages of Man. In *Worlds of Old Yiddish Literature*, ed. Simon Neuberg and Diana Matut, pp. 95–120. Cambridge: Legenda.

Roth, Cecil. 1928–31. The Jews of Malta. *Transactions of the Jewish Historical Society of England* 12:187–251.

———. 1946. *The History of the Jews of Italy*. Philadelphia: The Jewish Publication Society.

———. 1964. *A History of the Jews in England*, 3rd edn. Oxford: Clarendon.

Rubin, Aaron D. 2013. Hebrew Loanwords in American Creoles. In *Encyclopedia of Hebrew Language and Linguistics*, ed. Geoffrey Khan et al., vol. 1, pp. 98–100. Leiden: Brill.

———. 2016. *A Unique Hebrew Glossary from India: An Analysis of Judeo-Urdu*. Piscataway, NJ: Gorgias.

———. 2017. Judeo-Italian. In *Handbook of Jewish Languages*, revised and updated edn., ed. Lily Kahn and Aaron D. Rubin, pp. 298–365. Leiden: Brill.

Russell, James R. 2013a. On an Armenian Word List from the Cairo Geniza. *Iran and the Caucasus* 17:189–214.

———. 2013b. On an Armenian Magical Manuscript (Jewish Theological Seminary, New York, MS 10558). *Proceedings of the Israel Academy of Sciences and Humanities* 8:105–91.

Rzehak, Lutz. 2008. The Linguistic Challenge: Bukharan Jews and Soviet Language Policy. In *Bukharan Jews in the 20th Century*, ed. Ingeborg Baldauf, Moshe Grammer, and Thomas Loy, pp. 37–55. Wiesbaden: Reichert.

Sadock, Benjamin, and Alyssa Masor. 2018. Bobover Yiddish: "Polish" or "Hungarian"? *Journal of Jewish Languages* 6:89–110.

Sáenz-Badillos, Angel. 1993. *A History of the Hebrew Language*. Trans. John Elwolde. Cambridge: Cambridge University Press.

———. 2013. Medieval Hebrew. In *Encyclopedia of Hebrew Language and Linguistics*, ed. Geoffrey Khan et al., vol. 2, pp. 624–33. Leiden: Brill.

Salomon, H.P. 1982. The Earliest Known Document in Papiamentu Contextually Reconsidered. *Neophilologus* 66:367–76.

Šamić, Jasna. 1996. Qu'est-ce que "notre héritage": plus particulièrement sur un manuscript conserve au siege de la communauté juive ("Jevrejska opština") de Sarajevo. *Anali Gazi Husrev-begove biblioteke* 17–18:91–96.

Sarna, Jonathan. 2019. *American Judaism*, 2nd edn. New Haven: Yale University Press.

Saron, Gustav, and Louis Hotz. 1955. *The Jews in South Africa: A History*. Cape Town: Oxford University Press.

Schor, Esther. 2016. *Bridge of Words: Esperanto and the Dream of a Universal Language*. New York: Metropolitan.

Schwartz, Martin. 2014. Lotera'i: Jewish Jargon, Muslim Argot. In *The Jews of Iran*, ed. Houman Sarshar, pp. 32–56. London: Taurus.

Schwarzwald, Ora. 2018. Judeo-Spanish Throughout the Sephardic Diaspora. In *Languages in Jewish Communities, Past and Present*, ed. Sarah Bunin Benor and Benjamin Hary, pp. 145–84. Berlin: De Gruyter Mouton.

Segal, J.B. 1993. *A History of the Jews of Cochin*. London: Vallentine Mitchell.

Sermoneta, Giuseppe. 1969. *Un glossario filosofico ebraico-italiano del XIII secolo*. Rome: Edizioni dell'Ateneo.

Shapiro, Alexander. 2007. Provence. In *Encyclopaedia Judaica*, 2nd edn., ed. Michael Berenbaum and Fred Skolnik, vol. 16, pp. 636–39. Detroit: Macmillan Reference USA.

Shalem, Vitaly. 2018. Judeo-Tat in the Eastern Caucasus. In *Languages in Jewish Communities, Past and Present*, ed. Benjamin Hary and Sarah Bunin Benor, pp. 313–56. Berlin: De Gruyter Mouton.

Shavit, Yaacov. 1993. A Duty Too Heavy to Bear: Hebrew in the Berlin Haskalah, 1783–1819: Between Classic, Modern, and Romantic. In *Hebrew in Ashkenaz: A Language in Exile*, ed. Lewis Glinert, pp. 111–28. New York: Oxford University Press.

Shivtiel, Avihai. 2005. A Judaeo-Armenian and Judaeo-Arabic Word-list from the Cairo Genizah. In *Studia Semitica: The Journal of Semitic Studies Jubilee Volume*, ed. Philip S. Alexander et al., pp. 139–43. Oxford: Oxford University Press.

Silber, Michael K. 2018. The Making of Habsburg Jewry in the Long Eighteenth Century. In *The Cambridge History of Judaism. Volume VII: The Early Modern World, 1500–1815*, ed. Jonathan Karp and Adam Sutcliffe, pp. 763–97. Cambridge: Cambridge University Press.

Skippon, Philip. 1746. *An Account of a Journey Made thro' Part of the Low-Countries, Germany, Italy, and France*, 3rd edn. London.

Slapak, Orpa, ed. 2003. *The Jews of India: A Story of Three Communities*. Jerusalem: The Israel Museum.

Slutsky, Yehuda, and Judith Baskin. 2007. Haskalah. In *Encyclopaedia Judaica*, 2nd edn., ed. Michael Berenbaum and Fred Skolnik, vol. 8, pp. 434–43. Detroit: Macmillan Reference USA.

Sola-Solé, J.M., Samuel G. Armistead, and Joseph H. Silverman. 1980–84. *Hispania Judaica: Studies on the History, Language, and Literature of the Jews in the Hispanic World*, 3 vols. Barcelona: Puvill.

Soltes, Ori Z., et al. 2004. *Beyond the Golden Fleece: A Cultural History of the Jews of Georgia*. Bethesda, MD: Foundation for International Arts and Education.

Spolsky, Bernard. 2014. *The Languages of the Jews: A Sociolinguistic History*. Cambridge: Cambridge University Press.

Sproull, William O. 1890. Hebrew and Rabbinical Words in Present Use. *Hebraica* 7:72–74.

Staller, Franz. 2019. *Kritische Edition und sprachhistorische Analyse der Innsbrucker Fragmente eines hebräisch–altfranzösischen Bibelglossars (ULB Tirol, Frg. B 9)*. Innsbruck: Studia.

Steinlauf, Michael C. 2010. Yiddish Theater. In *YIVO Encyclopedia of the Jews in Eastern Europe*, online edn., ed. Jeffrey P. Edelstein et al. www.yivoencyclopedia.org.

Steinschneider, Moritz. 1967 [1857]. *Jewish Literature from the Eighth to Eighteenth Century with an Introduction on Talmud and Midrasch: A Historical Essay*. Hildesheim: Georg Olms.

Strack, H.L., and Günter Stemberger. 1996. *Introduction to the Talmud and Midrash*, 2nd edn. Trans. and ed. Markus Bockmuehl. Minneapolis: Fortress.

Strich, Adam, with George Jochnowitz. 2017. Judeo-Occitan (Judeo-Provençal). In *Handbook of Jewish Languages*, revised and updated edn., ed. Lily Kahn and Aaron D. Rubin, pp. 518–52. Leiden: Brill.

Strolovitch, Devon. 2017. Judeo-Portuguese. In *Handbook of Jewish Languages*, revised and updated edn., ed. Lily Kahn and Aaron D. Rubin, pp. 553–93. Leiden: Brill.

Szajkowski, Zosa. 2010. *La langue des juifs du pape*. Trans. Michel Alessio. Valence d'Albigeois: Vent Terral.

Tirosh-Becker, Ofra. 2011. לשונותיהם של יהודי אלג׳ריה [The Languages of Algerian Jewry]. In אלג׳ריה [*Algeria*], ed. Haim Saadoun, pp. 117–32. Jerusalem: Ben-Zvi Institute.

Tirosh-Becker, Ofra, and Lutz Edzard. 2021. *Jewish Languages: Text Specimens, Grammatical, Lexical, and Cultural Sketches*. Wiesbaden: Harrassowitz.

Tov, Emanuel. 2012. *Textual Criticism of the Hebrew Bible*, 3rd edn. Minneapolis: Fortress.

Turniansky, Chava. 1984. צרור איגרות ביידיש מירושלים משנות השישים של המאה השש-עשרה [A Correspondence in Yiddish from Jerusalem, Dating from the 1560s]. *Shalem* 4:149–210.

———, ed. 2019. *Glikl: Memoirs 1691–1719*. Trans. Sara Friedman. Waltham, MA: Brandeis University Press.

Ulrich, Eugene. 2010. *The Biblical Qumran Scrolls: Transcriptions and Textual Variants*. Leiden: Brill.

Valls i Pujol, Esperança. 2014. Hebrew Fragments as a Window of Economic Activity: Holdings in the Historical Archive of Girona (Arxiu Històric de Girona). In *Books Within Books: New Discoveries in Old Book Bindings*, ed. Andreas Lehnardt and Judith Olszowy-Schlanger, pp. 149–81. Leiden: Brill.

van de Kamp, Justus, and Jacob van der Wijk. 2006. *Koosjer Nederlands: Joodse woorden in de Nederlandse taal*. Amsterdam and Antwerp: Contact.

Verbickienė, Jurgita, ed. 2009. *Mokslas krikščioniškas zemaitiškai parašitas: Kunigo Jono Krizostomo Gintilos žemaitiškas katekizmas hebrajų rašmenimis* [Christian Science Laid Out in Samogitian: A Samogitian Catechism in Hebrew Characters by Reverend John Chrizostom Gintiłło]. Vilnius: Lietuvių kalbos institutas.

Verschik, Anna. 2017. Jewish Russian. In *Handbook of Jewish Languages*, revised and updated edn., ed. Lily Kahn and Aaron D. Rubin, pp. 594–99. Leiden: Brill.

———. 2018. Yiddish, Jewish Russian, and Jewish Lithuanian in the Former Soviet Union. In *Languages in Jewish Communities, Past and Present*, ed. Sarah Bunin Benor and Benjamin Hary, pp. 627–43. Berlin: De Gruyter Mouton.

Wagner, Esther-Miriam. 2013. Germanic Languages, Hebrew Loanwords in. In *Encyclopedia of Hebrew Language and Linguistics*, ed. Geoffrey Khan et al., vol. 2, pp. 57–60. Leiden: Brill.

Weil, Shalva. 2011. Cochin Jews. In *Cambridge Dictionary of Judaism and Jewish Culture*, ed. Judith R. Baskin, p. 107. New York: Cambridge University Press.

Weinreich, Uriel. 2007a. Yiddish Language. In *Encyclopaedia Judaica*, 2nd edn., ed. Michael Berenbaum and Fred Skolnik, vol. 21, pp. 332–38. Detroit: Macmillan Reference USA.

———. 2007b. Yiddish Literature. In *Encyclopedia Judaica*, 2nd edn., ed. Michael Berenbaum and Fred Skolnik, vol. 21, pp. 338–72. Detroit: Macmillan Reference USA.

Weiser, Chaim M. 1995. *Frumspeak: The First Dictionary of Yeshivish*. Northvale, NJ: Jason Aronson.

Wettinger, Godfrey. 1985. *The Jews of Malta in the Late Middle Ages*. Valletta: Midsea.

Wexler, Paul. 1985. Jewish Languages in Kaifeng, Henan Province, China (1163–1933). *Zeitschrift der Deutschen Morgenländischen Gesellschaft* 135:330–47.

White, William Charles. 1966. *Chinese Jews: A Compilation of Matters Relating to the Jews of K'ai-fēng Fu*, 2nd edn. New York: Paragon.

Wodziński, Marcin. 2018. *Historical Atlas of Hasidism*. Princeton, NJ: Princeton University Press.

Yadin, Azzan. 2013. Contact of Hebrew with Other Languages. In *Encyclopedia of Hebrew Language and Linguistics*, ed. Geoffrey Khan et al., vol. 1, pp. 597–601. Leiden: Brill.

Yardeni, Ada. 2002. *The Book of Hebrew Script: History, Palaeography, Script Styles, Calligraphy and Design*. London: British Library.

Yarshater, Ehsan. 1977. The Hybrid Language of the Jewish Community of Persia. *Journal of the American Oriental Society* 97:1–7.

Yelenevskaya, Maria. 2015. An Immigrant Language in a Multilingual State: Status and Group Competition (Russian in Israel). *Russian Journal of Communication* 7:193–207.

Yoda, Sumikazu. 2005. *The Arabic Dialect of the Jews of Tripoli (Libya): Grammar, Text and Glossary*. Wiesbaden: Harrassowitz.

Zand, Michael. 1985. The Literature of the Mountain Jews of the Caucasus (Part 1). *Soviet Jewish Affairs* 15(2):3–22.

———. 1986. The Literature of the Mountain Jews of the Caucasus (Part 2). *Soviet Jewish Affairs* 16(1):35–51.

———. 1991. Notes on the Culture of the Non-Ashkenazi Jewish Communities under Soviet Rule. In *Jewish Culture and Identity in the Soviet Union*, ed. Yaacov Ro'i and Avi Beker, pp. 378–444. New York: New York University Press.

———. 2007. Bukhara. In *Encyclopaedia Judaica*, 2nd edn., ed. Michael Berenbaum and Fred Skolnik, vol. 4, pp. 257–63. Detroit: Macmillan Reference USA.

Zand, Michael, Mordkhai Neishtat, and Michael Beizer. 2007. Georgia. In *Encyclopaedia Judaica*, 2nd edn., ed. Michael Berenbaum and Fred Skolnik, vol. 7, pp. 495–501. Detroit: Macmillan Reference USA.

Zinger, Oded. 2009. כאשר זאת שאתי אינה אתי: נישואי מרחק בגניזת קהיר [Long Distance Marriages in the Cairo Geniza]. *Pe'amim* 121:7–66.